The Realm of Reason

The Realm of Reason

CHRISTOPHER PEACOCKE

CLARENDON PRESS · OXFORD

OXFORD
UNIVERSITY PRESS

Great Clarendon Street, Oxford OX2 6DP

Oxford University Press is a department of the University of Oxford.
It furthers the University's objective of excellence in research, scholarship,
and education by publishing worldwide in

Oxford New York

Auckland Bangkok Buenos Aires Cape Town Chennai
Dar es Salaam Delhi Hong Kong Istanbul Karachi Kolkata
Kuala Lumpur Madrid Melbourne Mexico City Mumbai Nairobi
São Paulo Shanghai Taipei Tokyo Toronto

Oxford is a registered trade mark of Oxford University Press
in the UK and in certain other countries

Published in the United States
by Oxford University Press Inc., New York

British Library Cataloguing in Publication Data

Data available

Library of Congress Cataloging in Publication Data

Peacocke, Christopher.
The realm of reason / Christopher Peacocke.
p.cm
Includes bibliographical references and index.
1. Rationalism. I. Title.
BD181.P425 2004   121—dc22   2003060939

ISBN 0-19-927072-4

1 3 5 7 9 10 8 6 4 2

Typeset by Newgen Imaging Systems (P) Ltd., Chennai, India
Printed in Great Britain
on acid-free paper by
TJ International Ltd, Padstow, Cornwall

Preface

When I moved from Oxford to New York in 2000 a number of factors pressed me to think through a general position on the relations between content, entitlement, and the a priori. One was the arrival of the fiftieth anniversary of Quine's 'Two Dogmas of Empiricism', an anniversary which prompted several meetings that called for a review of where matters stand, and how they should stand, on the great issues raised in that famous paper. Another factor was a sense that I was moving to a country where there were very different attitudes about the relation between philosophy and the empirical than were prevalent in Britain and Europe, different to such an extent that the very idea of philosophy as a relatively a priori subject was at issue. This sense of difference is certainly partly illusory. Even the briefest examination of the positions held by the contributors to the collection on the a priori which I edited with Paul Boghossian will show that both in North America and in Europe almost as many flowers bloom on the topic of the a priori as there are writers on the subject.[1] This sociological fact does not, however, remove the intellectual demand that one have a developed, and insofar as it is possible and within one's ability, a systematic position on the relations between content, entitlement, and truth.

Though I had worked on issues about the a priori and entitlement over several earlier periods, it was the invitation to give the Whitehead Lectures at Harvard University in the academic year 2000–1 that prompted me to think and write about these issues on a somewhat larger scale. I am grateful for Harvard's invitation, and learned much from reflection on the excellent discussions I had there in April 2001. All the material presented there is included in the present volume. Some of the questions and discussions that April prompted me to push the development of a generalized rationalist position much harder and further than I had previously attempted. The present book is the result of these reflections. I am conscious

---

[1] P. Boghossian and C. Peacocke (eds.), *New Essays on the A Priori* (Oxford: Oxford University Press, 2000).

that if the theses of this work are in the right direction at all they constitute at best a preliminary survey of a vast territory, much of which remains unmapped. I hope this sketch of a map will be useful to, and encourage, others who want to enter this territory, to explore more—and no doubt to correct this sketch.

Several institutions and persons made this book possible. New York University ensured that in leaving Britain before the end of my Leverhulme Research Professorship I did not lose some precious research time. I thank NYU and the Leverhulme Trust for this valuable and most welcome support, and Paul Boghossian and Jess Benhabib of NYU for securing the arrangement. I have no idea when if ever this book would have been written without this help.

Earlier versions of this material were presented in seminars at NYU between January 2001 and December 2002, and I thank Paul Boghossian, Hartry Field, Robert Fogelin, Joseph Raz, Stephen Schiffer, Declan Smithies, and Roger White for many illuminating comments on these, as indeed on other, occasions. At the Whitehead Lectures and discussions I benefited from the comments of Alex Byrne, Richard Heck, Christine Korsgaard, James Pryor, Tim Scanlon, Susanna Siegel, Judy Thomson, and Ralph Wedgwood. As always, informal discussions with, and advice from, Tyler Burge have helped me substantially. Conversations with David Wiggins in London over the years have given me a valuable perspective on what would be needed to establish my claims. I also had the opportunity to present an early version of this material in lectures at a conference on my work in March 2002 organized jointly by the Department de Filologia i Filosofia at Girona University, in cooperation with the Càtedra Ferrater Mora (Girona University) and the Sociedad Española de Filosofía Analítica, in the dramatic setting of the Faculty of Arts in Girona University. For that memorable meeting, and the excellent discussions there, I thank Manuel Garcia Carpintero, José Díez, Paul Faulkner, Robert Hopkins, Carlos Moya, Lucy O'Brien, Josep Prades, Dan López da Sa, Anna Sherratt, and Mark Textor. An early version of the chapters on perceptual entitlement formed the basis of one of my presentations at the NEH Institute on Consciousness and Intentionality run by David Chalmers and David Hoy at the University of California at Santa Cruz in the summer of 2002, and there I learned from the comments of David Chalmers,

Fred Dretske, Scott Sturgeon, and Aaron Zimmerman. A later version was presented at the Rutgers Epistemology Conference of 2003, where I was helped by comments from Catherine Elgin, Gilbert Harman, Thomas Kelly, Anna-Sara Malmgren, James Pryor, Mark Richard, Joshua Schechter, and Timothy Williamson. I have also drawn on material in several recent papers in writing this book, and have extracted papers from the developing material as I worked. I repeat my thanks to those mentioned in these papers.[2] The two referees commissioned by Oxford University Press gave me a multitude of acute and thoughtful observations, both substantive and expository, and thereby greatly improved the final version. I thank them for going so far beyond the normal call of duty. Peter Momtchiloff's wise advice and support has again been important to me. It was his enthusiasm for developing my Whitehead Lectures into a book that was crucial in setting this project in motion, and I thank him warmly for it.

The title of this book was suggested by my children Alexander and Antonia, whose unedited amusement at the boring effect of the other titles I had in mind prevented this volume from having a deadly heading. The book is dedicated to my wife Teresa, the love of my life, who also saved my life.

Washington Square
New York City
June 2003

---

[2] 'Three Principles of Rationalism', *European Journal of Philosophy*, 10 (2002), 375–97; 'Explaining Perceptual Entitlement', in R. Schantz (ed.), *The Externalist Challenge* (Berlin: de Gruyter, 2003); 'The A Priori', in F. Jackson and M. Smith (eds.), *The Oxford Handbook of Contemporary Philosophy* (Oxford: Oxford University Press, 2004); 'Explaining the A Priori', in *New Essays on the A Priori*; 'Moralischer Rationalismus: Eine erste Skizze', *Deutsche Zeitschrift für Philosophie*, 49 (2001), 197–208.

Contents

Introduction
Reasons and Sense

Frege said that while all sciences have truth as their goal, it falls to logic to discern the laws of truth.[1] An analogous point can be made about reason in general. If we were to formulate the point in Frege's own grand style we would say: While reason applies to all things, it falls to philosophy to discern the laws of reason. Here, discerning these laws involves stating what it is for something to be a law of reason.

That it is possible simultaneously so to echo and to generalize Frege's remarks on truth and logic is no accident. A proper conception of reason has Frege's own conception of logic as a special case. Under Frege's conception of logic the laws of logic and rules of inference are justified by the truth-conditions assigned to the sentences in question, in accord with a truth-theoretic semantics for the expressions those sentences contain. Given Frege's semantics for the logical constants we can see how and why a premiss gives conclusive grounds for a conclusion that follows logically from it. If the truth-condition for the premiss is fulfilled, so also will be the truth-condition for the conclusion. Since, under Frege's conception, compositionally determined truth-conditions can be identified with sense, this is a theory under which the rationality of a logically valid transition is explicable in terms of the nature of the senses involved in the transition.

A generalization of Frege's conception of the correctness and rationality of a transition aims to explain how in other cases, beyond logic, the correctness and rationality of a transition is explicable in terms of the nature of the senses involved in the transition, where these senses are conceived truth-conditionally. The generalization should respect Frege's repeated strictures not to confuse the normative with mere psychological generalizations. And, just as Frege wrote that 'From the laws of truth, there follow prescriptions about asserting, judging,

---

[1] In *Logical Investigations*, trans. P. Geach and R. Stoothoff, ed. P. Geach (Oxford: Blackwell, 1977), 1. Other quotes from Frege in this and the next paragraph are from this page.

thinking, inferring', prescriptions about asserting, judging, thinking, and inferring will also follow from such laws of reason as we are capable of discerning.

The nexus of questions about interrelations between reasons on the one hand and sense, meaning, or content on the other constitute a classical territory of philosophy. So described, the problems in this territory were recognized, addressed, and answered in multiple different ways by (amongst others) Descartes, Leibniz, Hume, Kant, various idealists, the middle and later Wittgenstein, Quine, and by many twentieth-century philosophers in the two streams so misleadingly classified as 'analytical' and 'continental'.

The material in the present book constitutes a set of steps intended to move in the direction of an answer to these questions. The position I develop can be described as a 'generalized rationalism'. The position is a form of rationalism in part because it holds that some reasons—or better, some entitlements—for making judgements are a priori, justified independently of perception. It is also a form of rationalism in part because it holds that the status of these entitlements as a priori is founded in a particular way in the network of relations between understanding, truth, and entitlement. The position I develop is more specifically a generalized form of rationalism because it holds that, once the issues are properly formulated, all entitlement has a fundamentally a priori component. All these formulations involve terms of art that I aim to elaborate in this material.

Writing as an empiricist, Bas van Fraassen has recently said that 'no empiricism can be as it has been. The empiricist tradition, like any tradition, cannot live unless it renews itself. The empiricism we need now, if it is to be viable at all, must be as different from the various empiricisms of Cambridge, Vienna and Berlin as theirs were from Locke's or Hume's'.[2] I would say the same about a modern rationalism. No rationalism today can be as it has been, and the rationalist tradition must equally renew itself. I will be arguing for a modern rationalism that differs from those of Frege and Gödel, just as theirs differ from that of Leibniz.

Just what a modern rationalism should be, and what should be regarded as fruitful and worthy of development from the historical

---

[2] *The Empirical Stance* (New Haven, Conn.: Yale University Press, 2002), p. xviii.

tradition, and what should be rejected, is itself a matter of current philosophical disagreement. The position I try to elaborate here should certainly not be seen as the only large-scale option claiming to be a form of rationalism. Others, notably Robert Brandom, have moved in a rather different direction.[3] I have tried to motivate the distinctive features of my position, and to argue that they articulate elements properly present in the classical rationalists.

At various points in the historical development of a rationalism improvements in the articulation of the position have been made possible by the development, in some cases for the first time, of theories of notions on which the rationalist needs to draw in formulating his position. The prospects for a detailed articulation of a rationalist position about logic were enormously improved by Frege's formulation of a truth-theoretic semantics for a formal language containing logical operators. Against the background of a truth-theoretic semantics one could see clearly for the first time how a premiss could give experience-independent grounds for a conclusion that follows logically from it. More specifically, one could see why the premiss gives such experience-independent grounds on the basis of the nature of the senses involved in the transition.

Rationalist positions have always made claims about the relations between entitlements or reasons on the one hand and truth and understanding on the other. One needs adequate theories of each of these if a rationalist position is to be articulated in any convincing detail. It is the development in the past forty years, by many different people, of substantive theories of intentional content and of understanding that makes promising the attempt to articulate further a rationalist position and, if I am right, to do so in a generalized form. Substantive theories of intentional content and of understanding are as essential to developing the rationalist conception as are systematic formal theories of referential semantics and truth.

I aim to expound a generalized rationalism in this material by formulating a series of principles of rationalism. Taken collectively, these principles relate entitlement to truth, to the identity of states and their

---

[3] *Making It Explicit: Reasoning, Representing and Discursive Commitment* (Cambridge, Mass: Harvard University Press, 1994).

intentional contents, and to the a priori. A case in support of these principles has to move back and forth. The principles themselves are in the nature of the case highly general. They must also be tested and made plausible in part by detailed consideration of specific examples of circumstances in which thinkers are entitled to make particular judgements. So there has to be back and forth between generality and specific cases.

The principles also need to be made plausible as against rival treatments of the phenomena, non-rationalist treatments of the examples of the entitlements in question. It is part of the task of making a generalized rationalism plausible to identify some of the difficulties that attend alternative approaches to this territory. The back and forth movement has also to be a movement between rationalist approaches and their rivals. I have not, however, attempted to discuss every single kind of rival approach that can be found in the literature.

One could formulate a generalization about the circumstances in which thinkers are entitled to form a belief with a particular content, say a perceptual belief based on perceptual experience. One might be able to show by consideration of examples that this entitlement exists only when the intentional contents of the entitling perceptual experience are of a certain kind, a kind identified in the theory of intentional content. Perhaps one could even make it plausible that this kind of entitlement does not rest on any other perceptual beliefs. All of this would be worth doing—but there is a clear sense in which these achievements would remain at the level of description rather than explanation. One should aim also to explain why such an entitlement exists; the explanation should explain why it is restricted to certain kinds of case or content; and the explanation should square with one's general account of the relation between entitlement and truth. In developing a generalized rationalism I will try to articulate these explanatory requirements more precisely; and to meet them, so far as I am able to. It is clear that without meeting them we will lack a full philosophical understanding of why the entitlement relation holds in the cases in which it does.

It may be helpful if I briefly locate this book in relation to two of my previous works. The present book can be regarded as forming one element of a trilogy, the other elements being *A Study of Concepts* and *Being Known*.[4] *A Study of Concepts* proposed a general form for, and constraints on, the possession-conditions for particular concepts. It is an account in which the level of reference and truth-conditions play a substantive role. *Being Known* discussed how we should conceive of reasons and truth-conditions in various problematic domains, in the light of a good account of possession-conditions for concepts of those domains. In the present book I aim to speak of the nature of the reason-giving relation in general, across domains, both by drawing on substantive theories of concept possession, and by reliance on the relations between conditions for possession and contributions to truth-conditions. The three works thus have a cumulative and interrelated character.

---

[4] *A Study of Concepts* (Cambridge, Mass.: MIT Press, 1992); *Being Known* (Oxford: Oxford University Press, 1999).

CHAPTER I

Entitlement, Truth, and Content

How are good reasons for forming a particular belief connected with the conditions under which that belief is true? If there is such a connection, can we explain why it has the nature it does? What does the connection show us about the relation between reasons and meaning or content?

These are central questions for any theory of reasons and rationality. Radically divergent views are to be found on the matter. Some theorists hold that truth actually has no fundamental or ineliminable role to play in the elucidation of rationality. Amongst those who think truth has some such role there is still disagreement on what that role is and on its wider philosophical significance. In the course of this book I aim to address these questions, and the wider issues, by formulating and supporting three principles. Any one of these principles is endorsed by a variety of substantively different philosophical positions. Taken collectively, however, these three principles amount to an articulation of a distinctively rationalist position, in a sense to be made clearer as we proceed. This chapter focuses on the first of these principles, and the challenges to it posed by alternative approaches to rationality and content.

1.1 The First Principle of Rationalism

The three principles of rationalism that I propose in the course of this book are each framed as claims about the relation of entitlement. I follow Tyler Burge in according this notion a central place in epistemology; and thereby, on the views to be developed here, in the theory of meaning and content.[1] It will help to locate the notion of

---

[1] T. Burge, 'Content Preservation', *Philosophical Review,* 102/4 (1993), 457–88.

entitlement if we give some examples, and state some of the conditions it meets. Examples of transitions to which a thinker is entitled include the following: making logical inferences; basing observational judgements on perception; self-ascribing sensations when experiencing these sensations; taking memory at face value in specified circumstances. This is just a selection from many more.

The notion of entitlement also conforms to the following principles. A transition to which a thinker is entitled is a rational transition. A judgement is knowledge only if it is reached by a transition to which the judger is entitled. A thinker may be entitled to make a judgement without having the capacity to think about the states which entitle him to make the judgement. A child may be entitled to make an observational judgement by his perceptual experience without his having the concept of perceptual states. Entitlement also need not be conclusive. The transitions which we divide into those to which the thinker is entitled and those to which he is not could be given a canonical notation. It is a highly substantive matter what kinds of concepts a canonical notation should employ. Some first steps towards a canonical notation are found in the descriptions of Alvin Goldman's 'cognitive-state transitions' and Robert Nozick's 'methods'.[2]

Whenever a thinker is entitled to judge something there is an objective norm which implies that it is correct, or is likely to be correct, to make that judgement in the circumstances of the thinker. A theory of entitlement and a theory of norms are different approaches to a single object, the structure of epistemic relations. If we follow through the legal image of entitlement, it is the norms that provide the titles to the judgements a thinker makes when is he entitled to make them. A thinker is entitled to a transition that is an instance of a logical principle because of the objective normative principle that if the premiss is true the conclusion will be correct. Sometimes it is easiest to understand the character of some principle of entitlement when one comes to realize that by judging in accordance with that principle the thinker will be doing the best he can by way of respecting some norm. I will discuss this further in the case of the entitlement to make perceptual judgements (see Ch. 4, sect. 1(c)).

---

[2] A. Goldman, *Epistemology and Cognition* (Cambridge, Mass.: Harvard University Press, 1986), at 77–8; R. Nozick, *Philosophical Explanations* (Cambridge, Mass.: Harvard University Press, 1981), at 179–85.

Is the notion of entitlement that of being rationally permitted to judge something in given circumstances, or is it that of being rationally required to judge it, if the issue arises and one must decide one way or the other? If 'permission' in this question means what is rationally permitted outright, even that is too strong. Consider the entitlement to take the contents of certain experiences at face value. There is a perceptual experience as of being in front of one of Escher's impossible three-dimensional triangles. An object can be constructed (Penrose built one) which is not really impossible but from one angle has an appearance which includes these contents: corner a of the triangle is closer than corner b; corner b is closer than corner c; and corner c is closer than corner a. If entitlement is outright rational permission, the perceiving subject in these circumstances is outright permitted to judge that corner a is closer than corner b. He is also permitted to judge that corner b is closer than corner c; and equally that corner c is closer than corner a. He is also rationally permitted to use the rule of conjunction-introduction. It would be a poor account of entitlement that did not count uses of conjunction-introduction as ones to which the thinker is entitled. But then, if entitlement is outright rational permission, our subject has outright rational permission to judge that there are cases which show *closer than* to be an intransitive relation. There can be no such outright permission—or not at least solely on the basis of an experience such as this.

Against this it may be said that outright rational permission to judge something might be structurally analogous to the notion of it's being morally permitted to do something. It can be morally permissible not to give the medicine to person x and morally permissible not to give the medicine to person y. These facts are entirely consistent with it's not being morally permissible to give the medicine to neither x nor y; one may be morally obliged to give it to one or the other of x and y.[3] So, it may be argued, we should not regard the fact that it is outright rationally permissible to judge that a is closer than b, and to judge that b is close than c, and to judge that c is closer than a, as implying that it is rationally permissible to judge all three of these contents at once.

---

[3] I am indebted to Joseph Raz for mentioning the parallel with moral permissibility; he should not be taken to endorse it.

I dispute that the structures are parallel. It is indeed the case that aiming to act morally leaves one, in some circumstances, some degree of freedom as to which action to perform. But it seems to me that there are no cases in which in aiming to judge only what is true one is rationally permitted, in the light of one's total evidence and attitudes, both to judge p and to judge its negation. The considerations in favour of saying there are no such cases run as follows. Suppose, for instance, we know that either Jack or Jill stole the jewels, and that it could only have been one person who stole them (because the corridor to the safe is so narrow). Suppose that all our evidence leaves entirely open whether it was Jack or Jill who was the thief. That is not a case in which we are rationally permitted to judge that Jack did it, and rationally permitted to judge that Jill did it. That is rather a case in which we are rationally required to suspend judgement on which of the two is the thief.

The intuitive difference between outright moral permission and outright rational permissibility of judgement is that while there can be different ways of acting morally correctly, in the case of judgement and truth any given proposition p must be either true or false, or (possibly) indeterminate; and one's total evidence must on balance support one of these possibilities over the other two if one is to be outright rationally permitted to judge that p. It is not rationally permitted to rule out the other two possibilities in the absence of relevant evidence, or in the presence of evidence that is no stronger than the evidence for what one does judge.

Still, it may be replied, is not the case of varying degrees of inductive boldness between two thinkers one in which, when there is some but not conclusive evidence for p, one thinker may be rationally permitted to judge that p and the other rationally permitted to judge that not-p? This, however, does not seem to me to be a case in which the two subjects are in the same total epistemic or informational state. The two subjects disagree, either explicitly or implicitly, about how much evidence is needed to confirm a given kind of conclusion. This may be either an empirical or an a priori disagreement; but in either case it would not be correct to say that they have exactly the same attitudes on matters other than p. The example in any case does not seem to be one in which one thinker is outright permitted to judge a proposition and the other to judge its negation, rather than being one in which the one thinker is rationally permitted to judge a proposition whilst the other is not. Such cases do not take one as far as outright permission to judge each element of an inconsistent triad, such as that involving the relative closeness of the corners of the triangle.

In short, it is not possible that there exist a proposition p such that: given a fixed, total informational state and background attitudes it is outright rationally permissible given all those factors to judge that p and it is equally outright rationally permissible given all those same factors to judge that not-p. Doing A and doing something obviously incompatible with A may be equally maximally morally good ways of acting in the circumstances. But judging that p and judging that not-p cannot be equally good ways of fulfilling an aim of judging only the truth.

I will be taking it for the present that a proper statement of principles of entitlement will have a relativized, prima facie form. In the case of basic perceptual entitlement, which we will be discussing in much more detail in Chapter 3, we can say that for certain perceptual contents p, prima facie, given that x has an experience which represents it as being the case that p, x is rationally permitted to judge that p. Here the logical form, if we use Davidson's well-known notation,[4] is

Prima facie (x has an experience as of p, x is rationally permitted to judge that p).

As always, moving from this to an outright conclusion that the thinker is rationally permitted to judge that p requires more than just her having an experience as of p. The further conditions that must be met, which have to do with the subject's other perceptual and cognitive states, are not met in the example of the perception of the impossible triangle. The structure and laws governing prima facie rational permission, and entitlement, are rich topics meriting further study. For present purposes I will leave the characterization at this intuitive level.

The notion of entitlement is meant to be an articulation of a concept we already employ in ordinary non-philosophical epistemic

[4] D. Davidson, 'How is Weakness of the Will Possible?', repr. in his *Essays on Actions and Events*, 2nd edn. (Oxford: Oxford University Press, 2001).

assessment, in assessing a subject's beliefs as rational. I do not mean to imply that knowledge can be reductively elucidated in terms of entitlement and other notions. My own view is that there is a large circle of interrelated notions, including entitlement, knowledge, and even intentional content itself, each of whose elucidations ultimately involves the others.[5] For those who doubt that there is any notion of entitlement having all of these properties I ask them to take it as part of the present theory that there is such a notion, and to assess the total theory which has this claim as a part.

The first principle of rationalism I propose links entitlement and truth. While the principle is part of a rationalist conception, other positions than rationalist ones can also endorse it; and some other prominently held positions reject it.

> PRINCIPLE I: The Special Truth-Conduciveness Thesis
> A fundamental and irreducible part of what makes a transition one to which a thinker is entitled is that the transition tends to lead to true judgements (or, in case the transition relies on premises, tends to do so when its premises are true) in a distinctive way characteristic of rational transitions.

I will call the property suggested in this principle as a necessary condition for a transition to be one to which the thinker is entitled 'the property of being rationally truth-conducive'. All the examples of the relation of entitlement that I gave are intuitively rationally truth-conducive. What the distinctive way is that is characteristic of rational transitions I aim to say in Chapter 2.

If a theory of entitlement and a theory of norms are indeed equivalent ways of looking at the structure of epistemic relations, then Principle I also has consequences for the correct way of characterizing the objective norms which underlie entitlement. Principle I suggests that the nature of those norms has to be explained, irreducibly, in terms of truth and truth-preservation.

The property of a transition of tending to lead to true judgements (or to do so when its premises are true) is not by itself enough to make a transition entitling. Pure reliability of a transition is not by itself enough to make the transition entitling, as, in my judgement,

---

[5] For this claim about knowledge, see *Being Known*, ch. 2.

many examples in the discussion of pure reliabilism over the years have shown.[6] If I am wrong about this, and there is a form of pure reliabilism that can capture a rationality requirement, all well and good. For what it is worth, I myself am sceptical that any such form of reliabilism exists. William Alston, for instance, has suggested that examples that seem to show the need for a rationality requirement that goes beyond reliability can, after all, be reconciled with reliabilism by requiring that the subject's beliefs be based on some state accessible to the subject.[7] This would not be sufficient by itself to make the beliefs rational. The accessible states might be mere imaginings, which by themselves do not make judgements about the objective world rational. Even if they are experiences, they may not be ones that make the judgement rational.[8] If, nonetheless, there is a form of reliabilism that captures the rationality requirement, I am in agreement with a theorist who endorses it in holding that in the relevant cases of reliability rationality requirements for entitlement will need to be fulfilled. Such a theorist and I are both in disagreement with a third party who holds both that reliability of some specified kind is all that is needed for entitlement and that it does not involve rationality at all. Principle I is, then, opposed to what is sometimes called 'externalism' about justification in epistemology.

The term 'externalism' is used in a different way in the theory of intentional content.[9] In Chapters 2 through 4 I will in fact be arguing that the right way of developing a rationalist conception involves acceptance of externalism in the theory of intentional content.

Thinkers are entitled, prima facie, to take the content of their perceptual experiences at face value. But it seems that there could be a Cartesian evil demon ensuring that the contents of all of one's

[6] For support for this claim see L. BonJour, *The Structure of Empirical Knowledge* (Cambridge, Mass.: Harvard University Press, 1985), esp. ch. 3, 'Externalist Versions of Foundationalism'. For a contrary view see Goldman's *Epistemology and Cognition*, 109–21.

[7] W. Alston, 'An Internalist Externalism', *Synthese*, 74 (1988), 265–83. Alvin Plantinga, *Warrant: The Current Debate* (New York: Oxford University Press, 1993), 190–2. Alston's emphasis in his epistemological writings on truth-conduciveness is, however, very congenial to the rationalist stance I am developing.   [8] See Plantinga, *Warrant: The Current Debate*, 190–2.

[9] The classic sources on externalism in the theory of intentional content are H. Putnam 'The Meaning of "Meaning" ', in his *Mind, Language and Reality* (Cambridge: Cambridge University Press, 1975) and T. Burge, 'Individualism and the Mental', *Midwest Studies in Philosophy*, 4 (1979), 73–121.

perceptual experiences about the external world are false. Taking perceptual experience at face value will not lead to true belief in such an evil-demon world. How then can we include amongst the transitions to which one is entitled the transition from a perceptual experience to the correctness of some content it rationalizes?

I answer that the transition is required to be truth-preserving only in worlds of a kind which one has a prima facie, defeasible entitlement to believe one is in. For this reply to be more than an empty box, one must have some systematic and general account both of what one is entitled to presume, defeasibly, about one's circumstances and of why one is entitled to presume it. I take on that task in Chapters 3 and 4.

The intuitive attractions of Principle I lie in the internal relations between rationality, truth, and the aim of judgement. It is a constitutive aim of judgement that one tries to judge that p only if it is true that p. Rational ways of coming to make judgements must be ones that tend to lead to the truth.

Principle I can seem like a truism, as nothing more than a reiteration of those uncontroversial interrelations between rationality, truth, and judgement. But Principle I does not just state a necessary condition for a transition to be one to which a thinker is entitled. It is a constitutive thesis, about what makes the transition one to which the thinker is entitled. A theorist might agree with the truisms about rationality, truth, and the aim of judgement, and might also agree that there are necessary conditions having to do with truth-preservation that must be met for a transition to be one to which a thinker is entitled. But if this theorist thinks that reference and truth are explicable in other terms, and that the entitlement to a transition does not need to be explained in terms of irreducible notions of truth and reference, then he is committed to disagreeing with Principle I. Take, for example, a theorist who has no objection to the use of the notion of truth but thinks truth itself is explicable in terms of entitlement. He need have no objection to the idea—indeed he will endorse the idea—that some kind of truth-preservation is a necessary condition of a transition being one to which the thinker is entitled. But this theorist is committed to disputing Principle I, with its claim about what *makes* a transition one to which a thinker is entitled. Principle I is a substantive philosophical thesis, and not itself a truism.

Principle I needs some qualification; it also admits of some generalization. It needs qualification because transitions can still be rational when they involve contents for which there are no truth-conditions. Indicative conditionals provide a much-studied illustration. There is no plausible truth-conditional content for the indicative conditional.[10] If we explain rational acceptance of 'If *p* then *q*' in terms of a sufficiently high conditional probability of *q* given *p*, there is still a principled account of what makes some transitions between indicative conditions rational, and what makes others irrational. There is a plausible definition of probabilistic entailment.[11] The definition implies that the uncertainty of a proposition that is probabilistically entailed by a set of premises has an uncertainty that is no greater than the sum of the uncertainties of each of those premises. This is a highly intuitive characterization. It suffices for the existence of a practice of rational acceptance of indicative conditionals, and of rational transitions between contents involving indicative conditionals. Principle I, in speaking of truth, does then need restriction to the cases in which contents have truth-conditions.

I said that this is a qualification of Principle I. But the case of indicative conditionals also suggests a natural generalization of Principle I that covers the case of both contents that have truth-conditions and those that do not. The generalization states that if something is part of the aim of judgement of contents of a given kind then what makes a transition involving such contents a rational one has to be elucidated in terms of preservation of the property specified in that aim. That property involves truth in the case of many contents, and it involves sufficiently high probability in the case of some others. The qualification to Principle I, when understood in the light of this generalization, strengthens the conception underlying this first principle of rationalism. The qualified version for truth is instance of a more general principle relating the conditions for rationality to a fundamental aim of judgement.

    [10] See D. Lewis, 'Probabilities of Conditionals and Conditional Probabilities', *Philosophical Review*, 85 (1976), 297–315, and 'Probabilities of Conditionals and Conditional Probabilities II', *Philosophical Review*, 95 (1986), 581–9.
    [11] See E. Adams, *The Logic of Conditionals: An Application of Probability to Deductive Logic* (Dordrecht: Reidel, 1975), 57 ff.

1.2 Reference and Truth in the Explanation of Reasons

Principle I and its commitments are certainly controversial. One kind of pure conceptual role or inferentialist theory would say that truth and reference do not have any essential role to play in an account of reasons and rationality. Robert Brandom describes a group of theorists, of which he himself is one, who 'start with a notion of content as determining what is a *reason* for what, and understand truth and representation as features of ideas that are not only manifested in but actually *consist* in their role in reasoning'.[12] So we need to ask the question: Can we elucidate the rationality of a transition without alluding to truth and reference?

I suggest three reasons why we cannot. (This work seems committed to the German maxim that all good things come in threes.) The first reason I label the 'Adequacy Problem'. Any pure conceptual-role theory or inferentialist theory has to answer the following question, a question to be faced by every account of rationality: Is its account of rationality consistent with the fact that judgement aims at truth? Truth is certainly not the sole aim of judgement. But a mental relation to a content p is judgement that p only if the thinker aims to make this the case: that he stands in that relation to p only if it is the case that p. In the case of pure conceptual-role theories (within which I will henceforth include inferentialist theories) the more specific form this question takes is: *Why* should judging in accordance with certain specified roles tend to produce true judgements? This is the Adequacy Problem for pure conceptual-role theories.

A direct answer from these theorists to the Adequacy Problem would be to say: 'For a content to be true is for it either to be establishable by specified conceptual roles, or for all of its consequences to be establishable by specified conceptual roles'. This imagined answer is drafted to take into account that conceptual-role theorists quite properly include certain canonical relations of consequence, as

---

[12] R. Brandom, *Articulating Reasons: An Introduction to Inferentialism* (Cambridge, Mass.: Harvard University Press, 2000), 47. Brandom calls such theorists 'post-Cartesian rationalists'. See also his *Making It Explicit*, 93–4. The discussions in Sects 2.1 and 6.5 below give reasons for questioning whether historically rationalists have really had that attitude to truth.

well as canonical grounds, in their individuation of content.[13] The characterization of truth involved in this answer is, however, very heavily anti-realistic. It requires that in every case in which a past-tense content is true we can either establish it or it has consequences all of which are establishable. There is, intuitively, no problem with the idea of a past-tense truth that has no present traces, and hence no present consequences, at all. I would argue that this is a consequence of a proper understanding of the objectivity of past-tense statements, as saying the same about the past as their present-tense counter-parts.[14] Such a possibility of verification-transcendent truth for empirical statements about the past is not excisable without cutting out too much of what is involved in objectivity.

Alternatively, the pure conceptual-role theorist may say that for a past-tense statement to be true is for it to have been establishable at the relevant time in the past, by someone suitably situated. It can be true that it was verifiable consistently with there not being, either now or in the future, any traces at all that this was so. I suggest, however, that, for reasons that should by now be familiar, this account is either circular or inadequate. The problem arises from the case of past-tense truths that would not have held had an observer been present. The account of the truth of a past-tense content p in terms of what would have been establishable in the past is an account that works only if we add the qualification that the presence of the estab-lishing thinker would not have affected whether p was the case. But, far from explaining content in terms of establishability, this account presupposes some prior explanation of what it is for p to be the case and to be unaffected by the presence of the establishing subject. If we do not add the qualification, the account gives the wrong truth-conditions in the case in which the presence of the observer does affect whether p was the case.[15]

Yet another response to the Adequacy Problem might be to say that truth is a property that sometimes holds when there is some kind of canonical establishability, or establishability of each canonical consequence, but that also holds in some other cases. That is surely

[13] See M. Dummett, *Frege: Philosophy of Language* (London: Duckworth, 1973), 453 ff.; Brandom, *Making It Explicit*, 116–32.   [14] *Being Known*, ch. 3.
[15] There is further discussion of this in *Being Known*, ch. 3.

correct; but I doubt that we can say what captures these other cases unless we use notions of truth and reference which do not consist wholly in their role in reasoning. Intuitively these other cases of truth should be captured by the condition that in them too, for example, an object really but unestablishably has at the specified time the same property it is established as having when it does hold establishably. This is then an explication of truth and reference which does not consist wholly in citing roles in reasoning. This explication uses a substantial notion of truth, and of reference to individuals and to properties, precisely in order to elucidate features of truth which are not explicable solely in terms of reasoning.[16]

A different response to the Adequacy Problem, a response intended both to avoid the problems of the most recent proposal and to avoid a commitment to anti-realism, is to insist that establishability by canonical conceptual roles is at least a sufficient condition for truth (even if it is not a necessary condition). Could this be used by a pure conceptual-role theorist as a starting point for reconciling his position with the fact that judgement aims at truth? It seems to me to move the bump in the carpet to another corner. How are the contents recognized by this theorist as ones which can in some cases hold unestablishably? If none of them can ever hold unestablishably anti-realism has not been avoided. If some of them can the question remains of how truth and reference can be explained solely in terms of their role in reasoning.

The second problem I want to raise for accounts of rationality and reasons that make no essential reference to truth is given by the question of which sets of roles and principles determine genuine concepts or meanings. For any genuine sense it must be possible to individuate that sense by stating the fundamental condition for something to be the reference or semantic value of that sense.[17] Not

---

[16] Under impure conceptual-role theories some specified conceptual role contributes to the individuation of a meaning or a concept, but there are also substantial constraints, formulated at the level of truth and reference, upon genuine meanings or concepts. Such theories have in principle the resources for meeting the Adequacy Problem; whether they succeed depends upon their details.

[17] See especially M. Dummett, *The Interpretation of Frege's Philosophy* (Cambridge, Mass: Harvard University Press, 1981), esp. 249 ff. on the 'strong' interpretation of the doctrine that sense determines reference; and my *A Study of Concepts*, ch. 1 and 2. The thesis that a sense is individuated by the condition for something to be its reference does not imply that all singular senses are descriptive. The condition can concern the object that stands in a certain contextual and/or psychological relation to the thinker at a given time.

every set of roles or rules determines a meaning or concept, because some sets of roles or rules fail to determine even a coherent condition for something to be the semantic value of the purported sense or concept for which they are the roles or rules. In the particular case of any purported logical constant whose sense is exhausted by its primitive rules, those rules determine a genuine meaning only if there is a semantic value for which they are all truth-preserving.

Under the conception of sense as essentially something that can be individuated by the condition for something to be the reference or semantic value of the sense it is a mistake to think of rules as a means of explaining entitlement that does not involve truth. The conditions for a set of rules to be legitimate can be given only in terms of semantic value or reference; and semantic value or reference can be explained only as the contribution made to the determination of the truth-value of intentional contents in which the sense features. So the conditions for a set of roles or rules to determine a meaning involve the notion of truth.

The rival view of conceptual-role theorists, and some of their allies, is that the conditions for the legitimacy of a rule as fixing a meaning can be given in terms of a Conservative Extension requirement. Suppose we have a theory T formulated in a language not containing the expression N. Suppose we have a new rule R which contains the new expression N. The rule R is said to be conservative on T iff: for any set S of sentences not containing N, and any particular sentence A not containing N, A is derivable from S in T + R only if it is already derivable from S in T. That is, the new rule does not extend the relation of derivability-in-T on sentences formulated in the old, unextended language. The Conservative Extension requirement is endorsed in various forms by Nuel Belnap and Michael Dummett. It is also endorsed for the special case of logical vocabulary (but not for all vocabulary) by Robert Brandom.[18]

This is not the place for a detailed discussion of the issues in the literature, which was initiated by Prior's famous note on 'tonk'.[19]

---

[18] Brandom in *Making it Explicit* and *Articulating Reasons*.; N. Belnap, 'Tonk, Plonk and Plink', *Analysis*, 22 (1962), 130–4.

[19] A. Prior, 'The Runabout Inference-Ticket', *Analysis*, 21 (1960), 38–9. There is some further discussion in my paper 'Understanding Logical Constants: A Realist's Account', *Proceedings of the British Academy*, 73 (1987), 153–200, esp. sect. 5.

In summary, my view is that Conservative Extension is both too strong and too weak to rule out the undesirable cases, even when it is required only for the introduction of specifically logical vocabulary. Conservative Extension is also the wrong requirement as a matter of principle for realists. It is too weak, because there are examples in the literature of spurious operators the rules for which do not violate Conservative Extension. We can imagine a spurious operator *vel* which has the same introduction rules as classical alternation, has some arbitrarily restricted elimination rule (for instance, to premises less than a certain length), and for which these are said to be the totality of valid rules. These rules are conservative over any theory, since they are a subset of the rules for classical alternation. But I do not think we know what *vel* means. A *vel* B cannot mean 'A or B or *p*', for some condition *p*, or else additional introduction rules would be valid for it. But it cannot mean something as strong as 'A or B', for then the elimination rule would be unrestricted. Though *vel* has a specified consistent and conservative set of rules, I suggest that we do not know what it means.[20]

Conservative Extension is also too strong as a requirement for a set of rules to be meaning-determining, because there are clear violations of Conservative Extension which are positively desirable. Adding second-order quantifiers—new, specifically logical vocabulary—to a language for first-order arithmetic can allow one to prove the Gödel sentence for the unextended language and theory not containing second-order quantifiers. This is a consequence of the fact that the set of true first-order arithmetical sentences is definable in second-order arithmetic.[21] Adding such second-order quantifiers and rules for them is not fallacious, and it certainly does not involve a 'change of meaning' of the vocabulary used in proving the Gödel sentence for the first-order theory. Nor is this a case of an empirical theory that non-conservatively extends some prior theory. Second-order arithmetic is not an empirical theory.

[20] For further discussion see my critical survey 'The Philosophy of Language' in A. Grayling (ed.), *Philosophy 2. Further Through the Subject* (Oxford: Oxford University Press, 1998) and also the discussion of the spurious 'quantifier' Qx . . . x . . . in my 'Proof and Truth', in J. Haldane and C. Wright (eds.), *Reality, Representation, and Projection* (Oxford: Oxford University Press, 1993).

[21] For more details see G. Boolos and R. Jeffrey, *Computability and Logic* (Cambridge: Cambridge University Press, 1974), chs. 18 and 19. The second-order quantifiers come with an ontology too, of course; but I am taking it that the legitimacy of this ontology is not a merely empirical matter.

If an example which is purely from logic is wanted we could cite Pierce's law: $((p \supset q) \supset p) \supset p$. This is not provable in a system which has only rules or axioms for the conditional, for those rules are the same for classical and intuitionistic systems, and Pierce's law is not intuitionistically valid. To prove it classically we need the rules for classical negation, or something with the same expressive power as classical negation. Can that really be a demonstration by itself that the laws of classical negation are illegitimate, because they allow the proof of formulae not containing negation that were not provable in the system not containing negation or something permitting its definition? Even the most ardent constructivist will want more premises and restrictions before drawing that conclusion.

Some pure conceptual-role theorists and some inferentialists assert that violations of Conservative Extension must involve a change of meaning for the vocabulary in the old, unextended language. Thus Brandom:

From the point of view of the joint commitments to understanding conceptual content in terms of material inference and conceiving the distinctive role of logical vocabulary as making those content-conferring inferential connections explicit in the form of claims, this constraint [Conservative Extension] on the definition of logical particles by introduction and elimination rules makes perfect sense. For if those rules are not inferentially conservative, the introduction of the new vocabulary licenses new material inferences and so alters the contents associated with the old vocabulary.[22]

I agree that this is a consequence of the inferentialist view; but is the meaning of an expression in the unextended language completely exhausted by the methods of proving certain sentences containing it, and of proving certain consequences from it, in the unextended language and theory? Suppose a new expression, even a logical expression, and its rules violate Conservative Extension, and yet the rules are compelling, and the new expression is plausibly legitimate. If a sentence in the unextended language is newly provable after the introduction of some new vocabulary, and rules for it, that is a positively desirable state of affairs provided the sentence was already *true* under its meaning in the unextended language. That is the situation for the

---

[22] *Making It Explicit*, 125.

Gödel sentence for first-order arithmetic. Violations of Conservative Extension, a proof-theoretic notion, are unobjectionable as long as they are semantically conservative in that sense. There need be no change of meaning if meaning was not fully captured in the old rules of the unextended language. This seems to be an entirely plausible description of the case of the universal quantifier over natural numbers, which features in the Gödel sentence for first-order arithmetic.

Semantic conservativeness is, however, a notion that immediately involves truth. If semantic conservativeness is the right general criterion for the legitimacy of a set of rules for a new logical operator then one cannot characterize the boundaries of legitimate rules without relying essentially on the notion of truth.

This second reason for saying that rationality cannot be elucidated independently of reference and truth also tells against those pure conceptual-role theorists who say that only warranted assertibility, and not truth, is the aim of judgement. What I have argued equally implies that the roles that determine genuine warrant cannot be picked out unless we rely on reference and truth. Even if mere warranted assertibility were the aim of judgement we would still need to say which sets of rules determine genuine meanings and which do not. Unless this theorist has some new resource for ruling out spurious meanings he will need to rely on considerations having to do with reference, semantic value, and truth; and then his conceptual-role theory is no longer pure.

The third, and in some ways the most fundamental, reason that we cannot elucidate rationality without mention of truth and reference can be argued once it is granted that truth and reference cannot be explained in terms of reasons and entitlement. Truth is an aim of judgement of a content; truth depends on properties of the objects (and other entities) mentioned in the content; so rationality in judgement must be a matter of some complex relation of the content judged to properties and relations of the objects and other entities that are the subject matter, at the level of reference, of the content judged.

The point can be illustrated at the most basic level of conceptual thought. It seems to me very implausible that one can explain why one is entitled to make judgements in accordance with basic conceptual roles for perceptual demonstratives, or for recognitional concepts, without alluding to the fact that these are rational ways of finding out about the objects that are given in perception. Nor, it seems to me, could the full conceptual role be properly characterized without taking into account the conditions under which they refer to particular objects. Under what conditions am I entitled to judge 'That chair [perceptual demonstrative] is F' when that chair is not actually presented to me in perception as being F? If I know, for instance, that that chair is the one I carried in from the corridor, and know this by having kept track of it, I am entitled to judge 'That chair is the one I brought in from the corridor', even though that information is not given in my current perceptual state. There seems to me no plausible way of characterizing the conditions for such entitlement except in terms of the thinker's information about the object picked out by the perceptual demonstrative—that is, by its reference, and thus by the contribution it makes to truth-conditions.

Despite these three reasons in support of Principle I, some would still say that the notions of reference and truth cannot play a fundamental and ineliminable role in an account of reasons and the rational judgement of intentional contents, simply because no notion of reference or truth is available in advance of, or independently of, notions of concepts, sense, and the contents of intentional states. Robert Brandom would say of reference and truth what he says of representation more generally: 'It is not clear, however, that a suitable notion of representation can be made available in advance of thinking about the correct use of linguistic expressions and the role of intentional states in making behaviour intelligible.'[23] Here I agree with the claim that no notion of reference is available in advance of the network of notions involving intentional states and their content. I disagree that it follows from this point that the notions of reference and truth cannot be mentioned in constraints on the existence of intentional contents, or in accounts of reasons and rational judgement.

On the first point, of agreement, I would actually argue for an even stronger position than Brandom's. The notions of concept (sense, mode of presentation) and of reference are mutually interdependent in at least two respects. (a) There is no thinking of something without thinking of it in some particular way, under some mode of presentation.

---

[23] *Making It Explicit*, 69; and many subsequent passages.

(b) As I emphasized, what individuates a mode of presentation is the condition for something to be its reference. This interdependence of reference and sense is a special case of a more general interdependence of sense, possession condition, and reference. No one of these can be fully explicated philosophically without mentioning the other two. The account I offered in *A Study of Concepts* is one that emphasizes such interdependence. It is just one amongst many other such accounts.

On the point of disagreement, it does not follow from the fact that reference is a coordinate notion with sense and possession-conditions that there are not substantive constraints upon sense and rationality having to do with the level of reference. That would simply be ruling out constraints on one concept framed using another concept drawn from the same local holism as the first concept. Such constraints are not contrary to reason. The general phenomenon is ubiquitous in the ascription of intentional contents. As we saw in the case of spurious operators, the constraint that a genuine possession-condition must determine a condition for something to be its semantic value is a real one, ruling out various alleged concepts as spurious. Its status as a substantive constraint does not at all depend upon there being a notion of reference 'antecedently available' to notions of intentional content.

The claims I have been defending have a consequence for theories of what it is to be in a psychological state with a given intentional content—the study of pragmatics in the sense in which Brandom uses this word.[24] If the nature of intentional content can't be given without adverting to the level of reference, the same must be true of an account of what it is to be in a state with intentional content. If we can't explicate what it is to form a belief that *p* without taking into account the conditions under which the concepts in *p* refer (and indeed in some cases what they refer to), we can hardly hope to elucidate the role of any other mental state with intentional content without drawing on the conditions for reference of its constituents.

So much by way of an overview of the considerations in support of Principle I, the Special Truth-Conduciveness Thesis. Each of these considerations, in its own way, implicates a role for a substantial notion of truth and reference in the explication of rationality. Principle I is not by itself, however, exclusively and distinctively

[24] Ibid. 68.

a rationalist principle, even though it is, for reasons to be argued later, an essential part of a rationalist conception. Principle I could be endorsed by a theorist who holds a purely reliabilist view of why some truth-conducive methods are entitling. The other two Principles I will formulate in later chapters are, by contrast, distinctively rationalist.

1.3 The Significance of the Quinean Challenge

In the later sections of 'Two Dogmas of Empiricism' Quine sketches a broad vision of the relations between rationality, evidence, and meaning.[25] It is not one which denies that reasons for belief have something to do with meaning. On the contrary, as we shall see in more detail, Quine's view is that in so far as meaning is a legitimate notion at all it is to be explicated in terms of evidential conditions. Quine's conception of rationality in the formation of beliefs is that it is a matter of pragmatic adjustment to total experience. The conception, and Quine's reasons for it, are challenging in many respects, but two are most pertinent for the project of this book. First, insofar as Quine is giving an account of rationality in belief-formation, his description has to do not with the truth-conditions of the contents of beliefs but rather with evidential conditions. So, in the cases in which evidential conditions and truth-conditions are distinct, Quine stands opposed to any theory, rationalist or otherwise, which seeks to elucidate the validity of reasons at least partly in terms of truth-conditions. Second, the Quinean conception leaves little room for any philosophically significant application for the notion of an a priori proposition, or more generally for experience-independent justification. Both of these are central to any rationalist conception, in the way I will be developing and defending a rationalist view.

Before we can proceed any further we need to have at least a working, umbrella characterization of the a priori. For present purposes we can use this:

> A content is a priori if a thinker can be entitled to accept it without that entitlement being constitutively dependent upon

---

[25] 'Two Dogmas of Empiricism', repr. in Quine's *From a Logical Point of View* (Cambridge, Mass.: Harvard University Press, 1961).

the content or kind of her perceptual experiences or other conscious states.

The species of dependence in question here is normative, not causal. It is a question of what, constitutively, provides the entitlement, and not merely of what facilitates it. This is a distinction that has long been drawn by rationalists. The entitlement may, but need not, be conclusive. A thinker may also be mistaken about whether her entitlement is conclusive.

This simple characterization of the a priori contains the modal 'a thinker can be entitled to accept it'. We will be concerned later in this book with the nature of ways of coming to know propositions. It will at that point be very helpful to see this 'can' as an existential quantification over ways of coming to judge a content. The displayed characterization of the a priori can then be seen as holding that the a priori character of a content is derivative from the a priori character of a way of coming to judge that content. More specifically, we can say that a way W of coming to judge that p is an a priori way if the way W involves a rationale or justification for accepting that p which is not constitutively dependent upon the content or kind of the thinker's perceptual experiences or other conscious states. Such a priori ways, and what makes them a priori, will later become one of the targets of our investigation.

It is important to distinguish in thought between a way of coming to judge a proposition and its contained, or involved, rationale or justification for believing that proposition. These may not be one and the same. They can be, and that is one of the features of a posteriori knowledge. When I see that the light is coming from a certain direction my judgement that it is coming from that direction is made rational by my experiencing it as coming from that direction. This is obviously a matter of perceptual experience. But when I perceive a logical proof of a proposition written out on a piece of paper we can distinguish between the way I come to judge the proposition—by seeing a proof of it—and the contained, or involved, rationale, which is the proof of it from no premises (for example). The rationale or justification is the tree-structured proof, a structure of propositions or Fregean thoughts, and this rationale or justification does not involve perceptual experience at all.

There are many parameters in this first general characterization of the a priori that could be set differently. For some purposes it is important to consider different settings of these parameters. It is sometimes important, both for consideration of a subject matter itself and certainly for our understanding the historical development of the notion of the a priori, to relax the restriction to conscious states in general. Of particular interest is the parameter-setting in which we allow as a priori entitlement anything which does not involve ways of coming to judge whose rationales constitutively involve perceptual experience. Under this more generous characterization ways of coming to know can be a priori if they involve other conscious states, such as those of spatial imagination or kinds of spatial intuition, or even emotionally sympathetic imagination, provided that they do not involve perception itself. A generalized rationalism will, however, be concerned in the first instance with the possibility of a rationalism that employs the most general settings that I have used here. (Some variant notions will be considered in Chapter 6.) It will also be a consequence of what I will be arguing in this book that more relaxed notions of the a priori can apply only because the stricter notion does.

In addition to this outright, non-relative general characterization of the a priori, there is also a corresponding relativized notion, which applies not to contents outright but to transitions. We can say:

> A transition from one of the thinker's conscious states to a judged content is an a priori transition if the thinker is entitled to accept that content given that she is in that conscious state without this relative entitlement being dependent upon the content or kind of any of her other perceptual experiences or other conscious states.

Consider the demonstrative content 'That rod is curved', where the perceptual-demonstrative component *that rod* is made available to the thinker by her perception of the rod which she experiences as curved. This content is certainly not outright a priori. Nevertheless, given the occurrence of such an experience, taken at face value, the thinker does not need to rely upon the content or kind of any *further* experience in coming to make the judgement 'That rod is curved'. The transition itself is a priori. As we might equivalently say, the content is relatively a priori, is a priori relative to the given perceptual state.

The case contrasts sharply with the content 'That rod is bending from differential expansion in the heat'. This content is not even relatively a priori in relation to an experience, taken at face value, of the rod as curved. Any transition from such an experience, taken at face value, to the conclusion that the rod is bending from differential expansion in the heat is not a priori. Additional information and/or experiences in addition to the perception of the rod as curved are required before our thinker is entitled to accept the content that the rod is bending from differential expansion in the heat. Like the outright a priori, the relative a priori need not involve, and will not in general involve, conclusive entitlement.

Neither the outright nor the relative a priori need involve the idea of truth purely in virtue of meaning. Fourteen years before 'Two Dogmas' Quine had already in 'Truth by Convention' argued against the idea that any sentence could be true by convention, or indeed true purely in virtue of meaning alone. In my judgement, the arguments Quine gave there, and especially those given later in 'Carnap and Logical Truth', constitute one of his most enduring contributions to philosophy.[26] To make clear what it is that I will later be opposing to Quine's vision I should say that my own view, like that of several other current defenders of the a priori, is that Quine's arguments in 'Truth by Convention' and 'Carnap and Logical Truth' are decisive.[27] The strongest of those arguments are completely free of any commitment to behaviourism or to evidential theories of meaning. Contemporary theorists of the a priori should not be involved with the uninstantiated and uninstantiable notion of 'true purely in virtue of meaning'.[28]

The means by which we come to know outright a priori propositions in such areas as logic and mathematics may involve any or all

[26] Both papers are reprinted in Quine, *The Ways of Paradox and Other Essays*, rev. ed. (Cambridge, Mass.: Harvard University Press, 1976).

[27] See my 'How Are A Priori Truths Possible?', *European Journal of Philosophy*, 1 (1993), 175–99; P. Boghossian, 'Analyticity', in R. Hale and C. Wright, (eds.), *A Companion to the Philosophy of Language* (Oxford: Blackwell, 1997).

[28] In fairness to a possibly non-existent class of theorists, one should add that even the reductionist empiricist who accepts Quine's second dogma need not be a friend of the idea that some sentences are true purely in virtue of meaning. This reductionist thinks that certain statements are true come what may, because they are confirmed by every sequence of experience types that may be instantiated. He need not hold in addition that statements with this special property are 'true purely by virtue of meaning'. Quine believes that he still has an argument in 'Two Dogmas' against such a reductionist who also believes that some truths are a priori.

of the following: engaging in conversations and discussion with others; reading books which archive knowledge achieved many generations ago; working out mathematical or proof-theoretical sketches on paper; musing and reflecting on examples; using computer simulations and computer proofs; and much else. Many in this array of methods involve perception at some stage or other. Does this fact undermine the status of knowledge so reached as a priori?

It does not. There is a distinction between the entitling conditions involved in a priori knowledge and what gives us access to those entitling conditions. Possession of what the thinker knows to be a proof (a tree structure of contents) provides an a priori entitlement to accept a logical or an arithmetical proposition. Inscriptions, conversations, rough workings-out on paper may all help a thinker to appreciate that there is such a proof, and what it is. But these perception-involving activities merely facilitate: they are not the entitlement itself. Of two thinkers, one may discover a proof of a given proposition in his head and the other may have to work it out on paper. The two thinkers may nevertheless have the same justification for their common conclusion. Only their modes of access to that justification differ. Respect for the distinction between a justification or entitlement on the one hand and what makes it available on the other is essential to a proper understanding of the a priori.

The distinction between an entitlement and what makes it available operates at the social level as well as the level of the individual thinker. In his most recent discussion, after many years' consideration of the notion of the a priori, Philip Kitcher argues for what he calls the 'tradition-dependence' of contemporary mathematical knowledge. He holds that this tradition-dependence is incompatible with that knowledge having an a priori status.[29] For Kitcher, to say that a piece of knowledge is tradition-dependent is to say that its status as knowledge depends upon the history in the knower's society of such matters as the development and acquisition of various axioms and principles of reasoning, and the reliability of their developers' modes of thought. Whether someone now knows something can depend upon matters of intellectual history prior to his birth. The use of unreliable methods

---

[29] Philip Kitcher, 'A Priori Knowledge Revisited', in Boghossian and Peacocke (eds.), *New Essays on the A Priori*, esp. 80–5. For the influential views of his earlier self see his 'A Priori Knowledge', *Philosophical Review*, 89 (1980), 3–23.

or fallacious reasoning in earlier generations could, Kitcher emphasizes, undermine the status of present beliefs as knowledge.

The friend of the a priori should agree with the thesis of the
tradition-dependence of much mathematical knowledge; but he
should also insist that it does not make the notion of the a priori
inapplicable. It is an empirical matter which institutions, divisions of
labour, and more generally psychologically characterized modes of
acquiring, storing, and transmitting information result in beliefs for
which an a priori warrant exists. This does not make the notion of
an a priori warrant inapplicable. It means only that it is an empirical
matter which conditions are conducive to the acquisition and transmission of beliefs for which such warrants exist. It is also an empirical matter which conditions are conducive to the acquisition and
transmission of a priori warrants themselves.

Doubts about the applicability of the notion of the a priori can also
flow from doubts about the very notion of an a priori warrant or entitlement itself. Philip Kitcher argues that if we use only a defeasible
notion of a priori warrant—what he calls the 'weak' conception—
'We would have abandoned the traditional thought that a priori
knowledge can prescribe to experience, that when we know something a priori we don't have to be concerned about what future experiences may . . . bring'.[30] Only an indefeasible conception of a priori
entitlement will capture that function of the notion of the a priori;[31]
the weak conception 'abandons parts of the idea that a priori knowledge is independent of experience'.[32]

This argument, which also influenced Kitcher's earlier writings
on the subject, may seem compelling. Absolutely indefeasible entitlement is simply not to be had. There can always be some evidence that
would rationally make us think we had made a mistake in believing
something to be a proof. To have indefeasible grounds we would have
to be infallible, and indeed to have conclusive grounds that we are so.
So it may seem that in accepting there are a priori entitlements we are
committed to something either that is too strong or that is too weak
to be a philosophically interesting notion of the a priori. If Kitcher is
right, we are committed either to infallibility or else merely to defeasible entitlement that, he says, involves an empirical element.

---

[30] 'A Priori Knowledge Revisited', 77.   [31] Ibid.   [32] Ibid.

The friend of the a priori should dispute both halves of this dilemma. The first step in doing so is to distinguish two kinds of defeasibility, which I will call *defeasibility of identification* and *defeasibility of grounds*. A ground for accepting a proposition can be conclusive even though our entitlement to believe that we have identified such a ground is defeasible. Identifying something as a conclusive ground is one thing; its being a conclusive ground is another. My confidence that something is a proof can be rationally undermined by the report of mathematicians whose competence I have reason to believe far outstrips my own. Nonetheless, a proof is a conclusive ground. Here we have defeasibility in respect of identification but not defeasibility in respect of grounds.

By contrast, inductive evidence for a generalization, even evidence drawn from an extensive range of a wide variety of kinds of instance, is never conclusive. In this case we have defeasibility of grounds. If the generalization does not hold, that does not show that the inductive evidence did not hold. The corresponding conditional for proofs would not be true. If the last line of a sequence of propositions is false it cannot be a sound proof.

With this distinction in mind, we can return to the claim that only indefeasible entitlements can capture a traditional notion of independence from experience, or can 'prescribe to experience'. Consider the case in which we have a genuine proof but in which (as is arguably always so) we have defeasibility of identification. It is always possible that some mathematician tells us, mistakenly, that what we have is not a proof. It would then in those circumstances be reasonable for us to accept his word, and not believe that it is a proof. But how does this show that as things actually are we have not properly and knowledgeably identified the proof as a proof? It seems it does not; and if we have properly identified it as a proof, the proof itself provides an experience-independent derivation that its conclusion holds. Once again, we have to distinguish the nature of the entitlement from the question of what may be involved in identifying it as an entitlement. A notion of a priori warrant that displays defeasibility of identification need not import an empirical element into the entitlement for propositions that it counts as a priori.

An important corollary of these points is that a priori status does not imply unrevisability in the light of (apparent) information from other thinkers. If the position I am outlining is correct, there is no valid argument from the sensitivity of your belief that p to empirical information about the opinion of other experts to the conclusion that you do not have an a priori warrant for p.

What of defeasible a priori entitlements? Are they drained of philosophical interest on this approach? In my judgement, the relatively a priori character of some defeasible experience-based entitlements is essential to a transition in thought being rational at all. If the supporter of the defeasible a priori is pressed by Kitcher for an explanation of the philosophical significance of these cases his answer should be as follows. Defeasible entitlement is a notion that must be instantiated if rational thought is to get started at all. Not all warrants can be empirical, on pain of regress. Acceptance of this point does not involve a commitment to infallibility, certainty, or indefeasibility. Kitcher himself favours a purely reliabilist epistemology, and would find some place for defeasible a priori warrants in that reliabilist framework (Ibid. p. 74). By contrast, examples in the literature on epistemology seem to me to establish that pure reliability cannot capture the rationality required for a warrant or entitlement relation.[33]

With this outline before us of a notion of the a priori that seems to have instances we can return to Quine's argument. Despite the very extensive discussion over more than half a century of Quine's views on these matters, it seems to me that the significance of Quine's argument has been underappreciated. Correlatively, there has been insufficient elaboration and defence of an opposing position. I aim to say what the significance of the Quinean challenge is, and to argue that the challenge is meetable once we move to an approach built around a truth-conditional conception of meaning, in the way that the rationalist (though not only the rationalist) advocates.

Quine argued as follows:

> (a) Whatever meaning is, and whatever it is that has meaning—whether an individual sentence, group of sentences, or whole theory—meaning must be characterized in terms of the experiences or evidence that would support what it is that has meaning.
> (b) For a vast range of individual sentences, experiences or evidential conditions cannot be associated with those sentences

---

[33] BonJour, *The Structure of Empirical Knowledge*, esp. ch. 3.

one by one if the association is meant to capture the meaning of those individual sentences. What experiences one would expect to occur, and what evidence one would expect to exist, given that a particular sentence is true, are frequently heavily dependent upon which other auxiliary sentences are also true.

(c) In the general case, then, experiences or evidence can be associated only with a class of sentences, where the class contains the many auxiliary hypotheses upon which the experiential or evidential consequences of any given sentence also depend.

(d) Given the truth of (a)–(c), the whole idea of the meaning of an individual sentence being given by a range of supporting experiences or evidence is an illusion. A fortiori, the whole idea of the existence of sentences whose meaning-individuating associated experiential or evidential conditions are always confirmed by the evidence is equally illusory. There are no such meaning–individuating experiential or evidential conditions.

Quine's later writings acknowledge a limited class of sentences that are always confirmed, but this class is far narrower than any traditional conception of the a priori would allow. His own positive view was that rationality in belief-formation is not something constrained by the meaning of the individual sentences whose acceptance is in question. Rationality is rather a pragmatic matter of shaping what one accepts to fit experience or the evidence.

For anyone with even the faintest rationalist sympathies there is a pressing need to consider Quine's argument. It is extremely plausible that many sentences do indeed not have confirmation conditions considered one by one. If there really is a sound argument from this point about confirmation to a rejection of any interesting application for the a priori, any form of rationalism is a non-starter. Quine seems to have a wholly general argument against the possibility of theoretically significant a priori truth, an argument that applies whatever notion of evidence is used in the explication of meaning. The argument would reach far beyond the reductionist empiricism which forms the content of the second of the two dogmas Quine targets. If sound, his argument against a theoretically interesting notion of the a priori will get a grip in the context of every evidential theory of meaning.

On the limited and specific issue of whether there are a priori contents and a priori transitions, Quine's argument has a clear lacuna. Many of those who argue in favour of theoretically interesting forms of the a priori do not accept purely evidential theories of meaning. They will therefore not accept that an a priori content is one whose meaning-constituting evidential conditions are always confirmed by the evidence. Such a theorist may rather hold, for instance, that an outright a priori method of coming to accept a given content p is one with the following distinctive property. It is entailed by the possession-conditions for the concepts composing p, together with the way their semantic values are determined, and their mode of combination in the content p, that use of the given method guarantees that p will be true in any world in which the method is applied.[34] Such an approach to the a priori has no commitment to a purely evidential theory of meaning or content. A theorist supporting this approach may reasonably remark that in 'Two Dogmas' the argument from holism of confirmation to the rejection of the applicability of any interesting notion of the a priori proceeds so quickly because only purely evidential theories of meaning receive any serious consideration in that paper. Truth-conditional approaches which are not purely evidential may be developed in a form which permits application of an interesting notion of the a priori, and the possibility of such treatments seems not to be addressed by the Quinean argument. The approach to the a priori which appeals to what is guaranteed by the possession-conditions for the concepts composing a content can certainly be developed in the framework of a truth-conditional theory of meaning.

It would, however, be an extremely superficial reaction simply to note the gap in Quine's argument and to leave the matter there. First, Quine presents a broad, general vision of the relations between meaning and rationality in the formation of beliefs. Any non-Quinean alternative must propose an equally broad and general vision, and defend its correctness. Simply saying that some contents and transitions are a priori, and that Quine's argument has a gap, is not meeting that need. Second, if a purely evidential theory of content is wrong we need to know where and why it is wrong, and to draw on that knowledge in building a better general approach.

[34] See e.g. my 'How Are A Priori Truths Possible?'.

Lastly, it cannot simply be that evidence is wholly irrelevant to meaning and content. In fact, for anyone who employs a notion of content constrained by Fregean consideration of cognitive significance, it is a consequence of the very nature of intentional content that evidence cannot be completely irrelevant. If, when we hold background information constant, there is something that is evidence for p but not evidence for q, it follows that p and q are distinct Fregean Thoughts. If we apply Frege's classical test, someone with that evidence could rationally believe p but not believe q. Even if they do not exhaust meaning, and even if they are not fundamental, evidential factors cannot be excluded from any epistemically significant notion of content.

1.4 Evidence and Meaning: The Need for a Middle Way

What then is the role of evidence in the individuation of concepts and meanings? On this issue, like so many others, we seem to need a middle way between two extremes.

At one extreme is the view that evidence has no part at all to play in the individuation of concepts and meanings; that is, has no part to play in the individuation of senses or intentional contents. Though this view certainly exists in the recent literature, it is too strong. We have already given an argument of principle against this extreme at the end of the preceding section. Its implausibility can also be illustrated by examples. There certainly seems to be a wide range of concepts for which certain evidential relations are constitutive or individuative. I list briefly a few. Having a perception of a desk straight ahead of one seems to give grounds, in everyday circumstances, for the content 'that desk is straight ahead', and that it does so seems to be partially constitutive of the identity of the concepts in the content. The same holds more generally for perceptual experience in relation to observational contents and concepts; for certain forms of premiss as constitutive grounds for certain contents containing logical concepts; for certain kinds of sensations as grounds for the self-ascription of a sensation of that kind; and so forth.

At the opposite extreme lies the Quinean view that meaning is not merely partially, but is exclusively, a matter of certain evidential relations. Despite many other changes in his views over the years, this purely evidential view of meaning is one that Quine held at the time of 'Two Dogmas' and through his later writings. Here are two statements from *The Roots of Reference*, twenty-four years after 'Two Dogmas' was first delivered:

The two roles of observations, their role in the support of theory and their role in the learning of language, are inseparable. Observations are relevant as evidence for the support of theory because of those very associations, between observable events and theoretical vocabulary, whereby we learn the theoretical vocabulary in the first place.[35]

Most sentences do not admit separately of observational evidence. Sentences interlock. An observation may refute some chunk of theory comprising a cluster of sentences, and still leave us free to choose which of the component sentences to count as true and which to abandon. The evidence relation is thus intricate and indirect. The same, of course, is true of the semantical relation. The semantical relation of observation to the theoretical language is similarly intricate and indirect, since we learn the language only partly by associating terms or sentences directly with observation, and partly by linking them to one another. The evidence relation, in all its intricacy, and the semantical relation, are coextensive still. (Ibid.)

Yet it is highly problematic to suppose that meaning can be exclusively individuated in terms of evidence. (The same will apply to attempts at joint individuation in terms of consequences and evidence: the arguments I will offer below apply equally to such a mixed position.) I distinguish three interrelated problems for such an extreme, exclusively evidentialist, view. These are not the only problems, but they are problems that can be formulated without commitment to any heavy-duty competing philosophical theory. The problems can even be stated without explicitly mentioning the possibility of verification-transcendent truth, something which has always been a challenge for evidential theories of meaning. It is, however, plausible that the possibility of verification-transcendent truth has its source in the conception which the problems illustrate. In any case, the problems I will be raising for purely evidential views all seem to me to be ones that do not arise for a properly defended truth-conditional conception of meaning. The three problems can be described respectively as the problem of the informativeness of evidential relations; the

---

[35] *The Roots of Reference* (La Salle, Ill.: Open Court, 1974), 38.

problem of the source of evidential relations; and the problem of the insufficiency and parasitism of evidential relations.

Problem (i): The Informativeness of Evidential Relations

A thinker can often understand a sentence, or grasp a content, before knowing what would be evidence for it, or what consequences it would have, in the circumstances in which he finds himself. The thinker has, in short, to *work out* what would be evidence for the content. Contrary to Quine's assertion, such evidential relations cannot be the means 'whereby we learn the theoretical vocabulary in the first place'. Sometimes we have already fully learned the theoretical vocabulary when we are engaged in such working-out of what would be evidence for its application.

This point applies to many different kinds of content. It applies to hypotheses about currently unperceived but perceivable objects. I may have to think about what would be evidence that my friend is spending today in Boston. It applies at the more elevated level of hypotheses about the behaviour of theoretically postulated entities in relation to observables; and to hypotheses about one level of theoretically postulated entities in relation to another level. How might the properties of a newly postulated form of matter affect radio waves reaching earth? To answer this question may be a major intellectual achievement. The concepts of the new kind of matter, of radio waves, and of earth may be employed long before anyone has worked out the answer to it.

Could the proposed evidential sensitivity be captured by saying that it is sensitivity to evidence that there is a new form of matter with certain properties, without specifying what that evidence is? If this is supposed to be how the person who understands statements about the postulated new kind of matter thinks of the evidence, it is a way of thinking which clearly presupposes grasp of the hypothesis that there is such a new kind of matter, and cannot be used to explain philosophically what is involved in that grasp. If it is not supposed to be how the person thinks of the evidence, it is not an evidential sensitivity which is constitutive of understanding. In the sense of evidence on which someone can have evidence that there is a new form of matter without necessarily thinking of it as such evidence, the evidence in that sense can be staring someone in the face without his realizing that it is such evidence. A thinker's failure to recognize it as such does not impugn his understanding of sentences saying that there is a new form of matter with certain properties.

Problem (ii): The Source of Evidential Relations

It is a real question how these evidential patterns allegedly constitutive of the semantical properties of a large set of sentences are, or even could be, worked out on Quine's account. What are they worked out *from*? It is surely what they are worked out from that should be mentioned in the account of understanding and meaning.

There are infinitely many sets of sentences large enough to have experiential confirming or refuting conditions associated with them. Our minds are finite. How then do we grasp this association of evidential conditions with infinitely many sets of sentences? The association must be determined from some finite, graspable basis. What could that be? The association cannot, on Quine's view, be determined by the meanings of the individual sentences in the sets, and in turn from their finitely many components. Quine's thesis is that the sentences do not have meanings considered one by one.

This point applies however we conceive of the notion of evidence. It applies whether the evidential theorist favours sensory stimulations, perceptual experiences, or known truths about observable objects and events. The problem results from the evidential theory of meaning, together with the thesis that the assignments of evidential conditions are made only to large sets of sentences. This structural problem will then be present whatever our conception of evidence. In my judgement, when there is such an association of confirming or refuting conditions with a set of sentences it is determined by the members of the set, which are themselves built up from finitely many constituents.

Why has this problem, that a Quinean style of evidentialism is committed to understanding involving an association that is, by the lights of his theory, not finitely graspable, not been more generally recognized? I think there has sometimes been a failure to distinguish between what I will call *radical evidentialism* and *structured evidentialism*. In his well-known discussion 'The Significance of Quine's Indeterminacy Thesis' Michael Dummett considers the model of meaning found in the later sections of 'Two Dogmas' and in Quine's later writings.[36] Dummett says that under the model of 'Two Dogmas' some individuation of the meaning of an individual sentence is still possible. In the case of a non-observational sentence—a 'non-peripheral' sentence in Quine's image of the web—our understanding

consists in our knowledge that it can be established or refuted only by means of an inference of a certain kind. The sentences to which a non-peripheral sentence is directly linked will, in general, be further non-peripheral sentences, which will, in their turn, be linked with yet other sentences. In general, there will be a large number of different possible paths leading, by means of such links, from the periphery to any non-peripheral sentence, any such path representing the total process of verification or falsification of that sentence (p. 381).

That is a formulation of what we can call structured evidentialism.

It is not surprising that, if structured evidentialism is attributed to Quine, there is a severe problem—precisely the one Dummett identifies—of seeing how Quine can believe in the Thesis of the Indeterminacy of Translation. The translation of one sentence by another is correct if and only if the two sentences have meanings that are individuated by the same tree structures of possible paths of verification or falsification; and that they are so is subject to no more than normal inductive uncertainty. This prima facie incompatibility of structured evidentialism with the Indeterminacy Thesis should already make one suspect that Quine holds something different; and I think he does. Quine holds radical evidentialism, which states that the best we can do by way of giving meanings is to specify a meaning for a large set of sentences, and we do that by associating that set with evidential conditions. It is not that there is nothing to be said about how those evidential conditions are derived. There are associations between theoretical sentences and other theoretical sentences; and between theoretical and observational sentences. But these are, according to the radical evidentialist, simply non-constitutive means by which sets of sentences come to have some association with observational conditions. Any sentence other than an observational sentence simply features in a huge number of large sets to which confirming conditions are

[36] 'The Significance of Quine's Indeterminacy Thesis', repr. in Dummett's *Truth and Other Enigmas* (London: Duckworth, 1978).

assigned. There is no case in which for a non-observational sentence it is assigned confirming conditions or inferential patterns or tree structures by itself. The radical evidentialist will not deny that there are tree structures representing possible paths of confirmation of the sort Dummett describes. The radical evidentialist just denies that they are individuative of meaning: those tree structures themselves depend upon auxiliary hypotheses. According to the radical evidentialist meaning must be a matter of some relation, however complex, in which the sentence stands to observation or the favoured kind of evidence itself. For the radical evidentialist complexity of association of evidential conditions with linguistic items is to be captured not by associating more complex entities as the meanings, such as constitutive inference patterns, but by associating evidence of the favoured kind with more complex entities, large sets of sentences or even theories.

There are, besides his endorsement of the Indeterminacy Thesis, other strands in Quine that suggest that he holds radical evidentialism. When Quine writes, 'the evidence relation . . . and the semantical relation of observation to theory' are coextensive, even after we take into account all the intricacies of confirmation of whole sets of sentences, that certainly seems to imply: same confirming and refuting observations or evidence, same meaning.

Dummett's structured evidentialism may seem much more intuitive and more respectful than radical evidentialism of the nature of the meanings of non-observational sentences. Certainly structured evidentialism can avoid infinitary associations of evidential conditions. Canonical inference patterns which individuate a non-peripheral expression's meaning are associated with linguistic items one by one. The meaning of a complete sentence can be determined by the meaning of its constituents under structured evidentialism. But structured evidentialism still faces a challenge about the association of evidential conditions with complete sentences. The intuitive point that we can often understand an individual sentence without knowing what, in our actual circumstances, would be evidence for it, is one to which a structured evidentialist must equally respond. It cannot be correct to write into a Dummettian structured individuation of the meaning of a hypothesis those evidential relations that can be discovered only after hard thought, and after possibly years of understanding the hypothesis in question. I will be arguing soon that the correct explanation of this phenomenon—of the possibility of understanding of a sort that does not consist in, but allows one, if one is smart and lucky enough, to work out evidential conditions—is an explanation that is incompatible with purely evidential theories of meaning. It has deep realistic roots.

Problem (iii): The Insufficiency and Parasitism of Evidential Relations

Even in cases in which experience plays a role in understanding, as it does in observational concepts of the perceptible world, understanding also involves more. It involves showing in one's thought some appreciation of the possibility that the property of an object that in fact causes one's perception is a property which could be instantiated unperceived by oneself or by anyone else. To have this appreciation is, I suggest, to have some tacit conception of the observed property as something categorical.

The idea of a categorical property has been found extremely problematic by many philosophers. The claim that there are categorical properties can hardly be taken simply for granted. Is it the case that when we carefully examine any given allegedly categorical property it can be seen to be dispositional after all? This is a fundamental issue in metaphysics, and we need to spend some time on it if we are to appeal to categorical properties.

Many philosophers hold that apparently categorical properties can always be shown to be dispositional. Michael Dummett once asked: 'Are not the notions of distance (length), mass and temporal duration intrinsically connected with the means for measuring them?'.[37] Hugh Mellor writes:

Take the paradigm, molecular structure—a geometrical (for example, triangular) array of inertial masses. To be triangular is at least to be such that if the corners were (correctly) counted the result would be three. Inertial mass entails only subjunctive conditionals specifying acceleration under diverse forces. It is . . . nothing but a 'generic' disposition—that is, a conjunction of specific dispositions'.[38]

---

[37] Personal communication, 1997.

[38] 'In Defence of Dispositions', repr. in his *Matters of Metaphysics* (Cambridge: Cambridge University Press, 1991), 115.

Simon Blackburn holds that the categorical credentials of properties we are apt to think of as categorical grounds are poor. He says that 'science finds only dispositional properties, all the way down'.[39] Karl Popper and Peter Strawson express similar views.[40] Scepticism about the notion of the categorical seems to be a point of agreement amongst philosophers who would not agree on much else.

To address this scepticism we first need a better characterization of the categorical. To this end I offer three characteristics of the categorical.

Let us say that an *actual-world property* is a property whose holding or not of an object is settled only by the way the actual world is, and is not settled by the properties and relations of the object in counterfactual circumstances. A first characteristic of categorical properties (and relations, which I henceforth take to be included amongst properties) is this:

(1) Categorical properties are actual-world properties.

Characteristic (1) seems to me to state part of what is involved in the very idea of the categorical. It is in the spirit of Goodman's claim that to apply a 'non-dispositional, or manifest' predicate 'is to say that something actually happens with respect to the thing in question; while to apply a dispositional predicate is to speak only of what can happen'.[41] Goodman throws away some of the intuitions underlying the notion of the categorical in adding the remark that this characterization may be merely relative, as illustrating 'the general problem of construing dispositional predicates on the basis of whatever predicates may be chosen as manifest'.[42] He says that 'A predicate like "bends", for example, may be dispositional under a phenomenalistic system'.[43] By contrast, I offer Characteristic (1) as part of an absolute, non-relative characterization of the categorical.

Characteristic (2) concerns explanation:

(2) An adequate empirical explanation of why an object has a particular disposition must either cite or be committed to the

---

[39] 'Filling in Space', repr. in his *Essays in Quasi-Realism* (New York: Oxford University Press, 1993), 255.
[40] Karl Popper in *Observation and Interpretation in the Philosophy of Physics*, ed. S. Körner, (New York: Dover Publications, 1957), 70; P. Strawson, 'Reply to Evans', in Z. van Straaten (ed.), *Philosophical Subjects* (Oxford: Oxford University Press, 1980), 280.
[41] *Fact, Fiction and Forecast*, 2nd edn. (Indianapolis, Ind. Bobbs-Merrill, 1965), 41.
[42] Ibid. n. 7.   [43] Ibid.

existence of an underlying categorical state. The underlying categorical state explains the manifestation of the disposition when its antecedent triggering conditions are fulfilled.

Possession of this characteristic does not imply that it is a priori that any dispositions must be underlain by a categorical state. It says only what the explanation must be like *if* there is an explanation of the disposition. The characteristic is also not to be understood as a principle about the explanation of the acquisition by an object of a certain disposition. It is concerned not with the history of, or the antecedents of, possession of the disposition but with explanations which cite current properties of the object, which are capable of explaining why, as the object is now, it has that disposition now.

A third characteristic offers a rationale for the presence of the second characteristic, a rationale which links the second characteristic with the first. The third characteristic is given in this principle:

(3) Only actual-world properties can explain the manifestations of dispositions.

It is also tempting for the friend of the categorical to give a rationale for this characteristic itself. The rationale is that, amongst the properties, only actual-world properties can be explanatory of events. This applies to the special case of those events which are manifestations of dispositions. The rationale might be further elaborated by the claims that explanations of events must be causal explanations, and that causally explanatory properties must be actual-world properties— only the actual can be causally productive, it might be said.

This last argument could be spelled out in more detail thus. Explanation of the manifestation of a disposition by citing some ground of the disposition is a causal explanation. Causal explanations require a relation of causation between the events in question, and causation is itself an actual-world relation. This can be regarded as one of the lessons of the objections to counterfactual analyses of causation, such as the objection from interrupted blocking.[44] Now when one event causes another in virtue of the object's having

---

[44] See e.g. the examples in Jonathan Schaffer, 'Trumping Preemption', Ned Hall, 'Causation and the Price of Transitivity', John Collins, 'Preemptive Prevention', and L. A. Paul, 'Aspect Causation', in the special issue on causation of the *Journal of Philosophy*, 97/4 (Apr. 2000).

a certain property—the striking causes the breaking of the vase in virtue of the vase's crystalline structure, say—it would be highly puzzling if the property in virtue of which the event causes the manifestation were not an actual-world property. If the causal relation held between these events in virtue of a property which is not an actual-world property, it seems that causation would not really be an actual-world relation after all. Here I assume that if P is an actual-world property or relation, and holds in some particular case in virtue of an object's having property Q, Q is also an actual-world property.

We can now return to the sceptical objection that categorical properties are really dispositional. The three characteristics suggest the following answers to the objection.

(a) Contrary to the objection, a predication of a categorical property never has a counterfactual or dispositional equivalent, unless the proposed equivalent contains, or presupposes something about, some categorical property. (It need not be the same categorical property, but some categorical property or other must be involved for equivalence to be attained.) This point in reply to the objection we can label the Ineliminability Claim, and it can be illustrated as follows. Any definition of distance in terms of measurement by unit rods works only if we add or presume that the rods do not change their length when moved. This addition or presumption involves a spatial, categorical notion, that of length. An attempted definition of distance in terms of the time taken to traverse it works only if either we use the notion of 'uniform velocity', which is again explained in terms of categorical notions, or else we use some condition about clocks, and these in turn must be assumed to be operating uniformly with respect to time. A characterization of the mass of an object in terms of counterfactuals about the force required to change its acceleration works only if the application of force does not cause the object's mass to alter, one way or another. In all these cases the counterfactuals achieve equivalence with the predication of the categorical property only if we assume some categorical property is held constant between the actual and the relevant counterfactual situations.

There is a recipe for drafting counter-examples to dispositional analyses of counterfactuals, and that there is so is no accident. The Ineliminability Claim is not an ad hoc reply. Rather, the Ineliminability

Claim follows from the first characteristic, that categorical properties are actual-world properties. If any categorical property is an actual-world property it follows that it cannot be defined in counterfactual terms.

(b) This ineliminability ought to be unsurprising on other grounds, too. In fact, it is the opposite which would be surprising. If categorical properties are involved in explanation, how could we expect counterfactuals not mentioning them to capture what is involved in having a categorical property, when the explanation of phenomena cannot be achieved without mentioning them? If categorical properties are involved in explanation (and are not just definitional apparatus), no counterfactuals not mentioning or presupposing counterfactuals can be expected to be a priori equivalent to a predication of a categorical.

(c) In some cases connections exist between the meaning of a term for a categorical magnitude and the measurement procedures for assigning that magnitude a particular value. Investigations in the theory of measurement have enormously increased our understanding of some of these connections.[45] Sometimes we have relational structures identified in the theory of measurement of a magnitude which give sufficient conditions for the magnitude to take a certain value. These connections, though, should not be thought to support a case for explanation of the categorical in terms of the dispositional. There are two reasons they offer no such support. First, in establishing representation theorems in the theory of measurement it is important that there be relations such as *x matches y in length* or *the Goodmanian sum of x and y balances z on a true balance* which do not themselves involve the assignment of numbers. However, to say that a relation does not involve the assignment of numbers is not to say that it is not categorical. I think all the relations used in these representation theorems are categorical. Counterfactual explications of them are sometimes offered, but it is obvious that these are only rough equivalents which serve the purpose only if it is assumed that fulfilment of the antecedent of the counterfactual does not alter the underlying property—that bringing the object to a balance does not alter its mass, and so forth. That is the first reason that these points in the theory of measurement do not support a dispositional analysis of categoricals.

---

[45] See especially D. Krantz, R. Luce et al., *Foundations of Measurement* (New York: Academic Press, 1971). In their informal discussions in this classic work these authors do not always sufficiently distinguish epistemic and metaphysical issues.

A second reason they do not support a dispositional analysis is that the connections which are brought out by the theory of measurement should in any case be construed as reference-fixing rather than as metaphysically necessary. If we try to marshal these systems of relations used in the theory of measurement into an account of what it is to have given length, the result is not a metaphysical necessity, but a contingency. What we obtain by such marshalling is, for instance, that the mass of an object x in grams is 17.4 iff the unique function f meeting certain conditions formulated in terms of the relational structure, and also mapping the standard gram in Paris to the number 1, is such that $f(x)$ is 17.4. This biconditional is not a necessity. Its right-hand side could hold if the standard gram in Paris had a greater mass, but that would not mean that our object x would in those circumstances weigh 17.4 grams. It is no accident that Kripke originally introduced the distinction between reference-fixing and sustaining necessities in connection with standard measures.[46] On the present view, he was right to do so.

Why then have so many philosophers thought that a notion of the categorical that is irreducible to the dispositional cannot have any application? One major reason involves the idea that the relation between properties and laws forces the rejection of the applicability of a notion of the categorical of the sort I have tried to characterize. There is a hint of the view in the quotation from Mellor above, but it is Blackburn who states the view with full generality:

Just as the molecular theory gives us only things with dispositions, so any conceivable improvement in science will give us only a better pattern of dispositions and powers. That's the way physics works.

Is it the way it has to work? I believe so. A quick route to this conclusion is to see the theoretical terms of a science as defined functionally in terms of their place in a network of laws.[47] A slower route is to reflect on what is needed from physical thinking. What is needed is the use of concepts—energy, temperature, entropy—that cover changes of state, permitting the formulation of conservation laws. Such concepts in effect tell us what is the same about a changing system, in terms precisely of its powers and dispositions.[48]

[46] S. Kripke, *Naming and Necessity* (Oxford: Blackwell, 1980), 54 ff.
[47] Here Blackburn cites D. Lewis's paper 'How to Define Theoretical Terms', repr. in his *Philosophical Papers*, i (New York: Oxford University Press, 1983).   [48] Blackburn, 'Filling in Space', 256.

I agree that many properties, both amongst those identified in folk physics and amongst those identified in more advanced scientific theories, are individuated in part by their relations to other properties, and that the individuating relations are given by the laws which relate the former properties to the latter. It seems to me that nothing in this tells against the applicability of the notion of the categorical. In the first place, the laws frequently relate one categorical property to other categorical properties and relations. This seems to me true of Newton's three laws. It is wholly consistent to maintain that some physical property is individuated in part or whole by its relations to other categorical properties, in ways given by the laws relating them, without commitment to a dispositional analysis of that property. There is no good argument from relational individuation of a property to a dispositional analysis of that property.

In the second place, recognition of the point that many properties are relationally individuated, via laws involving them, in no way obviates the need, which I emphasized earlier, for assumptions about the actual world in drawing any counterfactual conclusions from a true predication of a categorical property. Perhaps the point is most sharply formulated in terms of possible worlds. The relational individuation of a property P implies that in any world in which P is possessed by an object that object will also have certain other complexes of properties, as determined by the laws. The property P and that complex of properties are instantiated together, if at all. It does not follow that for an object to have P in the actual world is for certain conditions involving that complex to hold in worlds close to the actual world.

Some friends of categorical properties have also held that the fundamental explanatory categorical properties are intrinsic properties. We can call this the Intrinsicness Thesis. It would be wrong to think that the phenomenon of relational individuation of properties is incompatible with the Intrinsicness Thesis. Let us say that an *autonomous* property is a property that is not individuated by its relations to other properties. It is an interesting question whether there are any autonomous properties amongst properties of spatiotemporal events and objects. If a categorical property is relationally individuated it is, trivially, not autonomous. It does not follow that the property is not intrinsic. The intuitive idea of an intrinsic property is that of a property whose possession by an object does not depend, constitutively, on that object's particular relations to other individuals wholly distinct from itself. An intrinsic property is thus one with respect to which a pair of duplicates cannot differ.[49] It is consistent to hold that mass is a categorical and relationally individuated magnitude whilst also holding that the mass of an object is one of its intrinsic features. If someone does hold this combination he will, incidentally, also identify a third objection to taking the biconditionals delivered by the theory of measurement as constitutive accounts of physical magnitudes. If mass is, though relationally individuated, an intrinsic magnitude of an object, a constitutive account of its nature should not mention other objects, neither the standard gram in Paris, nor its comparative mass-relations to other objects. These are all merely contingently related to the magnitude itself. They have epistemic significance in an account of how we latch on to the magnitude, but are not essential to the magnitude itself.

Many categorical properties are, however, extrinsic. The property of an object of resting on another physical object is evidently extrinsic. It can also enter explanations—it explains why an object falls when its supporting object is removed. The defender of the Intrinsicness Thesis will be inclined to hold that any such explanation which mentions extrinsic properties can be expanded into one which mentions only intrinsic properties of the objects involved, and the lawful relations between them. I will, however, be emphasizing the explanatory power of categorical spatial and temporal relations, and it is highly problematic to try to apply the notion of intrinsicness to spatial and temporal relations. Perhaps one could attempt to introduce a notion of intrinsicness which applies to relations between objects as well as to monadic

---

[49] For some time it was accepted, following Jaegwon Kim, that an intrinsic property is one which could belong to an object even if that object were the only thing in the universe (J. Kim, 'Psychophysical Supervenience', *Philosophical Studies*, 41 (1982), 51–70). Rae Langton and David Lewis pointed out that this is not quite right, as it includes the property of being unaccompanied. They recommend that we say that 'P is *independent of accompaniment* iff four different cases are possible: something accompanied may have P or lack P, something unaccompanied may have P or lack P. P is *basic intrinsic* iff (1) P and not-P are non-disjunctive and contingent, and (2) P is independent of accompaniment' ('Defining "Intrinsic" ', *Philosophy and Phenomenological Research*, 58 (1998), 333–45, from the abstract at p. 333). The intuitive formulation involving constitutive dependence in the text above could be accepted without commitment to these possibilities of lone existence.

properties. This could no doubt be done, but it would still be highly problematic whether any natural resulting characterization would count spatial and temporal relations as intrinsic. There will always be a good case to be made that the temporal relations between two events depend on the relations between the times at which those events occur. A corresponding point applies to the spatial relations between objects and the locations of those objects. The categorical does not, in the general case, have to be fundamentally intrinsic.

Another concern driving those sceptical about the categorical has been the worry that the friends of the categorical will make categorical properties unknowable. If we know categorical properties only by their dispositions and their powers, and yet categorical properties are distinct from those dispositions and powers, how can we ever know the nature of those categorical properties in themselves? The friend of the categorical should reject the antecedent of this conditional. We have already noted, at the end of the preceding section, that the acquisition of perceptual knowledge that an object has a categorical property should not be regarded merely as knowledge that the object has a disposition to produce certain experiences. In perceiving the shape of an object or the duration of an event, a person is perceiving the object or event to have certain categorical properties. It seems to me absurd to say that we know about shape or duration only by their effects, and do not know what they are in themselves. There may be more to learn scientifically about both; but we do not know them merely by their effects. To know of something only by its effects is precisely not to know it in the way in which, in perception, we know of spatial and temporal properties.

These are not all the arguments which have been mounted by sceptics about the categorical.[50] I conjecture, though, that the conception outlined in these points contains the resources for addressing those other arguments. Now we can return to our question about the role of evidence in understanding and ask this question. What would be experiential evidence, or any other kind of evidence, that this same property (as one now perceives) is instantiated at other places and times?

What would constitute such evidence is very much an empirical matter. It is the notion of a categorical property that forms the

---

[50] Blackburn in particular mounts several other arguments in 'Filling in Space'.

constitutive bridge between the perceived and unperceived cases. What *makes* something, in the context of other information, evidence that some property picked out by an observational concept is instantiated unperceived by the thinker? I suggest that what makes it so is that it is evidence that the same categorical property as is perceived to be instantiated in the perceived cases is instantiated also in the cases in which the thinker does not perceive the object in question.[51] I contend that this condition, formulated in terms of sameness of property and the metaphysics of the categorical, cannot be framed in terms of a purely evidential theory of meaning—or not in any way that is not parasitic on non-evidential matters.

Perhaps it may be said that this problem would not arise if an evidential theory of meaning were cast in terms of propositions about the objective perceptible world itself, instead of experience. Fair enough. But grasping such evidential conditions would itself then already involve some tacit appreciation of properties as categorical. For such a variant of evidentialism problem (i) above, of the informativeness of evidential relations, would also rearise yet again in the case of the relation between such evidence and theoretical notions. When a theorist has the idea that some particles' orbits are arranged in such-and-such shapes, what would be evidence for this again has to be worked out empirically. The understanding of the hypothesis involves a notion of shape as a categorical property.

1.5 How to Avoid the Problems

Taken collectively, the informativeness of evidential relations, the need for a finite source for evidential relations, and the role of the categorical in our appreciation of evidential relations pose insuperable obstacles for purely evidential conceptions of meaning and content. The point is further grist to the mill of those who, like Donald Davidson, want to free the theory of meaning and understanding of any scheme–content distinction.[52] All the preceding considerations

---

[51] This is why the verification-transcendent instantiations are not 'free standing', as Hilary Putnam rightly insists they cannot be (see his *Pragmatism* (Oxford: Blackwell, 1995), 12).

[52] 'On the Very Idea of a Conceptual Scheme', repr. in his *Inquiries into Truth and Interpretation* 2nd edn., (Oxford: Oxford University Press, 2001).

tell against the idea that meaning or intentional content is just a way of organizing experience or evidence.

Truth-conditional conceptions of content, by contrast, have the resources to solve all three of the problems faced by evidential theories of meaning. On a truth-conditional conception the phenomenon of the informativeness of evidential relations is explicable. It is the truth-conditions that can be grasped in advance of working out what can be evidence for a content. A thinker draws on his grasp of those truth-conditions in working out, in the context of additional information, what would be evidence for the truth of a particular content. The treatment I endorsed above of the meaning of observational statements may be seen as an elaboration of a truth-conditional treatment thereof, with the implicit grasp of the notion of the categorical contributing to the substantive account of what is involved in grasping truth-conditions of observational statements. The very statement of the problem of the insufficiency and parasitism of evidential relations was stated using a truth-conditional conception of the content grasped. As always, it is a task for the truth-conditional theorist to provide substantive theories of grasp or understanding that elaborate the nature of a thinker's appreciation of the truth-conditions of a given kind of content. The truth-conditional approach provides a framework and the possibility of solving the problems besetting purely evidential approaches; but for the possibility to be realized substantive theories of understanding must be developed in tandem with the truth-conditional conception.

The truth-conditional approach also provides a finite source for grasp of evidential conditions. The truth-conditions of sentences and of intentional contents are compositionally determined. The truth-conditions of a complex sentence or content are fixed by the mode of combination of its constituent expressions or concepts, together with the identity of the concepts so combined. The finite basis for grasp of the truth-conditions of whole sentences can then serve to provide, in the presence of additional empirical information, a finitely based source of evidential relations for any given content.

Quine's evidential conception of meaning and his radical holism was forged in reaction against Carnap's conception of meaning and its attendant account of the source of experience-independent justification. Though I have been disagreeing with Quine on some counts, the alternative I am in the course of developing is emphatically not a variant of a Carnapian approach. The alternative I propose is, I will later argue, rather an elaboration and generalization of the classical rationalist tradition present in different forms in Leibniz, Frege, and some parts of Gödel. This generalized rationalism diverges from Carnap on many issues. It diverges on the matter, already mentioned, of whether the notion of truth-purely-in-virtue-of-meaning has any application. It also diverges on the question of whether there are conventionalist elements in the acceptance of a priori principles, and on whether there is a substantial form of relativity to a language or to a framework in the acceptance of a priori principles. The conception of entitlement I am developing is not fundamentally conventionalist; nor will it involve any language-relativity.

CHAPTER 2

States, Contents, and the Source of Entitlement

2.1 The Second Principle of Rationalism

The next Principle I want to articulate is distinctively rationalist.

PRINCIPLE II: The Rationalist Dependence Thesis
The rational truth-conduciveness of any given transition to which a thinker is entitled is to be philosophically explained in terms of the nature of the intentional contents and states involved in the transition.

This principle, in speaking of any transition to which a thinker is entitled, goes vastly beyond what was discussed by the classical rationalists, whose concern was usually with the outright a priori. But I want to consider first what the classical rationalists held about transitions to which we are entitled independently of the content or kind of perceptual experience, and then to consider whether some generalization is possible, once we appreciate the conception they were expressing.

The claim that there is a dependence of the rationality of accepting certain principles upon the identity of the concepts they contain, and thereby a connection with understanding, is present in progressively more explicit forms in Leibniz, Frege, and Gödel. It is important to characterize the nature of the rationalist conception correctly. It is quite insufficient to say that a rationalist view is one that holds that there are a priori principles and holds that this a priori status is founded in the nature of the concepts in the principles and is available to anyone who possesses those concepts, or properly understands the expressions in the principles. As Quassim Cassam notes, conventionalists such as Carnap in 1937 and the Ayer of *Language, Truth and*

Logic (1946) meet that description.[1] Consider a conventionalist who holds this combination of views: any (consistent) set of principles determines a concept; to possess the concept is to know those principles for the concept; and the experience-independent truth of those principles involves no more than their conventional acceptance of those principles. A conventionalist holding this combination acknowledges the a priori status of certain principles, and also founds this status in concept-identity, and connects knowledge of the principles with understanding. But this is quite outside the letter and spirit of the position of several major rationalists, and outside the position I am in the course of developing.[2]

Part of what distinguishes a rationalist position as I shall develop it is not merely its acknowledgement of a priori principles, together with some link between that phenomenon on the one hand and concepts and understanding on the other. The present rationalism holds further that what it is for one of these principles to be true is not to be explained in conventionalist terms, but involves the application of a uniform notion of truth applicable to arbitrary contents. Understanding in turn consists in grasp of truth-conditions, given by applying this uniform notion of truth. A rationalist holds too that these principles are knowable through the use of reason.

Historically, rationalists have differed considerably on the question of how knowledge is attained through the use of reason. Leibniz emphasized that some principles to which we are entitled independently of the detailed content of perceptual experience are accessible by the use of reason. It would be anachronistic to attribute a systematic referential semantics to Leibniz. Nonetheless, it is clear that according to him in a huge range of cases the correctness of outright a priori principles can be traced back either to the law of identity or else to what we now call Leibniz's Law.[3] The principle that A = A and Leibniz's Law itself are principles which are implausible candidates for

---

[1] Q. Cassam 'Rationalism, Empiricism and the A Priori', in Boghossian and Peacocke (eds.) *New Essays on the A Priori;* R. Carnap, *The Logical Syntax of Language,* trans. A. Smeaton (New York: Harcourt Brace, 1937); A. Ayer, *Language, Truth and Logic,* 2nd edn., (London: Gollancz, 1946).

[2] For related points on inadequate characterizations of the opposition between rationalism and empiricism see Cassam's 'Rationalism, Empiricism and the A Priori'.

[3] See amongst many other passages Leibniz, *New Essays on Human Understanding,* trans. J. Bennett and P. Remnant (Cambridge: Cambridge University Press, 1981), bk. IV, 'Of Knowledge', esp. ch. 7, 'Of Maxims or Axioms'. On his own use of Leibniz's Law, see for instance pp. 413–14 of this same chapter.

a conventionalist treatment. To the best of my knowledge, Leibniz never suggested a conventionalist treatment of these basic laws.

Frege's treatment of the laws of his formal system in *Grundgesetze* is equally squarely rationalist in the sense I have been emphasizing. He aimed to give a justification of each of the laws of his logical system. The justifications he offered for the laws rely on principles about the reference of the expressions they contain. Consider Frege's Law I, which is (A ⊃ (B ⊃ A)) in modern notation. The statement of this law in Frege's text at §18 is immediately preceded by the German word *also*, meaning 'therefore'. What precedes the *also* is an argument from the truth-functional semantics for the conditional that Frege had given earlier, in §12, to the impossibility of this law ever having the truth-value 'false' (or denoting it, in the theory of that book).[4] Though Frege's philosophical writings in places endorse what certainly looks like a redundancy theory of truth, his actual practice in the *Grundgesetze*, which was meant to be an implementation of the project of tracing the laws of arithmetic back to their 'ultimate justification', gives a theory of reference and truth a much more substantial role.

In the case of Gödel, no one who has read his philosophical writings, and in particular the several versions of the explicitly anti-Carnapian 'Is Mathematics Syntax of Language?', could be left in any doubt as to his opposition to any form of conventionalist treatment of logic and mathematics.[5] Gödel's view was that any set of conventions must be consistent. Consistency itself is not a conventional matter, and to establish it involves citing substantive, mathematical propositions that are not merely counted as true by convention. As he summarizes his view: 'the syntactical [Carnapian] interpretation of mathematics does not relieve one of the necessity to acknowledge certain, by no means trivial, propositions of a mathematical character as true in a non-conventional sense'.[6] Gödel repeatedly wrote of the need for rational foundations for axioms that give one reasons to believe that they are true.[7] A modern rationalism can accept all this without endorsing Gödel's obscure quasi-perceptual and quasi-causal epistemology of mathematics and the abstract sciences. The ideas of

    [4] G. Frege, *Grundgesetze der Arithmetik* (Hildesheim: Olms, 1998) sect. 18, p. 34.
    [5] K. Gödel *Collected Works*, III, ed. S. Feferman, J. Dawson, jun., et al. (New York: Oxford University Press, 1995).   [6] Ibid. 358.
    [7] Ibid. 346–7.

understanding as consisting in some kind of appreciation of substantial truth-conditions and of a priori knowledge being explained by this understanding do not require the quasi-causal epistemology. They are better off without it. It is worth recalling that Gödel believed that 'mathematical propositions, as opposed to empirical ones, are true in virtue of the *concepts* occurring in them', something which already suggests resources for a non-causal a priori epistemology of the abstract sciences.

As against the account of the core of rationalism that I have been giving, Robert Brandom presents an opposition between empiricism on the one hand and a rationalism that develops an account of intentional content that is not subject to substantive constraints involving the notions of truth and reference on the other. He quotes Sellars's expression of a view that occurred early on to Sellars: 'What was needed was a functional theory of concepts which would make their role in reasoning, rather than supposed origin in experience, their primary feature'. Brandom continues: 'Put this way, the idea forms one of the mainstays of classical rationalism.'[8] Whilst I wholly agree that a certain role in reasoning is essential to the identity of a concept on rationalist views, and that that is an important insight of Brandom's, it does not follow that constraints involving reference and truth play no role in the individuation of concepts. I will make a few observations on Brandom's position, partly because that position is of interest in itself, and partly to sharpen the articulation of my own, different stance.

(a) Acknowledging constraints at the level of semantic value on the existence of genuine concepts need not involve any reversion to some general empiricism. Consider those logical concepts that are plausibly individuated by grasp of primitive introduction and elimination rules for them, such as conjunction. The fact that these rules determine a concept only if they fix a semantic value (a truth-function, in this case) for the constant they aim to define does not imply any empiricist account of either mastery of the logical concept in question or of the rationality of accepting the primitive introduction and elimination rules for the constant.

(b) Suppose we endorse a theory under which the existence of a concept is constrained by the principle that its possession-condition

----

[8] Both passages are from *Making It Explicit*, 93.

must, together with the world, determine a condition for something to be the semantic value of the concept. The theory of *A Study of Concepts* is such a theory. So too is the relaxation proposed by the recognition of implicit conceptions.[9] We can call such theories 'referentially constrained'. A referentially constrained theory can, and in my view should, accept the principle that if the concepts *C* and *D* have exactly the same role in the formation of judgements then *C* and *D* are one and the same concept. If concepts are individuated by their possession-conditions, as in *A Study of Concepts*, concepts with the same role in the formation of judgements will be identical. Referentially constrained theories are not merely consistent with acknowledgement of this fact. In my view, proper referentially constrained theories should be enthusiastic about it. A concept is individuated by its role in the formation of certain judgements, which aim at truth. Only what is relevant at the personal level to this referentially formulated aim is relevant to the identity of the concept.

I would argue this even for the representational content of perception. An experience has, for instance, a certain scenario content only if experiences with such contents contribute to the construction of the experiencer's conception of the layout of the spatial world around him. That is, they play a certain role in spatial reasoning and thought, broadly conceived. This condition can be met even by nonconceptual representational content.

Where Brandom sees a contrast between conceptual-role theories that do not make essential use of referential notions, and theories that rely on the notions of representation and truth, I see an entirely understandable intertwining of the ideas of individuation of concepts by their role in the formation of judgements and the presence of referential constraints on the existence of a genuine concept. Consider the Rationalist Dependence Thesis, Principle II of rationalism, as formulated at the start of this chapter. How is it verified by an inferential transition in thought involving, say, the rule of conjunction-elimination? In accordance with this second principle of rationalism, it is in the nature of possession of the concept of conjunction that someone is willing to make in thought transitions of the form of

---

[9] C. Peacocke, 'Implicit Conceptions, Understanding and Rationality', *Philosophical Issues*, 9, on 'concepts' ed. E. Villaneuva (1998), 43–88.

conjunction-elimination. Such transitions fulfil the aim of judging only what is true precisely because there is something which is the semantic value for which such transitions are guaranteed to be truth-preserving. If they were not truth-preserving, they would not contribute to a constitutive aim of judgement. They could not be truth-preserving if each component of the constituent intentional contents involved in the inference did not make a contribution to the truth-value of the intentional content in which it occurs. The transition would also not be one to which the thinker has the kind of entitlement he does to a primitive logical principle unless its truth-preserving character were guaranteed by the semantic value assigned to the logical constants involved.

Under the present rationalist conception all of the following inextricably involve one another: the possession-condition for a concept; the determination (together with the world) of a semantic value by that possession-condition; and the fact that truth is a constitutive aim of judgement. We could not excise reference and truth from this form of rationalist conception and be left with an intelligible aim for judgement and an intelligibly motivated conception of intentional content. Nor is it required in this account that truth and reference be antecedently available, if this means that we should be able to say what makes something have a given reference or a given truth-condition entirely independently of considerations at the level of sense. What makes something the reference of a concept has to be explained in terms of the possession-condition for that concept.

Reference and truth play no equally overarching, constraining role under Brandom's rival delineation of a rationalist view. I myself think Brandom is consistent, given his conception, to write of 'norm-instituting attitudes', and to endorse an inferentialist view which he describes as starting 'with inferences that are correct in the sense that they are accepted in the practice of a community'.[10] By contrast, on the exposition of a rationalist conception I am suggesting, within the realm of intentional content and judgement, attitudes and community practices cannot be norm-instituting by themselves. The norms, which are real, must be founded in constraints that

---

[10] *Making It Explicit*, 134, 137.

involve truth and reference. Their correctness is founded in a priori matters that have nothing to do with community practices.

In my judgement, the most basic rationalizing state, that of perceptual experience, already involves reference to objects, properties, and relations. The condition for correctness of a perception as of the phone being on the desk is that a certain object, the phone, stand in a certain relation to a second object, the desk. The ability to refer to material objects in demonstrative and recognitional thought is consitutively dependent upon the reference in perceptual states themselves to individual objects, to properties, and to relations. To attempt to explain such reference in perceptual states by community practices seems to me to reverse the correct order of philosophical explanation. It also makes it extremely difficult to give a plausible account of non-linguistic animal thought and reference.

The classical rationalists Leibniz, Frege, and Gödel were primarily concerned with contents that are outright a priori, and with ways of coming to know those contents. The generalization effected by the Rationalist Dependence Thesis (Principle II) moves from the rationalists' treatment of outright a priori contents to a corresponding conception of all transitions to which a thinker is entitled. The generalization is motivated by the idea that the grounding of the rational truth-conduciveness of a transition in the nature of the intentional contents and states involved in the transition is not something restricted to transitions to outright a priori contents, but rather applies quite generally.

Rational transitions to which Principle II applies include the following: from perceptual experiences to judgements about the material world around the thinker; from perceptual experiences to judgements about the actions and mental states of others; from the thinker's own subjective conscious states to self-ascriptions of those states; from memories about oneself and the world to judgements about oneself and the world in the past tense—amongst many others. These are not in general inferential transitions. As rational transitions which the thinker is entitled to make, the rationalist who accepts Principle II is committed to the existence of an explanation of this rationality in terms of the identity of the states and intentional contents involved in the transition. A full defence of the second principle of rationalism would evidently be a vast task. If the

Principle is correct a convincing case for its correctness in any one of these areas would itself be a major task, as well as being a contribution to philosophical understanding of thought about that area.

It is possible to divide parts of the task into broad segments. In some kinds of case the transition to which the thinker is entitled starts from a conscious mental state with a representational content. That is, it is in the nature of the state that it seems to one who is in that state that the world is a certain way. The state represents the world as being that way, and judgement may endorse or reject the content so represented. In these cases the judgement made rational by the occurrence of the state endorses part of the representational content of the conscious mental state. Some cases of entitlement to take perceptual experience or memory at face value fall under this general kind. It will be helpful to have a label for this kind, and I will call them *content-endorsing transitions*.

For the content-endorsing transitions involved in perceptual judgements, the task for the rationalist who supports Principle II is twofold. There is the content of the perceptual entitling state; and there is the content of the perceptual judgement based upon it. The first task is to show why the content of the perceptual entitling state will tend to be true. In accordance with Principle II, this explanation must draw on the nature of the intentional states and contents involved in the transition. The second task is to show why the transition to the judgement of the content made rational by the entitling perceptual state is truth-conducive when the entitling state has a correct content. Again, the explanation must draw on the nature of the states and intentional contents.

For some theorists these two tasks will collapse into one single task. John McDowell, for instance, holds that perceptual content is always conceptual content.[11] For such a conceptualist, in taking a perceptual experience at face value a person is endorsing in judgement the very content which the experience represents as correct. So the second task just distinguished is already incorporated into the first task.

[11] *Mind and World* (Cambridge, Mass.: Harvard University Press, 1994), esp. 'Lecture III' and 'Afterword Part II', also his 'Reply to Commentators', in *Philosophy and Phenomenological Research*, 58 (1998), 403–31, esp. 414–19.

For those who hold that at least some of the representational content of perception is non-conceptual the second task is a substantive one. Carrying out the task will involve appeal to the relations between non-conceptual contents and the conceptual contents of judgements that perceptions with those non-conceptual contents make rational. Suppose, for instance, the non-conceptual content of an experience as of something square is specified by contents concerning the right angles of some closed four-sided figure and the symmetry of that figure about the bisectors of its opposite sides. The holding of these contents is a priori sufficient for something to fall under the concept *square*, and is so as a matter of the possession-condition for the concept *square*. Such is the sort of argument one would develop in carrying out the second task.[12]

The greatest challenge, however, is carrying out the first task. To be clear on the nature of the task we have to distinguish three levels at which we can characterize the relation of entitlement. We need at this point to step back from the special case of content-endorsing transitions to consider entitlement in general, since these distinctions of level apply to entitlement without restriction. We will return to consider content-endorsing transitions to perceptual judgements after considering these levels more generally.

2.2 Entitlement: The Three Levels

The three levels at which we may characterize the entitlement relation are levels which we can distinguish for any property or relation. For any property or relation there is an increase in generality and explanatory power as one proceeds through these three levels of characterization.

Level (1). The first of the three levels I distinguish is simply the level of instances or examples of the entitlement relation. So characterizations at this level comprise true statements of the form 'a thinker in such-and-such circumstances with so-and-so background information is entitled to judge that *p*'. These examples involve a specification of types of circumstances in which an entitlement

---

[12] See my *A Study of Concepts*, ch. 3 at pp. 79–80, and the remarks on this enterprise in my 'Does Perception have a Nonconceptual Content?', *Journal of Philosophy*, 98 (2001), 239–64.

exists. The types may concern the thinker's environment, his other conscious states characterized in terms of content, and his general capacities. If a thinker is entitled to make the judgement, of a seen object, that it is curved, when he visually experiences it as curved, and when there is no reason for doubting his senses, then that would be a statement included at this first level of instances. So would statements about the entitlement to rely on apparent personal memory in making judgements about one's own past.

It is an important matter what we take to be the entitling state. We cannot take it to be something of the kind *perceiving that p*, since that state implies that its subject already believes (indeed arguably knows) that *p*. A transition with something of this kind as the specified entitling state would be vacuous as a means of rationally reaching new beliefs. It could be employed only if it were redundant. But there are kinds of perceptual states with the content that *p* that are factive (imply the truth of *p*) without implying that the subject already believes that *p*. One of these is the state *perceives x to be F*, or *perceives x and y to stand in relation R*. One can perceive the room to be square without believing it is square (one may falsely believe that one is subject to a perceptual illusion). Such a factive perceptual state can be the entitling state for a perceptual judgement without vacuity ensuing.

An alternative approach would be to take as the entitling states perceptual experiences whose contents can be false, such as *having an experience as of x being F*, or even *having an experience as of there being something in front of one that is F*.

Perceptual entitlement is often said to be defeasible. One's entitlement to judge, on the basis of an apparently perceptual state, that *p* can be defeated in the presence of further information, such as that one is in a room with strange lighting conditions, or that one is, unbeknownst, a participant in an experiment in the psychology of perception. Back in Chapter 1 Section 3 we distinguished between defeasibility of grounds and defeasibility of identification. To reactivate our memory traces: When something one thought to be a mathematical proof turns out not to be so one's identification of the object as a proof is defeated. What is in question in such cases is the correctness of the identification of something as a certain kind of ground. If something really is not a proof, it is not a proof all along, whatever we think about it. By contrast, in what I called 'defeasibility of grounds', defeating conditions show that the grounds one has are not strong enough.

Which kind of defeasibility one regards perceptual entitlement as possessing varies with whether one takes the entitling state to be factive or not. When the entitling state is factive the defeasibility of perceptual entitlement can consist only in defeasibility of identification, not defeasibility of grounds. If someone really does perceive x to be F, then it will be true that x is F. What can be defeated is only one's identification of one's own state as a perceiving x to be F. When the entitling state is not factive we have genuine defeasibility of grounds: an experience as of its being the case that p may be shown, in the light of further information, to coexist with its not being the case that p, or to be in the context entirely sufficient to make it rational to accept that p.

Much later in this work I will be arguing that there are good reasons for taking the entitlement as formulated using factive perceptual states to be more fundamental than those formulated using non-factive states of perceptual experience. For the moment we can remain neutral on the issue. Both the factive and the non-factive states seem, in the case of a range of representational contents that p, to give prima facie reason for judging that p, in the absence of corresponding defeating conditions.

Level (2). The second level is the level of generalizations about the entitlement relation. This level consists of true generalizations which, in the presence of additional information determined by the generalizations, have, or jointly entail, statements at level (1) as instances.

It may be helpful to think of the relation of this level to others as the same as that exhibited by tacitly known grammatical generalizations to other levels in the theory of grammars. In his 1965 theory Chomsky wrote that a grammar 'is *descriptively adequate* to the extent that it correctly describes the intrinsic competence of the idealized native speaker'.[13] In the same spirit as Chomsky's use of the term, we could call this second level 'the level of descriptive generalization'. A descriptively adequate grammar for a language will have theorems

---

[13] *Aspects of the Theory of Syntax* (Cambridge, Mass: MIT Press, 1965), 24. Competence *chez* Chomsky is of course already an explanatory notion. We can distinguish those grammatical generalizations that are psychologically real from those that are not.

specifying instances of the property of grammaticality for the language.

We equally operate at this second level of characterization when in developing a logic for some particular expression in natural language we move from particular valid transitions containing the expression but not containing schematic letters to the stage of formulating general schemata that are valid. That is a move to a level of descriptive adequacy. As in the other cases it can be an important step towards theoretical understandings. It is, for example, illuminating, and a step towards an explanatory theory, to note that though transitivity does not hold for the counterfactual conditional the schema 'If A were the case, then B would be the case; if A and B were the case, then C would be the case; so if A were the case, C would be the case' is generally valid.[14]

Level-(2) generalizations in the case of logic do not have to involve any reduction of normative notions to non-normative notions. Recognizing the existence of Level (2) does not involve any commitment to a reductionism, either in the logic case or elsewhere. On the contrary, a generalization to the effect that all instances of a certain schema are valid simply uses the notion of validity. It is entirely neutral on the question of its reducibility to anything else.

In the logic case, as in the grammar case, people are capable of making all sorts of mistakes about which are the correct generalizations at this second level. Vann McGee has argued that *modus ponens*, often taken by many philosophers as an example of an obviously valid rule, fails when the consequent of the conditional is itself a conditional.[15] It is one thing to make judgements for reasons which are entitling, in a variety of conditions. It is another to be able to articulate correctly generalizations about the conditions under which one is entitled to make judgements of a given kind. This is simply the application to the notion of an entitled transition of a point long recognized about the possible inability of those who correctly use the concept *chair* to offer a correct definition of the concept (even

---

[14] R. Stalnaker, 'A Theory of Conditionals', in N. Rescher (ed.), *Studies in Logical Theory* (Oxford: Blackwell, 1968); D. Lewis, *Counterfactuals* (Oxford: Blackwell, 1973), esp. 32–5.

[15] McGee's example: For someone speaking in 1980 of the then upcoming election in the United States utterances of the premisses 'If a Republican wins, then if Reagan doesn't win, Anderson will win' and 'A Republican will win' are true, but an utterance of 'If Reagan doesn't win, Anderson will win' is false (see Vann McGee, 'A Counterexample to Modus Ponens', *Journal of Philosophy*, 82 (1985), 462–71).

when there is one). Having a classificatory ability is one thing; it is another to be able to collect together correctly in thought in a non-trivial fashion some of the conditions under which the classification applies. What we need to be responsive to good reasons is an ability to respond to entitling conditions with appropriate judgements. Making correct generalizations about entitling conditions is a further ability, not implied by the former capacity.

The generalizations about the relation of entitlement at this second level may be more or less extensive, and correspondingly more or less illuminating. The generalizations may use theoretical notions in classifying circumstances, contents, and capacities. It is information about the extension of these classifying notions that one will need if one is to use the generalizations to derive truths at level (1) about instances of the entitlement relation.

Level (3). The third level is the level of explanation. This third level consists of explanations of the relevant true generalizations at level (2). If certain theoretical notions seem to be involved in capturing the correct generalizations at that second level, then one of the tasks at this third level is also to explain why they do so. In linguistic theory Chomsky distinguished a level of explanatory adequacy, that of univeral grammar, a level of theory at which one aims to explain why the child selects a particular descriptively adequate grammar.[16] Explanations at that level would be empirical explanations of acquisition in the linguistic case.

In the case of the development of a logic formulations of explanations at this third level would involve the development of a semantical theory that explains the patterns of validity and invalidity captured in the generalizations about schemata at the second level.

As these examples show, explanations at this third level may be either empirical or a priori, according to the nature of the explananda in the given case. In the case of the explanatory level for the entitlement relation we are concerned with philosophical explanations. In contrast at least with the linguistic case, the task of characterizing this third level for the relation of entitlement is that of explaining timeless generalizations rather than historical (extended) events of acquisition of a grammar. In the particular case of explaining the entitlements

---

[16] *Aspects*, 25–7.

provided by perception and memory the task is to explain the true generalizations about defeasible entitlement, and to say why those generalizations (and nothing weaker or stronger) capture the extension of the entitlement relation.

The development of a third-level characterization of the entitlement relation further divides into two parts. First, one must specify (with arguments) some very general property which is required for an arbitrary transition to be one to which the thinker is entitled. Earlier we specified truth-conduciveness under this heading; but one would equally need to make a specification of this first part under other approaches. This first part can be called *goal-specifying*. The second part of a characterization at this third level is then showing that, and showing why, generalizations about the entitlement relation at the second level have the general property specified in the first part. This second part can be described as *proof of fulfilment of the goal*. One would similarly distinguish these two parts in a level-three characterization of a logic. One would first specify a semantic property that a valid inference must possess; one would then show, in a semantic theory, why the general principles identified as intuitively valid at the second level have this property, and why the invalid ones lack it.

2.3 The Second Level for Perceptual Entitlement

How would we describe these three levels in more detail for the case of perceptual entitlement? At the level of examples I wrote, like James Pryor, of an entitlement to take the perceptual content of experience at face value, in the absence of reasons for doubting it.[17] For a wide range of perceptual contents there is such an entitlement. It exists for many spatial contents, temporal contents, contents relating to surface texture, colour, and illumination, and a range of material properties.

There are, however, also cases where it is much less plausible that perceptual experience alone can supply the entitlement. Consider furniture that looks Swedish; appliances that look like Mac computers; or the properties of looking sad or looking delighted. Are we entitled,

---

[17] J. Pryor, 'The Skeptic and the Dogmatist', *Noûs* 34/4 (2000), 517–49, at 536 ff. This position is in the same spirit for entitlement in perception as Burge's on the entitlement to accept the utterances of interlocutors (see Burge, 'Content Preservation').

in the absence of reasons for doubt, to judge on the basis of such experiences that some furniture we see is Swedish, that some presented object is a Mac computer; or that someone is sad or delighted? In some of these cases one can follow a strategy of divide and rule. One can explain the apparently perceptual phenomenon thus. There is some kind such that the thing or person appears to be of that kind, and the person judges that things of that kind are (say) Swedish people; or Mac computers. The perceptual entitlement holds only for the kind which is given in the content of perception, as opposed to the content of the judgement. But such a division is not plausibly available in all cases. It does not, for example, fit the case of perception of the expression of an emotion. To describe when seeing the face of a person the experience in which they look sad in non-emotional terms is not to capture its distinctive representational content. There is no kind described without reference to the emotions of which one can say that the facial expression appears to be of that kind and it is merely an additional judgement on the part of the person that people looking that way are sad.

It is tempting to say that the purely perceptual entitlement holds only for observational concepts. That may well be true; but it is hardly an illuminating generalization at Level (2), unless we have some independent account of observationality. We are in danger of moving in a circle, for it is only too plausible to say that observational concepts are those that can be applied with entitlement simply on the basis of perceptual experience, and without further information. Unless we have some characterization of observational concepts distinct from that, then to say that the perceptual entitlement holds only for observational concepts will become the vacuous claim that it holds for those contents for which it holds.

I will suggest later on that one by-product of a proper characterization of Level (2) for perceptual entitlement is a starting point for characterizing the relevant notion of observationality without circularity. Suppose we can formulate a sufficiently wide-reaching true generalized conditional about the conditions under which perceptual entitlement holds. It will have the form 'If such-and-such conditions hold for the content p and for the thinker's circumstances then the thinker is entitled to take the content p of his perceptual experience at face value'. One way to characterize the non-observational will be as contents not meeting the antecedent of that conditional.[18]

The task of formulating such a generalization about perceptual entitlement lies at the second of the three levels. So I aim to characterize, without using the notion of an observational concept, a relation which holds between a perceptual experience and a particular content p which it represents as being the case, a relation with the following property: The holding of that relation is sufficient for a subject who enjoys the experience to have a perceptual entitlement to judge that p, in the absence of reasons for doubt. Various other perceptual entitlements, I will later argue, have their status as such in virtue of the relations in which they stand to this sufficient condition.

In some cases, and to a first approximation, what is constitutive of an experience's having a certain representational content is that when the thinker's perceptual apparatus is functioning properly, in a normal environment, experiences with that content are caused by the holding of the condition which is in fact the correctness condition for that content. This is plausible for the spatial representational contents of perception: the representational contents concerning such matters as distance, direction, shape, and size. In *Being Known* I argued that the same is true for the temporal contents of perception.[19] When all is working properly, in a normal environment, and in the most fundamental cases, a subject's perception of temporal order and magnitude is caused by instances of those order-relations and temporal magnitudes. (The perception of temporal magnitudes, like the perception of spatial magnitudes, is commonly unit-free.)

Suppose we agree that it is constitutive of a particular kind of experience's having a spatial or temporal content that such experiences have certain causes in specified conditions. It does not follow that it is constitutive of that content that it feature in experiences of that kind in any perceiver capable of having states with that content. Experience of different kinds, in more than one sense modality, may have the same spatial representational content. A given subject may

---

[18] Pryor uses the notion of propositions which our experiences 'basically represent': these are propositions we seem to perceive to be so, but not in virtue of seeming to perceive other propositions to be so (p. 539). This will give a wider class of entitling states than results from application of the criterion of observationality outlined below.   [19] *Being Known*, ch. 3.

be capable of having experiences in only one of those modalities. Furthermore, the given content may also feature in proprioception. The feeling of moving one's arm in a straight line may involve the same content *straight line* as also features in visual or tactile experience. The spatial content *straight line* can also feature in the non-proprioceptive awareness of acting that can be present even when one's limbs are anesthetized. Indeed, the very fact that perceptual experiences with these contents are individuated in part by facts about their causes in certain circumstances opens up the possibility of the occurrence of such contents in other conscious states, both in perception and in action. The cause that is involved in the individuation may cause other experiences too. Equally, the state of affairs that is the cause may be mentioned in constitutive accounts in which it features as an effect, as in the non-proprioceptive awareness of action. In short, we must be careful not to overstate the constitutive principle which links the individuation of some perceptual contents with the holding of those contents in the perceiver's environment.

What is true, however, is that the spatial and temporal contents of experience are in a certain sense *constitutively basic* with respect to these experiences. That is, these experiences do not have these elements of their content in virtue of the experiences' having certain other relations to other states with the same contents. One can contrast this with contents of perceptual experience which seem to use such concepts as *soldier* or *judge*, as when one says that it looks as if there is a soldier guarding the building, or a judge speaking from the bench in a courtroom. Such experiences, if that is their literal content, have those contents by virtue of their having contents which also feature in the ability to come to believe that someone is a soldier or a judge; and these capacities in turn have to do with some knowledge, perhaps rudimentary, of what it is to be a soldier or a judge. Unlike the case of contents concerning the properties of being a soldier, or of being a judge, perceptual experience can provide a thinker's fundamental fix on spatial and temporal properties and relations.

The experiences of which I am writing are sometimes called externally or anti-individualistically individuated. For present purposes this is not an ideal label. For the essential characteristics of the phenomenon are present in, for instance, proprioception of limb position, and the disposition of one's own body in space. One has an awareness that represents one's limbs and body as being a certain way spatially. It is highly plausible that what gives this awareness the content it has is that, when all is functioning properly, an awareness as of one's arm being straight is caused by one's arm being straight. This is not a relation between conditions external to the perceiver's body and the perceiver's own mental states. So I prefer to speak of perceptions which are *instance-individuated* with respect to certain of their contents. What makes these perceptions have the content they do is the fact that when the subject is properly related to the world the holding of these contents causally explains such perceptual experiences of their holding.

One intuitive mark of the content of an experience being instance-individuated is that when a thinker takes it at face value and the resulting judgement is false one or other (or both) of two alternatives holds. Either the environment is abnormal—the light rays are bending, for instance—or else there is some error in the subject's specifically perceptual mechanisms and computations. This applies to false perceptually based judgements of basic shape, distance, direction, and spatial and temporal order and magnitudes. No such alternation follows for experiential contents that are not instance-individuated. An apparatus in a laboratory may look to a subject like a cathode-ray tube and not in fact be so even though the environment is quite normal and the subject's specifically perceptual mechanisms are not defective. *That is a cathode-ray tube* is not an instance-individuated content of an experience. Though the distinction certainly needs elaboration, the error of this subject is partly cognitive, rather than perceptual—even if the concept *cathode-ray tube* enters the content of his experience.

Even when the perceiver is properly connected to the world, and the environment is normal, still some instance-individuated spatial, temporal, and bodily contents of perceptions do misrepresent. There are some reliable illusions—such as the Müller-Lyer—which occur even in ordinary circumstances when the embedding of the subject is as proper as it is ever going to be. In these cases the experiences have the contents they do because of their relations to those experiences that are directly instance-individuated with respect to perception. These cases of illusion can be described as derivatively instance-individuated with respect to perception.

We can, then, formulate this generalization at the second level about the relation of entitlement:

> A perceptual experience which represents a content as correct and which is instance-individuated with respect to that content is also one which entitles a thinker to judge that content, in the absence of reasons for doubting that he is perceiving properly.

This needs some adaptation if perception has non-conceptual content. Suppose it does. Then for conceptual contents for which there is a perceptual entitlement to judgement there will be a range of non-conceptual contents of experience which generate an entitlement to judge such a conceptual content. Call these 'the range of non-conceptual contents which canonically correspond to the conceptual content'. The generalization at the second level would then be formulated by saying that:

> A perceptual experience which represents a non-conceptual content as correct and which is instance-individuated with respect to that non-conceptual content is one that entitles a thinker to judge a conceptual content as correct, in the absence of reasons for doubt, when the non-conceptual content is in the range which canonically corresponds to the conceptual content.

Under either variant the generalization at the second level is equivalent to something simple and intuitive. The generalization is in effect saying that when making perceptual judgements one is entitled to take it, in default of evidence to the contrary, that one is in the circumstances with respect to which one's perceptions are instance-individuated for the contents in question. So I will call this thesis about the second level 'the Individuation Thesis about Perceptual Entitlement'.

This Individuation Thesis suggests an approach to the issue of what makes something an observational concept. The intuitive idea is that a non-observational concept will not be instance-individuated, because it has commitments which go beyond what is involved in instance-individuation. An experience of something as a Mac computer, or as a PET scanner, cannot be purely instance-individuated, because that would not capture the commitments of these concepts, the commitment that objects falling under them are capable of carrying out certain functions.

Such a development of a criterion for observationality has to be carried out with some care, because instance-individuation is not to be taken as meaning that nothing more than causal interaction is involved in an experience's having a certain content. There is causal interaction in ordinary visual experience with patterns of light reaching the eye; with retinal stimulation patterns; and with the state of the optic nerve. None of these matters enters the representational content of ordinary visual experience. The representational contents of visual experience also serve as input to the subject's construction of a conception of the layout of the objective spatial world around him. This is a feature of perceptual experiences with instance-individuated contents. So the criterion for a concept to be non-observational might be better formulated thus: Non-observational concepts have commitments going beyond the minimal conditions for objective content which are met by the contents of experiences which are instance-individuated. I simply note the possibility of this approach to observationality, as one by-product of the Individuation Thesis about Perceptual Entitlement. It would take us too far off our main path to pursue here the further elaboration which would be necessary to develop the criterion in detail and with a rationale.

Our actual entitlement to perceptual judgements rests on far more than the Individuation Thesis alone, applied atomistically experience-by-experience. Consider a stream of experiences each of which entitles a thinker to believe some corresponding content. If these objective contents cohere, each being a spatial content of a perception reasonably expected to follow its predecessors, then the resulting entitlement to judge each content is massively greater than if each experience had occurred in isolation. Holism of confirmation is as pervasive in the sphere of perceptual judgements as it is in other areas. Even the proposition that objects have rears is something that requires perception from more than one angle, and cannot be confirmed by a single view.

All the same, it seems to me that this holism of confirmation serves to increase a prior level of entitlement that can already exist in the individual case before additional perceptions or evidence are brought in. The additional perceptions or evidence are important because they can give further reasons for thinking things are as an initial perception represents them as being. (They can also serve to show that certain kinds of defeating conditions do not hold.) In a sequence of coherent experiences the later experiences themselves give defeasible reasons for making certain judgements, independently of the occurrence of the earlier experiences. It is only because this is so that the later experiences can then give further confirmation of the judgements supported by the earlier experiences.

There is an abstract, structural argument that if rational, entitled thought is to be possible at all some concepts must be such that one is default-entitled to presume that one is in the circumstances in which they are individuated. Maybe there could be a concept whose possession-condition makes reference to applications in circumstances one is not default-entitled to presume are one's own. Perhaps there could be a concept which, as a matter of its nature, is to be applied to objects which look a certain way, but only under a certain kind of abnormal illumination. Any entitled application of this concept on the basis of experience will require inference, or some other entitled transition, to the conclusion that the illumination is of the special abnormal kind. Now could it always be that inference, or some other entitled transition, has to be made before we are entitled to apply a concept? It seems that this could not be so if entitled application is ever to get started.

This abstract, structural argument seems to me to be sound. But abstract arguments by themselves have only abstract conclusions. It is one thing to know that default entitlements must exist. It is another to explain how they are possible in the first place, and to explain why they have the particular character and contents they do. The abstract argument does not give us an understanding concerning any particular generalization about the entitlement relation of why it, rather than some other principle, holds. To move towards such understanding in the perceptual case is the purpose of my next question, which is at the third of the three levels I distinguished. The question is: If the Individuation Thesis about Perceptual Entitlement is a true generalization about entitlement, what explains its truth?

There would be no further task of answering this explanatory question if the Individuation Thesis about Perceptual Entitlement were derivable simply from the truths about the individuation of perceptual content together with principles about the nature of entitlement in general. But I cannot see what such a derivation from those premisses alone would be like. The generalization which is the Individuation Thesis about Perceptual Entitlement does not itself explain why one is in the default case entitled to accept what would hold in the circumstances with respect to which perceptual content is individuated. Those circumstances may be special from the standpoint of the theory of the individuation of content; but what is so special about them for epistemology and the theory of entitlement? Why is one entitled in the default case to form perceptual beliefs as if one were in the circumstances with respect to which the content of the perception is individuated? To achieve philosophical understanding of these issues we have to undertake the further substantive philosophical task of explaining the epistemic significance of facts about the individuation of perceptual content. It is part of the task of connecting the epistemology of the theory of content with its metaphysics.

CHAPTER 3

Explaining Perceptual Entitlement

3.1 The Argument Outlined

By the end of the preceding chapter we had come to the conclusion that there is an entitlement to take experiences with instance-individuated contents at face value. What is the philosophical explanation of the existence of this entitlement? This is a question at the third of the three levels I distinguished. In this chapter I address this philosophical question about explanation, and the theory I propose involves three steps.

> *Step 1* consists in the formulation and defence of a general principle about the explanation of complexity.
>
> *Step 2* is the claim that the general principle in Step 1 applies to the explanation of the occurrence of experiences with instance-individuated contents, and does so in such a way as to support the presumption that the contents of such experiences are correct.
>
> *Step 3* is the claim that this application to perceptual states provides the philosophical explanation, at Level (3), of why one is entitled to take experiences with instance-individuated contents at face value.

The argument has two extensions. The *first extension* applies the argument to all 'as-if' states—to all states which are states in which it as if some condition obtains. A *second extension*, even more general in character, applies the argument to all non-conclusive entitlements.

The argument is not intended to apply to all entitlement to take experiences at face value. As we actually are, we are entitled in ordinary circumstances to judge that a friend is happy when we see his happy facial expression. This is certainly some form of perceptual entitlement. But the content *happy* as a component of the intentional content of our experience when we see his face is not instance-individuated. There is far more to the capacity to be in states with such a content than merely having a certain kind of perception when the other person is sad (or even visibly sad). Such cases will need separate treatment that I will not be attempting here. But it is plausible that these cases are possible only because the entitlement present in cases of instance-individuation is possible; the case I will be discussing seems to be fundamental to perceptual entitlement.

3.2 The First Step: The Explanation of Complexity

Here are some illustrations of what I mean by complexity, with some discussion of each case.

(a) Snowflakes

I start with the humble example of the snowflake. Although no two snowflakes have the same shape, almost all exhibit sixfold symmetry. Figure 3.1 shows one of W. A. Bentley's famous series of photographs of snowflakes.

Each undamaged snowflake repeats a pattern around its centre, with a repeat at each sixty-degree segment. This is an example of complexity or order that needs explanation. The problem of what the explanation is attracted the attention of Kepler, who wrote a pamphlet about it.[1]

The explanation is as beautiful as the patterns it explains.[2] It is well known that the most efficient way of packing spheres on a plane results in a hexagonal arrangement (see Fig. 3.2).

---

[1] J. Kepler, *The Six-Cornered Snowflake,* trans. C. Hardie (Oxford: Oxford University Press, 1976).

[2] For an overview see I. Stewart, *Life's Other Secret: The New Mathematics of the Living World* (Allen Lane: London, 1998), 30–5; and for further details R. Davey and D. Stanley, 'All About Ice', *New Scientist*, 140, 18 Dec. 1993, 33–7.

Figure 3.1   The Hexagonal Symmetry of Snowflakes

Source: W. A. Bentley, *Snowflakes in Photographs* (Mineola, NY: Dover, 2000), 51.

Oxygen molecules in frozen water are roughly spherical and they are arranged on a plane. The frozen crystals grow in a way that minimizes energy. They do not grow in solid hexagons, however, because long sides tend to break. Growing arms also develop other arms, by the same principles (Figure 3.3).

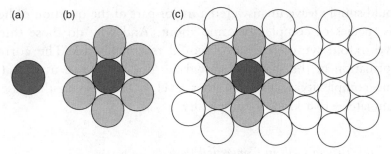

Figure 3.2 Packing Spheres on a Plane

Source: Ian Stewart, *Life's Other Secret* (London: Penguin, 1998), 32.

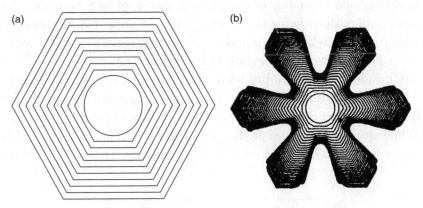

Figure 3.3 The Formation of Arms in a Snowflake

Source: Stewart, *Life's Other Secret*, 33.

The differences between individual snowflakes are explained by the varying conditions of temperature, moisture flow, and so forth in which they are formed.

What matters for present purposes about this explanation is that the complexity or order at the level of the whole snowflake is explained in a way that does not simply presuppose a similar complexity or order in the states or conditions that do the explaining. There is no appeal here in the explanation to objects that themselves exhibit a similar sixfold symmetry that is simply taken for granted; and it would hardly provide a satisfying explanation if there were. Any such alleged explanation, for instance one saying that snowflakes are built on skeletons that themselves exhibit sixfold symmetry, would simply leave unanswered a major part of the question of how this species of complexity came about. 'And why do those things have sixfold symmetry?', one would reasonably ask. The correct explanation of the shape of snowflakes does not leave us with the same complexity again at another level. It reduces—in this case it eliminates—that kind of complexity.

(b) Bénard Cells in Convection Patterns

A second example concerns convection currents in heated liquids. Take a closed volume of a liquid that receives heat from a source below it. Within a certain range of quantities of heat applied from below, this liquid will reliably divide into a set of what are known as Bénard cells, within each of which the liquid circulates in a rotating pattern, when one takes a vertical cross section of the liquid (Figure 3.4).

Consider a small quantity within the fluid that is moving upwards. This small quantity enters a cooler region of greater density than it has itself, and so is buoyed further upwards. The opposite applies to a falling quantity. Particles at the top of the liquid are constrained to move horizontally by the top of the container. There are multiple

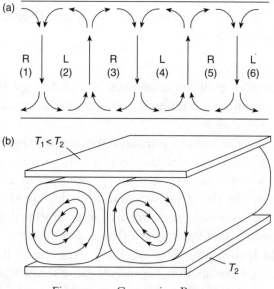

Figure 3.4   Convection Patterns

cells because a quantity moving at the top of the container cools, and eventually falls again.[3]

This explanation of how the convection cells arise does not appeal to any prior division of the liquid into cells or volumes. The complexity or order is explained in a way that does not beg any questions.

(c) Amoebic Behaviour: Order Over Time

Sometimes the complexity or order to be explained has to be characterized in terms of the environmental relations of the system or object in question. A group of amoebae whose supply of nutrients is reduced tend to aggregate into a single multicellular body. This environmentally described regularity needs explanation.

The explanation is that starved amoebae emit a chemical (cAMP). This chemical attracts other amoebae to it, and it also causes them to emit the same substance.[4]

This explanation does not appeal to any principle that starved organisms tend to coalesce. No such principle is true. Even if it were, it would still need explanation of why it is true. The correct explanation shows why the complex coalescence occurs without leaving a residue of unexplained complexity.

It of course needs explanation why organisms displaying such complexity survive, and why this behaviour is adaptive. That is a good question, but a different one, and it can equally be answered. One needs both an explanation of how complexity occurs and another— and different—explanation of why objects or organisms which display such complexity continue to exist and reproduce.

These three initial examples give a first fix on the notion of complexity or order, and what is needed for a satisfactory explanation of particular instances of complexity. The general phenomenon of order needing a certain kind of explanation has illustrations in widely diverse areas. Illustrations range from the biochemical phenomenon of replication of a molecule, through biological phenomena of reproduction, to such economic phenomena as economic cycles of growth and

---

[3] G. Nicolis and I. Prigogine, *Exploring Complexity: An Introduction* (New York: Freeman, 1989), 8–15.
[4] Ibid. 31–6.

recession. All of these involve a kind of order. All the satisfying explanations of these cases of order do not simply reproduce the complexity to be explained. But can we say something general about the nature of this complexity? What is it, and why does it have to have a certain kind of explanation?

The kind of complexity which needs explanation cannot be a matter of the improbability of the particular arrangement of particles whose distribution constitutes the complex state on a given occasion. The instantaneous distribution of particles at a given moment in a case of convection currents in Bénard cells is no less improbable than an equally detailed specification of the distribution of particles in a case of random Brownian motion. The same applies to sequences of such distributions over time. Correspondingly, the task of explaining this kind of complexity should not be described merely as the task of explaining the occurrence of the very improbable.

Nor does complexity consist in the objective improbability of the occurrence of the particular *kind* of arrangement of particles that makes us classify a case as one involving complexity. On the contrary: a good explanation of the sixfold symmetry of snowflakes shows that that kind of pattern is highly likely, almost inevitably occurs. A good empirical explanation of the characteristic feature of a particular instance of complexity can hardly be one that shows the case is not one of complexity after all.

Both the preceding attempts to explain complexity in terms of improbability misarticulate what seems to me the correct account of the phenomenon exemplified in the initial examples. The improbability in question is apparent, rather than real. Complex phenomena are ones which instantiate kinds that are apparently improbable; but in fact there is an explanation of why those kinds are instantiated. The challenge is to say what the explanation is. An explanation must consist in showing how what seems unlikely can in fact come about with less difficulty than seemed to be the case. It may be almost inevitable, as with the symmetry of snowflakes. The explanation shows why the empirically possible—as opposed to geometrically possible—shapes for a snowflake all exhibit sixfold symmetry. All the examples of complexity and their explanations that we have considered so far conform to the following description: There is a wide variety of apparently possible states for some object, event, or process, but there is an explanation of why the actual instances all fall within some restricted, specifiable narrow range of this wide variety of apparently possible states.

The fact that all of the many undamaged snowflakes exhibit sixfold symmetry is evidence that there is some underlying uniform explanation. But frequency of occurrence should not be written into the characterization of what complexity is, or into the conditions under which we need an explanation of it. As Roger White remarked to me, even if there were only one snowflake ever in the universe, there could and would in fact still be an explanation of its sixfold symmetry. When complexity has an explanation, the explanation can apply equally whether the instances are frequent or whether they are rare.

The complexity which has an explanation (if it is not merely coincidental) is not a merely mind-dependent property. It is true that the sixfold symmetry of snowflakes is perceptually salient, and that Bénard cells correspond to perceptual groupings when they are illustrated. But complexity can exist, and we can have evidence that it exists and has an explanation, even when it is not perceptually salient. The Fibonacci series is widely exemplified in nature, so widely that it is plausible that there will be an explanation, or explanations, of why it is so. But one does not need to be able to perceive the locations or angles at which (for instance) new shoots grow as instances of the Fibonacci series for the phenomenon to need explanation. The instantiation of a complex property can have, and need, an explanation whether or not that property is perceptually salient. When there is an explanation of a complex property of some object or event, there is an explanation of why the object or event has a property which falls within a narrow range of the space of possible properties of that object or event. Shapes with hexagonal symmetry form a small subset of the geometrically possible shapes for a quantity of a frozen liquid. What needs to be explained is why the shapes of actual snowflakes fall within that narrow subset. In this description of the task neither what is to be explained nor what it is to be an explanation of it seems to me to be mind-dependent.[5]

---

[5] Presented with this characterization of complexity one could be forgiven for remarking that what (following quite standard usage) I have called complexity is really a kind of simplicity. For more on this, see Sect. 3 of this chapter.

In this account 'ease' and 'complexity' are not being interdefined. It's not the case that anything that could easily come about is not really complex after all. Snowflakes really are complex. We continue to classify them as complex after we know the explanation that shows that hexagonal symmetry is almost inevitable, given the physical principles that are at work. Conversely (and to repeat), something displaying hexagonal symmetry would still be complex even if generated by a program that drew on a series of random numbers, or was a result of an explosion in a factory. Such an occurrence is not impossible; rather, it is fantastically improbable.

The notion of complexity I am using is not the only extant notion, nor the only significant one. Peter Godfrey-Smith, for example, explains a notion of complexity which is intuitively a notion of heterogeneity, and puts it to good theoretical use.[6] This is just a different notion from complexity as a certain kind of order in the range of actual phenomena, which is the notion I am pursuing. The range of geometrically possible shapes which might be taken by a solid built from water molecules (independently of minimization of use of energy and considerations of rigidity) goes vastly beyond those with sixfold symmetry. That is, it is more heterogeneous than the actual range of shapes of snowflakes, and so more complex in Godfrey-Smith's sense. But the actual range, with its orderliness, is more complex in the sense with which I am concerned, the sense which has been intended in the many scientific writings in the tradition in which Nicolis and Prigogine, for instance, are writing.

Any explanation of complexity as I am conceiving it must explain more complex states by less complex states. An explanation which did not do so would not have shown how the apparently unlikely could easily come about. If a proposed explanation simply reproduces the complexity to be explained, one will have explained the apparently unlikely in terms of the equally apparently unlikely. One will not have shown how the complexity could easily have come about. Similarly, in cases in which a complex kind is frequently instantiated one will not have shown why it should be so frequently instantiated.

---

[6] See his *Complexity and the Function of Mind in Nature* (Cambridge: Cambridge University Press, 1996), at 24–8.

I summarize this point in the Complexity Reduction Principle:

Other things equal, good explanations of complex phenomena explain the more complex in terms of the less complex; they reduce complexity.

Correspondingly, I also suggest:

Other things equal, it is more probable that a complex phenomenon has a complexity-reducing explanation than that it has no explanation, or that it has one that does not reduce complexity.

This is, obviously, a probabilistic principle. It does not imply that there is an outright sufficient reason for everything, or for every complex thing, that occurs. It permits that some states of affairs may have come about randomly, or as a result of massive coincidence. But the Complexity Reduction Principle is fairly described as some variant of the idea underlying Principles of Sufficient Reason that have been presented by past writers. It is a Qualified Principle of Sufficient Reason. It would not have satisfied Leibniz, for it does not imply that there is an outright sufficient reason for everything of a certain kind that actually occurs. To repeat, it is not part of my position that things always come about in easier, rather than less easy, ways. My position is rather that it's more likely that they come about in easier ways, and that it is correspondingly more rational to hold, other things equal, that they have come about in an easy, rather than in a highly improbable, way.

That it is rational to hold that things have come about in a way in which they are more likely to have come about seems to me an a priori principle. It is not something extracted from any particular science, but is presupposed in all empirical sciences.

What various empirical sciences tell us is not that things tend to come about in the easier ways. Rather, the empirical sciences give us more information about which ways are the easier ways. Which ways are the easier ways is largely an empirical matter. Particular sciences may have surprises about which ways are the easier ways.

It is an objective matter how easy it is for an event or state of affairs of a given kind to occur in given circumstances. It is not an epistemic matter. In making judgements about easiness we should be aiming to get this objective matter right. One way is an easier way than a second for a certain state of affairs to come about if the first way is exemplified in a wider range of initial conditions that could bring about the state of affairs—where this 'could' is empirical (rather than being the 'could' of pure metaphysical possibility). In assessing how easy it is for an event of a given kind to occur in given circumstances we have to draw on all sorts of information about those circumstances. The easiest way for a piece of inanimate matter in outer space to move may be for it to be pushed by some other piece of matter, and not for it to be controlled by states with informational content. But for a piece of matter such as a human arm, that we know is under the control of states with intentional content, the easiest way for it to move in given circumstances is for its owner to move it. This is a simple case that shows the need for the qualification 'other things equal' that I have inserted in the Complexity Reduction Principle and the Qualified Principle of Sufficient Reason.

When we succeed in giving a complexity-reducing explanation of some phenomenon, the phenomenon is no longer surprising in the sense elegantly analysed by Paul Horwich.[7] As Horwich notes, and as all the examples above confirm, the property of being surprising should not be identified with that of having a low probability (either subjective or objective). Improbable things happen all the time—the particular lottery ticket that wins, the particular pattern of traffic over time in Manhattan on a particular day—and they neither do nor should surprise us. Let E be a surprising states of affairs and let C specify the believed circumstances of its production. Horwich's point is that the fact that E is surprising consists in the fact that the subjective probability of C given E is much lower than the probability of C. Before we had any idea of the explanation of the hexagonal symmetry of snowflakes, and given our belief that the circumstances of their production do not involve laws which primitively give some special place to hexagonal symmetry, the subjective probability of laws not specifically mentioning hexagonal symmetry given the existence of hexagonal snowflakes is lower than the probability of such laws outright. Once we have Kepler's explanation of the symmetry we obtain new beliefs about the circumstances of their production (namely the consequences of our accepted laws) which result in a new subjective probability for our accepted physical laws given the occurrence of

---

[7] *Probability and Evidence* (Cambridge: Cambridge University Press, 1982), 101–4.

hexagonally symmetrical snowflakes. Correspondingly, the occurrence of hexagonally symmetrical snowflakes is no longer surprising.

I do not imply that the removal of surprise is what good explanation here consists in. Surprise disappears rationally only when constraints on good explanation are met, and nothing I have said here undermines the views that good explanation is not a mind-dependent matter, and that rational reduction of surprise is answerable to it. What is true, however, is that Horwich's account gives a good theory of the epistemic changes involved in the transition from first not having to then possessing a good explanation of some complex phenomenon.

In giving examples of the explanation of complexity I considered the illustrations provided by complex spatial patterns, at a given time or over time, and by complex behaviour, relationally characterized, over time (as in the case of the amoebae). In some cases complexity is encoded or implicit in some relatively simply described state. Many psychological states with intentional content are like that. The state is simply specified by giving the kind of state in question, together with its intentional content. For a state to have a given intentional content, however, it must stand in an extremely complex network of relations to other states and to the subject's environment. Any explanation of how the subject comes to be in that state, an explanation that accounts empirically for the presence of this complexity, must not simply presuppose similar intentional complexity.

It is for this reason that the spuriousness is so widely acknowledged of a purported explanation of someone's ability to recognize his grandmother by postulating a 'grandmother' neuron. In fact, the whole methodology described by Dennett in 'Artificial Intelligence as Psychology and as Philosophy' of explaining intelligent capacities in terms of less intelligent ones can be regarded as the application, to the special case of certain psychological capacities, of the Complexity Reduction Principle.[8] This methodology, both in artificial intelligence and in psychology, involves the explanation of rich intellectual capacities in terms of the activities of subsystems involving progressively less intelligence, until we eventually reach a level at which the subsystems involved have no more capacities than can be explained in physical terms such as the firing of assemblies of neurons in response to certain

[8] In his *Brainstorms* (Bradford Books: Montgomery, 1978).

patterns of stimulation of those assemblies. A purported explanation that contained an ineliminable violation of this reduction in intellectual capacities would also be a violation of the Complexity Reduction Principle. It would be offering an explanation of some intellectual, or more generally content-involving, capacity in terms that presupposed that capacities of a similar degree of intellectual richness were already present. This would involve unreduced, unexplained complexity given the relatively uncontroversial premise that possession of some intellectual capacity is a complex state needing explanation. We can no more accept intellectual capacity as an unexplained, primitive feature of an organism than we could accept primitive, unexplained sixfold symmetry of certain arrangements of matter in a purported explanation of the shape of snowflakes.

In the case of evolutionary biology the appeal to step-by-step evolution to explain such matters as the existence of as complex and subtle an organ as the eye and more generally the ability of organisms to survive and reproduce equally involve an application of the Complexity Reduction Principle. Richard Dawkins is explicit about some aspects of this methodology (I have demurred from the point in the following passage about probability, which he himself later qualifies.):

A complicated thing is one whose existence we do not feel inclined to take for granted, because it is too 'improbable'. It could not have come into existence in a single act of chance. We shall explain its coming into existence as a consequence of gradual, cumulative, step-by-step transformations from simpler things . . .[9]

Dawkins's 'could not' here is that of empirical implausibility, rather than that of metaphysical impossibility.

3.3 The Second Step: The Application to Perceptual Experience

Consider a particular occurrence of a perceptual experience with an instance-individuated content that p. This is an event of considerable complexity. Its complexity is in part relational, in two respects.

First, to have this instance-individuated content that p the experience must be of a kind which, when the subject is properly connected

---

[9] R. Dawkins, *The Blind Watchmaker* (Harlow: Longman, 1986), 14.

to the world, has its instances caused by the fact that p (or else it is derivatively instance-individuated), in the sense discussed in Chapter 2. The spatial and temporal experience of organisms, even relatively primitive ones, with well-developed perceptual systems will in fact have many contents concerning spatial and temporal properties and relations that are instance-individuated in this sense. There is much about the particular experience under this first head alone that requires empirical explanation.

There is a second respect in which this experience displays a relational complexity. An experience with spatial representational content, for instance, must be one whose content is capable of contributing to its subject's conception of the spatial layout of the world around him. Without this the experience would not have a spatial content at all. The content of the experience must be capable of integrating with other spatial representations in confirming or disconfirming the subject's conception of the layout of the world. The same applies *pari passu* to the temporal contents of perceptual experience and to their role in building up simultaneously the subject's conception of his history and the history of the world around him. So in these spatial and temporal examples the requirement of causal sensitivity to instances of the properties and relations represented as instantiated is only a necessary condition for a perception to have a content of one of these kinds. It is not a sufficient condition. These most recent holistic elements in the possession of spatial and temporal perceptual content all contribute further to the complexity of the property of having an experience with a given spatial representational content that p.

Taking both these kinds of complexity together we have another case of complexity that needs empirical explanation; and the Complexity Reduction Principle will apply here too.

I suggest that the explanation of the occurrence of a perceptual experience with the instance-individuated content that p which most reduces complexity is that the experience is produced by a device which has evolved by natural selection to represent the world to the subject. This involves, other things being equal, the perceptual experiences produced in such a subject being predominantly correct. The occurrence of an experience with the representational content that p would hardly be a coincidence if its representational content held of the world, and the subject had a properly functioning perceptual system whose holistic complexities were adapted to its spatial embedding in the world. For a subject with such a perceptual system its being the case that p would in the predominance of cases then explain the occurrence of an experience with whatever complex relational property is involved in representing it as being the case that p.

It is a relatively a priori truth that since subjects rely substantially on their perceptual systems in the formation of belief there will be selection for roughly accurate perceptual systems. As always in evolution by natural selection, there are trade-offs. Some, perhaps considerable, inaccuracy may be traded for speed or range of representations. But perceptual states generated by a system produced and sustained by natural selection can be expected to be in large part correct in their representational contents.

The explanation by natural selection of the existence of roughly accurate perceptual systems reduces complexity. The explanation succeeds by citing states of affairs of lesser complexity than that which is to be explained. The explanation does not postulate the occurrence of other intentional states in the production of the perceptual experience. Nor does it postulate other unexplained states of the same relational complexity as those to be explained.

Why does the explanation of entitlement apply only to the contents of instance-individuated perceptual experiences? It would not be a satisfying answer to this question to say: 'The entitlement does not, when we consider the cases intuitively, apply beyond the instance-individuated.' If the proposed complexity reduction explanation really were to apply also beyond the instance-individuated cases, that would then constitute a serious objection to this theory. For by the lights of the complexity-reduction account there ought also to be a corresponding purely perceptual entitlement in the cases of contents of experience that are not instance-individuated—when actually there is no such entitlement.

In fact, it seems to be intrinsic to the complexity-reduction account that it applies only to the instance-individuated cases. The complexity displayed by experiences with instance-individuated contents is one which involves a causal sensitivity, when the subject is properly connected to the world, to instances of the very properties and relations represented in the experience. This is not true of those elements of the representational content of the experience which are not instance-individuated, such as *soldier, clock,* or *computer.*

It is neither necessary nor sufficient for an experience to represent someone as being a soldier, or something as being a clock, or a computer, that experiences of that kind be caused, when the subject is properly connected to the world, by soldiers, or clocks, or computers. It is entirely sufficient that the perceived features which also cause the subject to perceive something as a soldier, clock, or computer be ones which the subject has evidence, good or bad, are sufficient for something to be a soldier, clock, or computer, and whose sufficiency for this has been, by some general mechanism, absorbed into the content of the perception itself, so that things are perceived as being soldiers, clocks, or computers. This is certainly an easy way for an experience to come to have the complex property of having a representational content involving these concepts *soldier, clock,* or *computer.* This is an explanation which does not, in itself, imply that experiences with these representational contents are likely to be veridical. It is neutral on that issue (though it does not preclude that further arguments to that conclusion could be developed).

The same explanation could not, in the nature of the case, be given for the occurrence of experiences with instance-individuated contents. In these cases it cannot be true that the perceiver has evidence (good or bad) that certain perceived features are sufficient for something's being straight, or curved, or, for instance, for it to be moving slowly. There is no further, more fundamental level of representational content of which it is true that things represented as being certain ways at that level of content are also, as an empirical matter, straight, or curved, or moving slowly. We are, at the instance-individuated level, already at the most basic level of representational content. There is nothing more primitive to fall back upon, and which might be merely empirically associated with these instance-individuated contents. This is why the complexity-reducing explanation that appeals to selection of roughly accurate perceptual mechanisms really is limited to the instance-individuated cases. For experiences with contents that are not instance-individuated, that need not be the explanation that most successfully reduces complexity.[10]

---

[10] On the perception of the expression of emotions I've equally said that there is no fall-back, more primitive level. This could be seen as a demonstration that the easiest way for these experiences to come about involves not just causation by instances but the subject's capacity to experience the same emotion, and to express it.

I will be arguing that the various sceptical hypotheses fail to reduce complexity. My thesis will be that it is not a good explanation, one reducing complexity, to suppose, in the absence of specific information to the contrary, that an experience with the complex property of having instance-individuated representational contents occurs without experiences of its kind being predominantly explained by the correctness of their representational contents.

Sceptical hypotheses about the explanation of perceptual experience can be divided initially into two broad classes. There are those that hypothesize that some agent is intentionally causing non-veridical experiences. Descartes's evil demon and the scientist who controls your brain in a vat fall into this first class. The other class of hypotheses do not involve any intentional production of illusions, but suggest either random or coincidental physical events that result in combinations of matter that produce illusory experiences; or else they suppose, for instance, that the universe has always consisted of one or more envatted brains.

Sceptical hypotheses that postulate intentional agents as the source of the experiences cannot reduce complexity. If the agents producing the illusions themselves have experiences, complexity is manifestly not reduced. The explaining states are as complex as those whose complexity is in need of empirical explanation. If the agents have other complex attitudes, or attitude-like states, without having experiences themselves, these attitudes still display a form of relational complexity that needs empirical explanation. The actual emergence of propositional attitudes other than experience can be given in evolutionary theory and its by-products, in a way that does not leave a residue of empirically unexplained complexity.

The sceptical hypotheses as normally formulated do not offer such empirical, complexity-reducing explanations of the emergence of the attitudes of the deceivers. It would of course be possible to modify them to provide such an empirical explanation of the complexity of the hallucination-producer's own states. But if that is then counted as an improved explanation because it reduces complexity it seems that a greater improvement would be made by not introducing the sceptical hypothesis in the first place.

What of the sceptical hypotheses in which the hallucinations are not intentionally produced? The aim of complexity reduction in explanation is to show how the apparently unlikely can easily come about after all. This aim can hardly be met by the hypothesis of chance or coincidental motions of matter that produce hallucinations. This is to explain the apparently unlikely in terms of the genuinely unlikely.

What of the hypothesis that the universe has always consisted of one or more envatted brains? Although this does not involve an unlikely kind of event or a coincidence at a particular moment, this still involves initial conditions in the universe that are highly complex. Why should the initial conditions (vats producing hallucinations) involve conscious events with the complex relational properties we described? This remains a case of empirically unexplained complexity.

The hypothesis of a world in which there are and always have been permanently envatted brains does raise another challenge for the present account. Wouldn't it be true of such a world that the easiest way for a perceptual experience to occur is for it to be caused by stimulation of one of the brains in the vats? Such an experience would be a hallucination. Doesn't this point mean that the whole approach to explaining perceptual entitlement by means of the notion of the easiest way in which something can come about, and by complexity reduction, is undermined?

I agree that there is a reading under which it is true that in the world of permanently and eternally envatted brains the easiest way for it to come about that a perceptual experience occurs will make that experience a hallucination. It would also completely undermine the present approach, or else lead to scepticism, if one were to reply to this point by drawing on empirical knowledge that the world is not in fact that way. That response has two defects. First, it cannot fully explain the empirical entitlement for the knowledge that the world is not in fact that way—its status as knowledge is just taken for granted in this response, rather than being explained. In the face of the objection appeal to the easiest way in which something can come about would be begging the question. Second, any such response would not leave the status of perceptual entitlement as relatively a priori. It would rather be empirical; and then it would not be clear how one could become entitled to believe anything about the observable world at all.

A better response is to distinguish what can easily be the case given that certain conditions hold from what can easily be the case absolutely, without such relativization to certain conditions. The easiest way for it to come about that an experience occurs given that the universe contains permanently envatted brains is for one of these brains to experience a hallucination. It does not follow that the easiest way for a perceptual experience to occur given no information about the conditions in the world is for there to be envatted brains and for an experience to occur in one of them. That is precisely what I have been arguing against.

There are many other cases in which we would draw the distinction between the unrelativized and relativized statements of the easiest way for something to come about. Given that DNA molecules already exist, both in natural organisms and in laboratories, the easiest way for a molecule of a specified type of DNA to come into existence is for one of the existing molecules to be copied, with a certain modification. Without relativization to the condition that DNA molecules already exist, the easiest way for the specified kind of molecule to come into existence is by some kind of chemical evolution.

There is similarly relativization to various conditions in statements of apparently non-epistemic, objective probabilities; for instance, statements about radioactive decay. The objective probability that an alpha particle will be emitted in a given time interval from a given quantity of matter is greatly increased relative to the condition that the matter is plutonium, rather than being some naturally occurring substance.

This relativization to specified conditions should not be taken to show that the notion of the easiest way for something to come about is epistemic. The relativization merely cuts down the range of worlds one considers in assessing how easy it is for a given condition to be met. Within that restricted range it is still a non-epistemic matter how easy it is for the condition to be fulfilled.

It is a claim of the unrelativized kind I intend when I say that the easiest way for a perceptual experience to occur is one in which it is unlikely to be a hallucination. The case for this claim, whether right or wrong, is made on philosophical grounds, and does not rely for its justification on empirical information attained by perception. There is no relativization in this claim to conditions which are known to hold only on empirical grounds.

It has been noted in several discussions of sceptical hypotheses, and emphasized particularly by Jonathan Vogel, that there are many arbitrary elements as these sceptical hypotheses are filled out in more detail.[11] There are so many 'unexplained explainers': Why should someone want to deceive undetectably? What is their history? Why should there be these envatted brains from eternity? On the present account this excess of unexplained explainers, this general lack of constraint, is a consequence of failing to respect the requirement of complexity reduction in good explanations. Once that requirement is abandoned the proposed explanation of the occurrence of perceptual experiences may be arbitrarily baroque. By contrast, there is a parameter that is not adjustable on natural-selection explanations of the emergence of perceptual systems. The explanation, now, of the occurrence of a range of experiences with instance-individuated contents is that the world is, predominantly, as they represent it to be.

This talk of an excessive number of adjustable parameters in the sceptical hypotheses may remind one of the Akaike theorem about the distance from the truth of a family of curves in the curve-fitting problem.[12] Akaike's measure of the distance from the truth of a family of curves contains a term $2k\sigma^2$ where k is the number of adjustable parameters in the equation for the family of curves in question and σ^2 is the variance of the distribution of errors around the true curve. It may be tempting to elucidate all my talk of reduction in complexity in terms of reduction in the number of adjustable parameters in a range of theories. The Akaike result is of great interest, and there may be further connections to be elucidated between what I am talking about and his parameter k—but I do not think they can be quite the same thing. There is a sensitivity of the measure of the distance from the truth in Akaike's measure only in the case in which σ^2 is not zero—that is, in the case in which there are some errors in the data points. But as far as I can see the intuitive notion of complexity reduction I have been emphasizing gets a grip even when we entirely prescind from errors in our data points. Even if we have a set of true statements about experiences, with no errors about which experiences are occurring, still there is a truth-related reason to prefer theories

[11] 'Cartesian Skepticism and Inference to the Best Explanation', *Journal of Philosophy*, 87 (1990), 658–66.
[12] For an exposition for philosophers see M. Forster and E. Sober, 'How to Tell When Simpler, More Unified, or Less *Ad Hoc* Theories will Provide More Accurate Predictions', *British Journal for the Philosophy of Science*, 45 (1991), 1–35. See also sect. 4 of E. Sober's article 'Simplicity (in Scientific Theories)' in E. Craig (ed.), *Routledge Encyclopedia of Philosophy* (Routledge: London, 1998).

which reduce complexity—in this case, theories which explain the relational complexity of experiences. Sceptical hypotheses do have excessive numbers of parameters compared with their non-sceptical competitors, and in the case in which there are errors in our data about which experiences occur a family of sceptical hypotheses will, other things equal, thereby be further from the truth than some families of non-sceptical hypotheses under the Akaike measure. But I do not think this gives us an account of what it *is* for a theory to fail to reduce complexity, as opposed to a consequence of such failure.

Alternatively, it may be said that all I have shown in the argument so far is that the sceptical explanations are not ones we count as 'scientific', and not that they are less likely than real-world explanations. I reply that 'explanation' is univocal. There are certainly various kinds of explanation, but these are distinguished by such differences as their differing explananda; or the level of generality in their various explaining conditions; and so forth. What I reject is the idea that there are kinds of explanation so radically different that something can be explained by one condition in an explanation of one kind whilst also being explained by something incompatible with that first condition in an explanation of some other kind. There could not be two correct explanations like that. If an experience is explained by properties of objects and events of which it is a genuine perception, it cannot also be a mere hallucination produced by a brain in a vat. Transcendental idealism and doctrines modelled upon it may recognize two senses of 'explain', but this is a problem for such doctrines, rather than one of its virtues.

The claims I have made about the easiest way in which perceptual experiences with instance-individuated contents may come about seem to put me in disagreement with at least part of what is intended in two widely held theses about simplicity and confirmation. They are widely held amongst thinkers who disagree on much else.

> Thesis 1 on Simplicity: Simplicity is irrelevant to confirming something as true.

Thesis 1 on simplicity is held by Bas van Fraassen and William Lycan, amongst many others. Van Fraassen regards simplicity of a theory as a pragmatic virtue, one speaking specifically to human concerns. Of the pragmatic virtues in general he writes that: 'In so far as they go beyond consistency, empirical adequacy, and empirical strength, they do not concern the relation between the theory and the world, but rather the use and usefulness of the theory; they provide reasons to prefer the theory independently of questions of truth'.[13] Lycan writes: 'Simplicity? Absence of mess? Why not prettiness and niceness? Why should these virtually *aesthetic* properties, which smack in any case of laziness and corner-cutting, be thought to count in any way towards *truth* (John Keats notwithstanding)?'.[14] One could quote many other writers to similar effect.

If an explanation reduces complexity it is natural to regard it as simpler than one that does not reduce complexity. I have argued that, other things equal, complexity-reducing explanations of complex phenomena are more likely to be true than those that do not reduce complexity. If both these points are correct, then, contrary to Thesis 1, there is some subspecies of simplicity that is relevant to confirming something as true.

It is also important, however, to distinguish simplicity in an explanation from simplicity of a state of affairs. In particular, a simple explanation need not cite an explaining condition whose truth consists in a simple state of affairs. In a good explanation of some complex phenomenon the cited explaining conditions are, other things equal, less complex than those being explained in the sense of complexity I tried to elucidate earlier. All the same, the explaining condition in an explanation that reduces complexity may not be a simple state of affairs on all intuitive notions of simplicity. In fact, in some cases it would be problematic were it to be simple on an intuitive notion of a simple state of affairs. All of the following are simple states of affairs in an intuitive sense: the state of affairs of the northern half of a globe being entirely covered with ocean and the southern half being entirely dry land; the state of affairs of a plane surface containing just one black square, the rest being entirely white; the emission of a particle of a given kind at regular one-second intervals by some quantity of matter. These are all orderly states of affairs. They would be counted as simple on the account of simplicity given by Elliot Sober.[15] In the sense of complexity we were relying on earlier all of these simple states of affairs

---

[13] *The Scientific Image*, 88.

[14] *Judgement and Justification* (Cambridge: Cambridge University Press, 1988), 134.

[15] *Simplicity* (Oxford: Oxford University Press, 1975).

are certainly complex! In the range of all possible states of the entities involved they instantiate a natural property found in only some of those possible states. Such simple states meet the earlier characterization of complexity, and their occurrence requires explanation. For those who regard complexity as a kind of orderliness, given that simplicity is itself a kind of orderliness, it is clear that complexity and simplicity in a state of affairs must in many, if indeed not all, cases overlap.

Is our preference for complexity-reducing explanations merely aesthetic or pragmatic? Consider the reduction in complexity, and corresponding simplicity of explanation, in the explanation of the sixfold symmetry of snowflakes. It is credible that this explanation is preferred merely on aesthetic or pragmatic grounds only if there would be merely something aesthetically or pragmatically inferior about an explanation which took hexagonal symmetry for granted in the explaining conditions. But to treat hexagonal symmetry that way seems to leave it unexplained, rather than to give us an inelegant or pragmatically inferior explanation. This point seems to go to the heart of the nature of explanation itself, rather than being dependent upon something speaking merely to human concerns. I am therefore in disagreement with those writers on simplicity quoted earlier if their views do entail that the simplicity of the explanations in the snowflake or Bénard-cell examples is something mind-dependent.

A second widely held thesis about simplicity has two connected parts.

> Thesis 2a on Simplicity: Only truth-relevant relations can bear upon confirmation.
> And hence:
> Thesis 2b on Simplicity: Sceptical hypotheses are as well con-firmed as the standard real-world explanations of an individual's experiences.

William Lycan calls Thesis 2a the 'spartan view' of confirmation. He writes:

It is also the spartan view that drives evil-demon scepticism about the external world: by hypothesis, the evil-demon theory makes exactly the same observational predictions as does the realist external-world theory, so both are equally probable or well-confirmed on our evidence, so we have no reason to believe the external-world theory to the exclusion of the other . . .[16]

The position I have been defending is entirely consistent with the Spartan View. What I do dispute is that the Spartan View must always omit anything to do with simplicity as relevant to confirmation. (So I also dispute the 'hence' linking 2*a* with 2*b*.) If what I have argued is correct, the fact that an explanation reduces complexity counts in favour of its confirmation, because it is an explanation that does not make it hard or excessively improbable for the postulated explaining condition to be true. Complexity reduction is a truth-relevant consideration, and can be acknowledged as such under the Spartan View. Two theories that have the same consequences for experience need not be equally well-confirmed under the Spartan View, if they differ in their explanations of complexity. A theory that involves extreme improbability of the states of affairs it postulates, or which does not explain complexity at all, is less likely to be true than a theory that explains the complexity involved in the occurrence of experiences. A good theory must not only explain the occurrence of experiences; it should also explain without extreme improbability and without pushing the question back why there is instantiation of just that complex network of relations involved in those experiences having the contents they do.

3.4 The Third Step: The Philosophical Explanation of Perceptual Entitlement

The third step of the argument is that the preceding considerations in Steps 1 and 2 provide the philosophical explanation of a thinker's entitlement to take at face value the instance-individuated content of a perceptual experience. Explanations that reduce complexity are more likely, other things equal, than those that do not. What explains the entitlement in question is the fact that explanations of the occurrence of experiences with instance-individuated contents which

---

[16] 'Theoretical (Epistemic) Virtues', in Craig (ed.), *Routledge Encyclopedia of Philosophy*, ix. 341. Crispin Wright has also argued in seminars at NYU that the evil-demon hypothesis is equally well confirmed as the real-world hypothesis.

succeed in reducing complexity will also result in the representational contents of those instance-individuated experiences being predominantly correct. Such representational contents are predominantly correct in the case that is most likely, that of the complexity-reducing explanation which appeals to the evolution of a perceptual system through natural selection.

The argument is open-ended in that I have not shown that explanations by natural selection of the existence of perceptual systems provide the only satisfactory explanation of complexity that succeeds in reducing complexity. I have not proved that there are no others: I have merely not been able to construct any. It is, however, striking that the wide range of sceptical hypotheses that have been presented over many centuries now do not seem to succeed in reducing complexity. Complexity-reducing hypotheses other than those that lead to predominantly genuine perception of the world have not been easy to come by.

The complexity-reduction explanation of the entitlement to take certain perceptual experiences at face value has two properties that we should require of any such explanation. First, it is a priori. The Level-(3) explanation I have offered has not been that since we are creatures of a kind that has evolved through natural selection our experiences are likely to be veridical on the whole. It is an empirical fact that we are members of a kind that has evolved through natural selection. Our knowledge of that fact rests on various pieces of evidence, which in turn rely ultimately on our perceptions. No a priori Level-(3) explanation could be extracted from this source. Our argument has rather been this:

> Experiences are complex events.
> As such, experiences are in need of complexity-reducing explanations.
> A natural-selection explanation of their occurrence meets the requirement of complexity reduction, and it is not clear that there is any other that does.
> The natural-selection explanation makes the contents of the experiences it explains by and large correct.

This argument does not have the truth of the wholly empirical biological theory of evolution by natural selection as one of its premises.

Second, as required, the Level-(3) explanation I am proposing also explains the defeasibility of perceptual entitlement. Complex states may in fact have complex explanations. What is less likely is not thereby impossible. Further information that makes it rational no longer to take a perceptual experience at face value is information which also shows that the complexity of the perceptual experience does not have a maximally complexity-reducing explanation.

Perceptual states have specifically representational (not merely intentional) content. In this they differ from states such as imagining or wishing, which have intentional content but not representational content. In being in a state with representational content the subject of the state is thereby under the impression that the world is a certain way. Intuitively it seems essential to the entitling character of perceptual states that their content is representational. But has this specifically representational character featured in the explanation offered at Level (3) of perceptual entitlement?

This feature is playing an essential role in the explanation. The complexity-reducing explanation of the occurrence of perceptual states invokes the adaptive advantages of having roughly correct perceptual states. But this is an advantage only if the representational content of these states is indeed taken at face value. The states would have no adaptive advantage otherwise if their contents were not taken at face value. But it is only because they have representational content at all that perceptual states even have a 'face value'.

Our task was to explain empirically the complexity of perceptual experiences with representational content. The kind of explanation possible for these states will not be available for states without representational content. For states without that sort of content, some additional mechanism, involving inference or some other operation, would have to be invoked before any adaptive advantage can be established. I should note that in making this feature of representational content part of the Level-(3) explanation of perceptual entitlement I am assuming that it is a priori that perceptual experiences, in default of reasons to the contrary, tend to produce corresponding acceptance of their representational contents. Only to the extent that this is a priori is the present explanation of perceptual entitlement also a priori.

It is one thing to hold that complexity reduction and its consequences provide a Level-(3) explanation of the entitlement to make perceptual judgements in the case of instance-individuated experiences. It would be another, and in my view false, to claim that ordinary thinkers who make judgements in an entitled way must know that this is the explanation of the entitlement (or even know these points about complexity reduction without knowing that they explain entitlement). This is partially parallel to the case of valid transitions involving certain operators in logic. Ordinary thinkers are entitled to make certain transitions involving logical constants, or the counterfactual conditional, and so forth. They will recognize instances of certain transitions as valid, and others as invalid. It does not follow that they can state the explanation of why transitions of these various forms are valid or are invalid. For that, as we noted, a semantic theory is required.

One difference stands out from the logical case. A case can be made that ordinary thinkers have some form of tacit knowledge of the axioms of a semantic theory, have (as I would say) implicit conceptions whose content is that of the axioms of a recursive semantic theory. Ordinary thinkers have the following actual abilities: to evaluate certain sentences as true or as false with respect to certain circumstances; to assess certain argument forms as valid and others as invalid; to appreciate the validity of new primitive forms of transition. These abilities are best explained by the postulation of tacit knowledge of the semantic contribution made by an expression to the truth-conditions of the complex sentences in which it occurs.[17]

Corresponding points do not apply to the explanation I have offered of the entitlement to take the contents of certain perceptual experiences at face value. What are the capacities or judgements of a thinker whose best explanation would be tacit knowledge of those points about complexity-reducing explanations? Of course thinkers will offer some kind of reaction when presented with sceptical hypotheses. But what they say in such circumstances is likely to have as little, or even less, to do with the explanation of why they are entitled to make perceptual judgements as the ordinary thinker's stabs at the formulation of grammatical rules have to do with the correct explanation of his grammatical and semantic competence. We should note also that the Level-(3) explanations of entitlement have to do

[17] Peacocke, 'Implicit Conceptions, Understanding and Rationality', 43–88.

with the philosophical explanation of normative truths, rather than the explanation of the de facto capacities of thinkers.

What then is the explanation of the difference between the logical case and the observational case? A straightforward answer is that the possession-condition for the logical concept requires the thinker to have an implicit conception with a certain semantic content, while there is no such requirement for the existence of an implicit conception on the part of the thinker in the possession-condition for the observational concept. This seems to me to be a true answer—but there is a good point behind the question that needs addressing. Rational transitions are ones that are rational from the thinker's own point of view. A good theory must have that consequence, and elucidate its holding. If not all explanations at Level (3) are known to thinkers, not even tacitly known, then this requirement of rationality from the thinker's own point of view must, at least in some cases, be met in some way other than by the thinker's knowledge of the Level-(3) explanation of an entitlement. I return to give a more positive account of this rationality requirement, and how it is met under the present approach, in Chapter 6, Section 4.

We can now return to issues about the particular account of perceptual entitlement I offered. The argument I have developed applies only to experiences with instance-individuated representational contents. But is there not equally an entitlement to take at face value the content of experiences that represent something as a soldier, as a clock, or as a computer? There certainly is such an entitlement as things actually are; but on my view that entitlement does not have the same source as the entitlement to take instance-individuated contents at face value. We already noted towards the end of Chapter 2 that there can be more than one source of an entitlement to take a given component of the representational content of an experience at face value. In more detail, I would distinguish at least the following varieties of perceptual entitlement.

(1) There is *basic* perceptual entitlement, which exists for cases in which the thinker takes an instance-individuated content of an experience at face value.

(2) There is *sequentially corroborative* perceptual entitlement. As we noted earlier, a sequence of experiences, even a sequence with purely

instance-individuated contents, can give a thinker additional entitlement to take its later members at face value simply because the later
members are as one would expect them to be if indeed the contents
of the earlier members of the sequence are veridical.

(3) There is *informational* entitlement. This is a wide category, cov-
ering many different subtypes. In the case of contents that are not
instance-individuated a thinker may have memories, knowledge
from which he can make inferences, testimony, and any variety of
background information and informational states that make it reasonable to believe that what is in front of him is, say, a real computer,
or a real clock, and not, for instance, a stage prop. It is information of
this breadth James Cornman was drawing on when he wrote:

a common explanation of why I have a visual experience of mail in my box,
and, indeed, see this mail, is that a postman puts mail in my box in the morning whenever he has mail for my address, and this morning a postman had
mail for my address . . . because it has remained there till now when I am
looking in the box, I have now a visual experience of mail in the box.[18]

Although informational entitlement for the veridicality of an
experience can come from virtually any background knowledge, we
ought to distinguish in thought between one's entitlement to think
that one's environment is a certain way and one's entitlement to think
that it has come to be that way as a result of a certain history. One can
be entitled to think, and can know, that one's environment is a certain
way without having any idea of how it came to be that way. The principles one uses in establishing how one's environment came to be the
way it actually is will depend on the use of general-purpose entitlements concerning testimony, memory, and other sources of information that are not specific to perceptual content. Basic perceptual
entitlement, by contrast, involves principles of entitlement that are
specific to the instance-individuated content in question.

I suggest that as things actually are we are indeed entitled to take a
wide range of representational contents of our experiences at face
value even when those contents are not instance-individuated; but this
is so only because there is informational entitlement, in the sense displayed above, to take such contents at face value. This seems to me to

---

[18] *Skepticism, Justification and Explanation* (Dordrecht: Reidel, 1980), 255–6.

correspond to an intuitive distinction. It is a highly intuitive position that while you can tell just by looking that some line is curved you need more background information to be entitled to judge that the thing you see in front of you is designed to carry out the functions of a computer. You need yet more information to be entitled to accept a particular explanation of how there came to be a computer at that location.

This is one of the many points at which my position differs from those who offer entirely undiscriminating arguments to the effect that the best explanation of the occurrence of our experiences is that they are veridical. Bertrand Russell famously, and admittedly briefly, developed such a position in *The Problems of Philosophy*.[19] As against his view, I do not think that there is any sound unrestricted argument, applicable to an arbitrary component of the representational content of experience, however theoretical, to the conclusion that the simplest explanation of why such experiences occur is that their contents are correct. Such a conclusion always needs some additional information when we move beyond the instance-individuated contents. This point applies equally to several other varieties of explanationist epistemologies.

A rather different kind of objection claiming that the account of perceptual entitlement I have given is too restricted appeals to a different kind of case. These are cases in which it is not plausible that the way in which the experience represents something involves further commitments like the *soldier* or *computer* case. The cases in question are also ones in which additionally, because the property represented as instantiated is regarded purely dispositionally, it is not possible to hold that experiences in which the property is represented as instantiated are caused, in any cases, by its instantiation. Some have held such purely dispositional views of colour properties, but a more plausible range of such cases is given by such a property as *sparkling*, as when one sees the sunlight sparkling on the lake. It is very plausible that there is a defeasible entitlement to take such experiences at face value. It is quite implausible that this entitlement relies on informational entitlement of the general kind mentioned in (3) above. For the light to be sparkling does not require the holding of further commitments about

[19] *The Problems of Philosophy* (Oxford: Oxford University Press, 1973), 10–11.

function, structure, or the like that require additional information before there exists an entitlement to judge, on the basis of perceptual experience, that the light is sparkling on the water. Yet it is plausible to treat the property of sparkling as purely dispositional: it is no more than the property of producing such experiences as of sparkling in properly perceiving subjects. The same arguably applies to various taste properties, and certain other sensory properties. If that is so then the presence of the pure disposition cannot be a causal explanation of manifestations of the disposition. It follows that experiences of something as sparkling are not instance-individuated in the meaning given, since that requires precisely such causal explanation when the perceiver is properly connected to the world. So the question arises of whether the entitlement to take such contents at face value has been accounted for adequately.

I think this entitlement does exist, and is purely perceptual, and that it can be captured consequentially under the present approach. It is a consequence of what I have been arguing that the thinker is entitled to accept, in the absence of reasons for doubt, that he is perceiving properly. But if he is perceiving and has an experience in which some surface is represented as sparkling then under the dispositional account of this property it will be true that the perceived surface is sparkling. So the thinker will in these circumstances be entitled to the judgement that the presented object is sparkling. This explanation draws, in the rationalist spirit, on the truth-condition for 'That surface is sparkling'. This reasoning is available both to those who think that these dispositional properties involve some species of non-representational properties of experience, like the so-called 'sensational' properties of my *Sense and Content*, and to those who think that the relevant properties of experience are purely representational.[20] All that matters for the point is the dispositional nature of the property, not the nature of the properties of experience that are manifestations of that disposition.

As promised I note two extensions of the argument of this section so far. The first extension is to a wider range of 'as-if' states. Suppose a state or kind S of event is individuated by the relations in which its instances stand to other events and objects. Suppose also that we can draw a distinction between genuine instances of the state S, instances that stand in the required relations, and 'merely as-if' states or events

---

[20] *Sense and Content: Experience, Thought, and Their Relations* (Oxford: Oxford University Press, 1983).

which are in a quite specific sense qualitatively similar to and parasitic upon those genuine instances. The 'merely as-if' states do not stand in those same relations as things actually are. They are also parasitic in the sense that they are given as states which although they do not in fact stand in the required relations it is as if they do. For illustration we can use a helpful example of Crispin Wright's.[21] Suppose, remarkably, a group of people ran around kicking a ball for ninety minutes without any idea or intention of playing soccer but engaging in the same bodily movements that would be involved in a game of soccer. We can say that their movements are as if they are playing soccer, even though those movements do not have the right relations to their own and to others' mental states for it to be a game of soccer. Similarly, a visual hallucination does not stand in the right relations to things in the environment to be a genuine perception; but it is, subjectively, as if it were so related. On the way I will use the terms here, we will say that genuine soccer games and genuine perceptions are as-if states, though of course they are not merely as-if states.

The first extension of the argument I propose then states this: In a significant range of cases given just the information that an as-if state qualitatively similar to an instance of S occurs the easiest way for this to be the case is for it to be a genuine instance of S, and not a mere as-if state. For it to be a genuine instance of S is the explanation that most successfully reduces complexity. Let us take Wright's soccer example again. (We will in fact end up with a very different position on the issues from Wright's, and I will eventually be drawing different conclusions from his own examples.) For the movements of a set of twenty-two people to replicate those of a soccer match without their having any idea of soccer is not metaphysically impossible. It would, however, involve a massive, extraordinary series of coincidences. An explanation that proposes that there is accidental replication of movements of the same kind as would occur in a real soccer match is a much less simple explanation than that they are playing soccer, and that their bodily movements are controlled by the intentions that are made understandable by their meaning to play the soccer.

It would not be a coincidence that the agents' movements matched those of a game in the other case Wright mentions, that in

---

[21] '(Anti-)Sceptics Simple and Subtle: G. E. Moore and John McDowell', forthcoming in *Philosophy and Phenomenological Research*.

which they are under the control of a movie director who wants his movie to represent a game taking place. But the hypothesis, given only that people are moving as if playing soccer, that they are under the control of a movie director seems to me more complex, to demand more of the world, than that they are simply playing soccer. It demands not just that the agents have the notion of soccer, but that they all be influenced by some further individual.

A second extension of the argument, which I leave as a conjecture until we consider it further in Chapter 5 on induction, is that the argument I have been developing is applicable to all non-conclusive a priori entitlement. The idea is that in every case in which we have a non-conclusive a priori entitlement to make a certain judgement on the basis of certain states or evidence this is so because the easiest way for those states to come about or for that evidence to obtain is for the content judged to be true. This would assimilate the philosophical explanation of sound inductive argument to the same model that we have applied in the non-conclusive, defeasible perceptual case.

3.5 Features of the Treatment

(1) The approach does not say that it is a priori that hallucinations are rare, nor that an evil-demon world is impossible. Hallucinations may be frequent, and there are genuinely possible worlds in which there is a deceiving evil demon. The present position is only that the explanations of the experiences in those worlds do not reduce complexity in the way that complexity is reduced in the explanation that the experiences occur because they predominantly represent the world correctly, and occur in a perceptual system that has evolved by natural selection.

(2) The argument I have offered goes far beyond the very modest position which states that *if* we're going to commit ourselves to anything about the relations of experience to the non-mental world the perceptual hypothesis is best, but that it is preferable outright just to remain neutral on whether the experience stands in any such relations at all. This very modest position offers no explanation at all of the complexity involved in the occurrence of an experience with a representational content. The conclusion of our argument is not just that *if* we say anything at all about the environmental relations of the experience then

the explanation that most reduces complexity is one that entails that perceptual experiences are likely to be predominantly veridical. What needs explanation is that a perceptual experience with a certain representational content occurs at all, with the complex of relations to the non-mental world this requires in the case in which its subject is properly connected to the world (and the complex of relations to other mental states whether or not the subject is so connected). Remaining neutral on the experience's relations to the environment is no explanation of these relations at all. Correct application of the Complexity Reduction Principle takes us all the way from the mental world to the non-mental, unconditionally—though, as always, defeasibly.

If this approach is correct it suggests that a widely accepted dichotomy is false. The dichotomy is well expressed by John Pollock, though he is by no means unique in accepting it. He writes:

According to internalism, the justifiedness of a belief is a function exclusively of internal considerations, so internalism implies the denial of both belief and norm externalism. That is, the internalist maintains that epistemic norms must be formulated in terms of relations between beliefs or between beliefs and nondoxastic internal states (e.g., perceptual states), and he denies that these norms are subject to evaluation in terms of external considerations.[22]

The argument I have offered suggests that what Pollock counts as an internal state, an experience as of something's being so, can in some cases give defeasible reason for thinking that something holds of the world outside the mind of the thinker. If this is so, norms formulated in terms of perceptual experience may help towards the fulfilment of goals which are formulated externally, in particular in terms of truth. If the dichotomy is false the possibility opens up of a general accommodation of norms which mention internal states in Pollock's sense and an overarching aim of judging only what is true.

(3) If the argument of this chapter is correct the following passage from Daniel Dennett seems prescient. It concerns what Dennett calls 'skyhooks'—procedures, capacities, or information that are not conceived as resulting from earlier selection processes and testing of the sort envisaged in natural selection. Dennett writes: 'The renunciation of skyhooks is, I think, the deepest and most important legacy of Darwin

[22] *Contemporary Theories of Knowledge* (Totowa, NJ: Rowman and Littlefield, 1986), 126.

in philosophy, and it has a huge domain of influence, extending far beyond the skirmishes of evolutionary epistemology and evolutionary ethics.'[23] If the theses of the present chapter are right, the Darwinian legacy is of significance even in the relatively a priori domain of theories about the normative notion of entitlement. This significance does not result from a confusing of the normative and the descriptive. Rather, the claim is that a proper philosophical explanation of certain truths about the normative—the entitlement relation—must be accounted for by the special explanatory status of Darwinian mechanisms. What has been important for the argument is not the empirical truth of Darwinian hypotheses but the special, complexity-reducing status of explanations by some natural-selection mechanism.

(4) How can the Complexity Reduction Principle be the basis of perceptual entitlement when, for instance, it seems to be so different from the notion of validity which underlies logical transitions to which one is entitled? I offer three remarks in reply. First, we should consider other transitions to which a thinker is entitled but which are not conclusive. In Chapter 5 I will argue that the Level-(3) explanation of the validity of enumerative induction should appeal to the easiest way in which something can come about. Complexity reduction in the explanation of perceptual entitlement and the explanation of the validity of enumerative induction are unified by their reliance upon the easiest way in which something can come about. Second, I will be arguing in the next chapter that a range of non-perceptual entitlements that involve relying on psychological states are also ones in which the Complexity Reduction Principle is implicated. If this is right the perceptual case is not unique. Third, if we see a spectrum of cases ranging from conclusive entitlement through strong but non-conclusive to weaker non-conclusive cases we can see conclusive entitlement as the special case in which the entitling grounds give a sufficient condition of truth without needing to appeal to easiness in our philosophical explanations. With the non-conclusive, complexity reduction needs to be brought into the philosophical account, but it is still serving a purpose which is uniform across the conclusive and the non-conclusive cases. It contributes to the determination of which grounds really are reasons for thinking something to be true.

[23] 'In Darwin's Wake, Where am I?', *Proceeedings and Addresses of the American Philosophical Association*, 75 (2001), at 23.

CHAPTER 4

Extensions and Consequences

The resources employed in the previous chapter in the explanation of the character and source of perceptual entitlement raise many questions. They also have applications beyond the case of perceptual entitlement. Here I trace out some of these ramifications and applications.

4.1 Applications

(a) The Complexity Reduction Principle is pertinent to wider issues about the relations between rationality and truth. It can be deployed in arguments over the issue of whether such notions as the default entitlement or default reasonableness of a method or rule can be elucidated in terms of its tendency to yield true beliefs. Hartry Field regards such a truth-based elucidation as 'thoroughly implausible, on numerous grounds'.[1] One of his grounds is

> The standard 'internalist' criticism: it is implausible to hold that our methods (assuming them reliable in the actual world) would be straightforwardly unreasonable in a 'demon world' (a world designed to make those methods unreliable, but undetectably so). (p. 125).

The treatment I have been proposing still permits a truth-based elucidation of default reasonableness for the practice of taking certain experiential contents at face value. Although this method is certainly not productive of truths in a demon world, we argued that that world provides a more complex explanation of why there are experiences than does a world in which there is no such demon. The default reasonableness of taking certain perceptual experiences at face value can be elucidated in terms of the tendency of doing so to produce true

---

[1] 'Apriority as an Evaluative Notion', in Boghossian and Peacocke (eds.), *New Essays on the A Priori*, at 124.

beliefs in the worlds which have the least complex explanation of why such an experience occurs, the ones in which it comes about in an easy way that there is such a perceptual experience. This is only the first step in accounting for default reasonableness in terms of a more elaborate relation to the production of true beliefs, but it is an essential first step.

(b) On the treatment of perception I have offered a thinker is entitled in the absence of good reasons for doubt to take certain perceptual experiences that represent it as being the case that *p* at face value, and to judge that *p*. In the right circumstances this judgement can be knowledge. Under this account the transition is from perceptual experience to knowledge. The thinker does not rely on a premiss to the effect that this experience, or experiences of some kind under which it falls, is perceptual.

If there were such reliance it is not clear that perceptual knowledge would ever be possible at all. If the transition to perceptual knowledge were even partly inferential it could yield knowledge only if the premisses of the inference were also known. But how is the premiss that this experience is a perception to be known? It is not known a priori. If it is known a posteriori it must rest on other cases of perceptual knowledge. But how are these other cases of perceptual knowledge to be attained if they themselves rely on some premiss to the effect that the experiences they involve are perceptual? This way lies infinite regress. Entitlement will never be attained unless some perceptual entitlement is non-inferential.

Gilbert Harman has argued a contrary case. His thesis is that examples that he regards as Gettier cases in the domain of perceptual knowledge give us reason to say that ordinary perceptual beliefs are based on inference. He writes: 'If we were to suppose that direct perceptual knowledge does not involve inference, these Gettier examples would require special treatment of an obscure sort'.[2] The kind of case Harman cites is that in which someone looks, has an experience as of a candle ahead of him, and comes to believe that there is a candle ahead of him. There is a candle ahead of him, but it cannot be seen because it is behind a mirror, which is reflecting a similar candle off to the right. This thinker is justified in believing that there is a candle

[2] *Thought* (Princeton, NJ: Princeton University Press, 1973), 174.

in front of him, and the belief is true, but it is not knowledge. Harman's diagnosis of why this is not knowledge is that the belief is reached inferentially, by a false premiss about explanation. He writes of this thinker:

He infers that it looks to him as if there were a candle before him because there is a candle there and because of the normal connection between the way things look and the way things are. Since that explanation is essential to his conclusion but is false, he does not come to know that there is a candle before him even though his belief is justified and true.[3]

There is an alternative explanation of why the belief that there is a candle in front of him is not knowledge. The subject's belief in the existentially quantified content 'There is a candle in front of me' rests on his perceptual-demonstrative belief 'That candle is in front of me', where the perceptual-demonstrative 'that candle' refers to the candle he sees—which is the one off to the right. But *that* candle, the one presented in his perception and demonstratively thought about, is not in front of him. So his existentially quantified belief that there is a candle in front of him does indeed rest on a false belief, about the candle off to the right, a belief to the effect that it is in front of him. The false belief upon which it rests is not, however, a hypothesis about the explanation of his perceptual state.

Far from this account of the example being of some obscure sort, this explanation of why the belief is not knowledge appeals to the same compelling principle that Harman himself famously identified and deployed, his 'no false lemmas' requirement to the effect that a belief which is inferred from a false premiss is not knowledge.[4]

If the mirror interposed between the subject and the candle in front of him reflected a second mirror, which in turn reflected that candle, then the subject's belief 'That candle is in front of me' would after all refer to the candle that is in front of him. The belief would be true, and the 'no false lemmas' requirement would not apply. But the defeasible entitlement to take perceptual experience at face value holds only in normal circumstances, and such an arrangement of

---

[3] Ibid. Examples of this kind—though used for a different purpose—trace back at least to H. P. Grice, 'The Causal Theory of Perception', repr. in G. Warnock (ed.), *The Philosophy of Perception* (Oxford: Oxford University Press, 1967): see especially his example (at p. 104) of the pillar ahead of the perceiver, obscured by a mirror which reflects a numerically distinct though similar pillar.
[4] *Thought*, ch. 3, sec. 6.

mirrors makes the circumstances abnormal. Once again, this is not to imply that normality of the circumstances is a premiss on which observational beliefs rest. On the contrary, if it were a premiss it would need empirical support—and regress would again be threatened. Quite generally, the conditions under which an entitlement exists should not be identified with premisses used by the thinker in judging in accordance with that entitlement.

(c) If perceptual knowledge is not inferential that fact bears on the correct diagnosis of what is wrong with the most famous argument of G. E. Moore's 'Proof of an External World'.[5] Moore wrote:

I can prove now, for instance, that two human hands exist. How? By holding up my two hands, and saying, as I make a certain gesture with the right hand, 'Here is one hand', and adding, as I make a certain gesture with the left, 'and here is another'. And if, by doing this, I have proved *ipso facto* the existence of external things, you will all see that I can also do it now in numbers of other ways: there is no need to multiply examples.[6]

This 'proof' is sometimes criticized on the ground that Moore's own perceptual experience entitles him to judge 'This is a hand' only in the presence of the additional premiss that his experience is produced (in the right way) by the external world.[7] Under this diagnosis, since this is what the sceptic is questioning Moore's 'proof' fails because its conclusion is already taken for granted in one of the argument's (suppressed) premisses. If what I have said is right this cannot be the correct diagnosis. Perceptual entitlement does not rely on such additional premisses.

Does this mean that the present approach is committed to accepting Moore's 'proof' as successful? Here we must distinguish between the existence of an entitlement and having a dialectically effective reply to the sceptic. If there are not in fact any good reasons for Moore to doubt his perceptual experience he is entitled to judge that he has two hands, and to move from this to the conclusion that material objects exist. Entitlement is preserved throughout Moore's line of thought.

---

[5] In Moore's *Philosophical Papers* (London: George Allen & Unwin, 1959), and repr. in *G. E. Moore: Selected Writings*, ed. T. Baldwin (London: Routledge, 1993). Page references are to Baldwin's collection.
[6] 'Proof of an External World', 165–6.   [7] Wright, '(Anti-)Sceptics'.

If, however, the sceptic is challenging whether there really is an entitlement to rely on perceptual experience then to offer Moore's reasoning and nothing more is to beg the question. One needs at the very least to say more about why there is an entitlement to rely on perceptual experience. If the sceptic has more specific grounds for doubt those too must be addressed. The important point is that it is entirely consistent to acknowledge that Moore's argument should not by itself rationally convince the sceptic whilst also holding that an entitlement to perceptual judgement is not a matter of inference.

For any given application we make of the earlier claims about entitlement we can ask: Is that application dependent only upon the first level of characterization, or is it additionally dependent upon the second level, or upon the third as well? If an application depends only upon a given level, that application is neutral on theses about the deeper levels. Theories that disagree on correct characterizations at the later levels may still agree on the application in question. In these initial remarks about the diagnosis of Moore's 'proof' the application depends only on the idea that there is defeasible perceptual entitlement of a non-inferential nature. This particular application is not dependent upon any one theory of the second and third levels. Theorists who disagree about those levels may nevertheless agree on a diagnosis of Moore's 'proof' which does not construe perceptual knowledge as inferential (and does not attribute that construction to Moore either).

There is, however, a puzzle on some conceptions of how perceptual experience can, under this approach, entitle one to think that there are material objects in front of one. The puzzle has been articulated, in the form of an objection, by Stephen Schiffer.[8] Suppose I have a certain subjective probability that I will not be suffering a perceptual illusion in my present circumstances. There will certainly be circumstances in which having a very ordinary experience, as of a flat surface in front of me, will not alter this subjective probability. (Extraordinary experiences would be a different matter.) Now suppose I have an experience as of a flat surface in front of me. This entitles me to judge that there is a flat surface there. From this it follows, and I know that it follows, that I am not hallucinating a flat

---

[8] 'Skepticism and the Vagaries of Justified Belief', forthcoming in *Philosophical Studies*.

surface there. So it seems that I am equally entitled to judge that I am not hallucinating a flat surface there. But how can my perceptual experience be crucial in yielding my entitlement to judge that I am not hallucinating? For my degree of entitlement cannot, rationally, be any greater than my antecedent probability that I am not suffering a perceptual illusion in my present circumstances. It seems that to whatever degree I am entitled to judge that I am not hallucinating that degree can be no greater after having the perceptual experience than my initial subjective probability that I am not experiencing an illusion in my present circumstances. Whatever degree of confidence I have in that proposition was present prior to the experience. It seems from the description of the case that my confidence cannot be rationally enhanced simply from the enjoyment of the experience itself. Is this point not in conflict with my treatment of entitlement by experiences with instance-individuated contents, and with the above treatment of Moore?

I reply that the default entitlement to take instance-individuated perceptual experience at face value in the absence of good reasons for doubt should be located in a theory of outright, all-or-nothing, propositional attitudes. These are more fundamental than degree-theoretic attitudes, and I doubt that the outright attitudes can be elucidated in terms of degree-theoretic attitudes. A thinker may simply have no attitudes in advance about the likelihood of his being subject to perceptual illusions in his present circumstances. For such a thinker his enjoyment of an experience of a flat surface in front of him will not only entitle him to think that there is a flat surface in front of him. It will, by inference, give him an entitlement to think that he is not subject to an illusion, an entitlement that he did not have antecedently to his having the experience.

Some may suggest that having no outright view in advance can be identified with having the degree of partial belief of 0.5. I am sceptical of such identifications. The procedures offered for identifying degrees of partial belief, such as betting or insurance arrangements that the thinker will accept, seem to me not to tap degrees of belief at all. What those procedures do identify depends on the details of the proposed procedure. In the case of the insurance offers that he will accept it does not identify degrees of a first-order attitude but is rather sensitive to what he knows that he knows. A specified procedure will identify something. Whether it identifies something that is a first-order attitude of a familiar sort, and which is operative outside the context of the procedure, is another matter.

In the particular sort of case before us—perceptual entitlement provided by experiences with instance-individuated contents—it also matters that outright judgement in these cases aims at knowledge. If I have a positive subjective probability that I may be experiencing a perceptual illusion and I think that this corresponds to a genuine objective probability I cannot rationally judge something on the basis of an experience with an instance-individuated content. It is rational of me to think that such a judgement cannot be knowledge, and I ought not to make the outright judgement in those circumstances. I can rationally make an outright probability judgement, but that is a different matter. On this conception the description of Schiffer's example does not fit those ordinary cases in which perceptual judgement aims at knowledge and often succeeds. Such success cannot be identified with high subjective probability, however high we set the bar.

(d) The generalization I formulated about the conditions under which a thinker is entitled to take for granted the representational content of his perceptual experience bears on the relationship between entitlement and factive states. I suggest that the generalization I formulated at Level (2) supports the view that we can in some cases formulate the conditions under which a thinker is entitled to make a judgement in terms of his sensitivity to factive states, such as genuinely perceiving something to be thus and so, rather than formulating them in terms of a sensitivity to experiences whose content may or may not be correct.

Let us take an observational content *Fa* and consider the conditions under which a thinker has a perceptual entitlement to accept it. We have so far been considering a defeasible rule concerning the non-factive state of perceptual experience (D):

(D) Non-factive-defeasible:
Judge *Fa*, where *Fa* is observational, if the question arises, when perceptual experience represents it as being so, in the absence of good reasons for doubting you are perceiving properly.

How should we formulate a rule that mentions a factive state? There may be an initial temptation to say this: A thinker is entitled *tout court* to judge *Fa*, where *Fa* is observational, if he perceives *a* (so given) to be *F*. That is, however, an implausible conditional when we consider the case in which the thinker is perceiving *a* to be *F* but does not realize he is and also has good (though misleading) grounds for thinking that he may well be hallucinating. In those circumstances he is, contrary to this formulation, not entitled to judge that *Fa*, even though he perceives *a* to be *F*. Nonetheless, he is all the same trying to follow the rule that if he perceives something to be *F* then he should judge it to be *F* if the question arises. That is, he is trying to follow this rule (O), which mentions factive epistemic states:

> (O) Factive-outright:
> When you perceive *a* (so given) to be *F*, then, if the question arises, judge that *a* is *F*.

What is the relation between the factive-outright rule (O) and the defeasible rule (D)? In the domain of rules in general—not just epistemic rules—we can distinguish between an objective rule and its subjective counterpart. The objective rule for making a chicken casserole has the form: obtain chicken and vegetables, then prepare them and cook them in a certain way. The subjective counterpart of this rule is: obtain what you believe to be chicken and vegetables, then do what seems to you to be preparing them and cooking them in the specified way. Someone who aims to follow the objective rule will also be conforming to its subjective counterpart, since doing so is the best he can do by way of trying to obey the objective rule. But the only rationale he would have for following a subjectively formulated counterpart rule is precisely that it would be a way he could hope to follow the objective rule. The subjective rule has no relevant rationale independently of that fact. A rule formulated in subjective terms that was not the reflection of some objective rule would, in particular, have no connection with the goal of making only true judgements. For these reasons the objective rule is explanatorily more fundamental than its subjective counterpart.

I suggest the same is true of the relation between the objective factive-outright rule (O) and the non-factive-defeasible rule (D). The latter is the subjective counterpart of the former, and has a rationale only in so far as judging in accordance with it will respect the object-ive rule (O). The complexity of (D) is precisely what one would

expect if the thinker were aiming to make his judgements sensitive
to his genuinely perceptual states. It is not as if one would find intelligible a statement of perceptual entitlement that had defeating
clauses relating not to reasons for thinking that one is not perceiving
properly but rather to some other arbitrary condition not having to
do with one's perceptual mechanisms. The practice of taking one's
perceptual states at face value is the practice of taking it that they are
delivering factual information about the world. Anything that makes
it rational not to take them at face value must be something which
undermines the proposition that one's senses are delivering factual
information about the world.

This is confirmed by the point that the qualification in (D), that
the thinker is entitled only if he has no reason for doubting he is perceiving properly, could not be replaced by something more general
to the effect that there is no reason for doubting that Fa. If that were
a correct formulation of a principle about entitlement one could
never be entitled to set to rest one's doubts about whether it is the
case that Fa by coming to perceive a to be F. One is frequently
entitled to do just that. Doing so seems to be a paradigm of rationality.
The qualification in the correct formulation of (D) concerns reasons
for doubting that one's experiences are genuinely perceptual; it further highlights the fact that this defeasible condition is simply aiming
to make judgements to which it counts one as entitled sensitive to
whether one's experiences are genuine perceptions of the way the
world is.

There is an argument that, under the Level-2 generalization I formulated, the non-factive-defeasible rule (D) and the factive-outright
rule (O) are in a certain sense equivalent. That sense is this: A thinker
is entitled to judge the observational content Fa in exactly the same
circumstances whether he is following the defeasible rule (D) or the
factive-outright rule (O).

We consider two cases, according as the thinker (1) does not or (2)
does have reasons for doubting his perceptual states. In case (1),
where the thinker has no reasons for such doubts, consider the case
in which he judges that Fa by rule (D). Then, by our earlier arguments, he is entitled to assume he is in the circumstances with respect
to which the observational content of his experience is individuated,
and these, I argued earlier, are circumstances in which his experience

is a genuine perception. So in the absence of reasons for doubt our thinker is entitled to treat his experience as perceptual. Hence he will equally be entitled to judge that *Fa* if he is following rule (O).

Conversely, and trivially, if our thinker is entitled to judge *Fa* when following rule (O) he must be entitled to take it that he is perceiving, which he would not be if there were good reasons for doubt. So he will equally be entitled to judge *Fa* if following rule (D). If there were any reasons for doubting that he is perceiving then he would not be entitled to judge *Fa* under rule (O) either.

In case (2), where the thinker has reasons for doubting that he is perceiving properly, he will not be entitled to judge *Fa* under either rule.

The argument could be refined, without essential alteration, to treat the case in which the thinker has reasons for doubting just certain of his perceptual states. We would just consider separately the two cases according as states with the perceptual content *Fa* are in the doubtful category or not.

The claim of equivalence for (D) and (O) will have analogues for other informational states in cases in which there are contents which stand to those states as observational content stands to perceptual states.

It is a plausible principle that what a thinker is entitled to judge, and what is justified and what is rational, depends only on what seems to the thinker to be the case, and not on which factive states he stands in. The truth of this principle (if it is true) does not imply that principles of entitlement, justification, and rationality cannot mention factive states.[9] It does not follow, because the thinker who responds to seeming, non-factive states may be doing so because he thinks or takes for granted that they are perceptual. The rules he is trying to follow may still mention factive states.

If the claim of equivalence of (D) and (O) is correct then at least some entitlement rules mentioning only non-factive states are equivalent to rules mentioning factive states. If the equivalence holds, it must be false that there are entitlements which are captured by rules mentioning non-factive states, but not by rules mentioning factive states.

(e) The above explanation of perceptual entitlement bears upon the theses of my book *Being Known*. There I argued that certain concepts can be individuated by the conditions under which certain

[9] Contrast R. Wedgwood, 'Internalism Explained', *Philosophy and Phenomenological Research*, 65 (2002), 349–69.

contents containing them are not merely rationally judged but are known. This was part of the 'Linking Thesis' of Chapter 2 of that work. The idea was, for instance, that the concept a Babylonian expressed by 'Hesperus' is distinct from the concept he expressed by 'Phosphorus' because there are certain circumstances in which he can come to know that Hesperus is F without thereby being in a position to know that Phosphorus is F. Now if a sceptic questions whether a thinker is entitled to take perceptual experience at face value his scepticism will extend to this Linking Thesis too. If perceptual knowledge is not possible it follows that it is not possible to know by perception that Hesperus has some property without knowing that Phosphorus has it. Much of the discussion of *Being Known* would then collapse. One would be left only with sceptical responses to the challenge of integrating metaphysics and epistemology, rather than the ones attempted in that book which aimed to show that we really do know much of what we think we know, and without weakening our conception of truth for the propositions in question.

Being Known thus presupposed that some answer to scepticism exists, without actually supplying that answer. I take the theses about perceptual entitlement at the third level of explanation to be the start of such an answer. They can be seen as a contribution to the task of explaining why, in the perceptual cases, the Linking Thesis is true. In a discussion essay written after *Being Known* I spoke of a 'Second Linking Thesis', linking instance-individuation with entitlement and, thereby, with knowledge.[10] The theses at the second and third levels in the present work certainly say more than the Linking Thesis of *Being Known*. They are, however, contributions to the tasks of explaining the conditions under which the Linking Thesis is true and of explaining why it is true, rather than being an autonomous, additional thesis.

The claims of the present argument also bear on the somewhat creaky discussion of the 'rationally non-discretionary' in *Being Known*. The rationality of judging an observational content on the basis of perceptual experience requires the rationality of two things: the rationality of moving from the content of the perceptual experience

---

[10] 'The Past, Necessity, Externalism and Entitlement', contribution to a symposium on *Being Known*, *Philosophical Books*, 42 (2001), 106–17.

to the content of the observational judgement (in theories under which these are distinct contents), and the rationality of taking perceptual experience at face value in the first place. What I have been offering is an explanation of why this second thing is rational; the approach of *Being Known* is incomplete without it.

(f) The existence of defeasible but non-inferential entitlement structures goes far beyond such cases as perception and the various forms of memory, and possibly testimony.[11] The existence of defeasible, non-inferential entitlement relations can also provide more room for manœuvre in the philosophical account of some areas of moral thought. One example is provided by the discussion in an important recent paper by Allan Gibbard, 'Normative and Recognitional Concepts'.[12] In the part of his paper concerned with 'Thick Recognition' Gibbard observes that one's understanding of a situation may be 'heavy with demands for action' (p. 163). One may, for instance, perceive an unjust act as demanding rectification. Such cases pose a problem for views that sharply separate how things are and what to do. Gibbard observes, acutely, that it would be completely unacceptable to think that the thing to do is to act on every impression that the situation demands a certain action. We are all subject to prejudices, and there can be illusions of demands. He says that 'the principle we'd need to accept' in order to take the apparent demands at face value is 'appalling' if it means we should act on any impression of any demand. His conclusion is that we should just take it as part of our situation that we have this sense, and this is 'a psychological aspect, not plan-laden in itself' (p. 164).

These cannot be the only two possibilities, if defeasible but non-inferential entitlement structures exist. Taking the seeming demands of a situation at face value in deciding what to do may be something to which one is prima facie entitled, an entitlement which can be defeated if the seeming demands are promoting a course of action one has reason to think is morally wrong. The 'appalling' principle Gibbard cites is the analogue of the epistemically wholly unacceptable principle that one should always take perceptual experience at face value—even an experience one knows to be of a perfect *trompe l'oeil*, or knows to have an inconsistent content. Putting the fact that

---

[11] On testimony see Burge, 'Content Preservation'.
[12] 'Normative and Recognitional Concepts', *Philosophy and Phenomenological Research*, 64 (2002), 151–67.

there are certain seeming demands into the specification of one's situation is the analogue, for the practical case, of the treatment of perception that says one has a premiss to the effect that one is having an experience of a certain kind. That approach has made it impossible to see how perceptual knowledge could be attained. The believer in the importance of thick concepts can and should insist that the apprehension of demands for action should not be assimilated to a model that has proved unworkable in the perceptual case. The defender of thick concepts and their significance should invoke the structure of a defeasible, non-inferential entitlement relation. I am not necessarily endorsing this position: my point is just that a defeasible, non-inferential entitlement relation makes available this position in logical space.

4.2 An Extension to the Philosophy of Action

Some of the features of this account of perceptual entitlement generalize beyond perception to cases in which the direction of the relation of causation between world and mind is the opposite of that in perception. It is not crucial to the general form of the account of entitlement I outlined in the perceptual case that the entitling mental state be caused by the conditions to which one is entitled. The general structure of the account can still get a grip provided that the mental state is individuated by certain of its relations to the conditions mentioned in a statement of the entitlement. In my view, this applies in the case of action—as one might well expect from the many symmetries, now widely recognized, between perception and action.

For basic bodily-action types φ the mental-event kind of trying to φ is individuated by the fact that events of that kind tend to produce φ-ings, when the subject's central control system is properly connected to his body. Now thinkers normally know what they are doing. In fact, they have a distinctive phenomenology of action. It can seem to the subject that he is φ-ing, and this apparent awareness can be present even in the subject who is acting with an anaesthetized or damaged limb from which there is no proprioceptive feedback (nor any illusion of such perceptual states). In such cases the distinctive apparent awareness a subject has of his own actions seems to be a result of his tryings. The fact that he tries to φ causally explains his impression that he is φ-ing.

Apparent awareness of one's φ-ing can be produced by one's trying to φ, even when one is not in fact φ-ing, and even when the limb in question is neither anaesthetized nor damaged. Some striking experiments by Tony Marcel have made this plausible.[13] The experimenter induces in the subject an illusion about the location of his hand. The subject is then asked to move his hand to a new location. This new location is chosen in such a way that for his hand to move to it from its actual present location it has to move in one direction (clockwise, say); while it is in an opposite direction (anticlockwise) that it would have to move if his hand were at its apparent initial location. Subjects succeed in moving their hand to the new location but they have the impression that they have moved it in the opposite (anticlockwise) direction, a direction in which of course they have not so moved it. The content of their trying (or some event causally related to it) seems to cause the content of their impression of action, even though the actual motor instruction issued requires, and produces, movement in the opposite direction.

The question then arises: How can this distinctive awareness yield knowledge on the part of the subject that he is acting a certain way? A reliabilist would say that in circumstances in which the agent does know trying to φ is reliably correlated with φ-ing. But there are strong objections in other cases to pure reliabilism. Is there some explanation of how we have knowledge of what we are doing which is not dependent upon perception of ourselves, or upon proprioceptive feedback, but which does not involve a reversion to reliabilism? I suggest that there is, and that it relies on a generalized version of the principle which we have given in the account of perceptual entitlement. The event type of trying to φ is individuated by its relation to φ-ings in the case in which the agent's control centre is properly connected with his body. The thinker is entitled to take it that he is in the circumstances with respect to which these event types are individuated. (Again, an explanation at Level (3) in terms of complexity reduction could be

---

[13] See the description of his vibro-tactile experiments in his paper 'The Sense of Agency—Ownership and Awareness of Action', in J. Roessler and N. Eilan (eds.), *Agency and Self-Awareness* (Oxford: Oxford University Press, 2003). For further philosophical discussion of the issues see also my paper 'Action: Awareness, Ownership, and Knowledge' in the same volume.

given of why he is so entitled, though the present argument for knowledge of action requires only that such an entitlement exists.) But in
these circumstances tryings to φ do produce φ-ings. The awareness that
is produced by the trying to φ can then, with entitlement, be taken at
face value. In suitable circumstances this can yield knowledge on the
subject's part that he is φ-ing. If we reject this approach it would be a
real task to explain philosophically how we have knowledge of actions
we are performing, without reverting to mere reliabilism. One cannot
simply apply the perceptual model straight since, as we saw, it is not the
bodily action itself that causes the apparent awareness of action.

It is tempting to apply the same generalization to other cases too,
outside the realm of perception and action. Consider, for instance,
the entitlement to self-ascribe beliefs on the basis of one's own
judgements. Judgement is individuated as an event of a kind which,
when all is working properly, leads to belief. So one can explain how
one can know what beliefs one has by making self-ascriptions that
are sensitive to one's own judgements—even though this is certainly
a fallible method. This explanation does not involve a reversion to
pure reliabilism. The method is a rational one. Again, too, one could
develop an appeal to complexity reduction to explain why the entitlement exists given the complex relations an event must stand in if
it is to be a judgement with a given intentional content.

4.3 Rationality and External Individuation

The materials on which we have drawn in presenting a rationalist
approach to entitlement suggest a general, abstract argument for this
principle:

> Only mental states with externally individuated contents can
> make judgements about the external, mind-independent world
> rational.

For brevity, I call the displayed principle 'the Requirement'. The argument I will offer for this requirement is independent of the Complexity
Reduction Principle and of any role it may play in Level-(3) explanations. The argument of Chapter 3 may be just one way of spelling out
in more detail how the Requirement is met in the perceptual case.

Judgement aims at truth of the content judged (at least). The truth of an intentional content depends upon how things are with the references of its constituents. If something referred to in the intentional content of the judgement is external to the thinker (is not mind-dependent) then the rationality of a judgement, necessarily and a priori, depends in part on the relations of that judgement to the external world. It follows that the rationality of a judgement is necessarily Janus-faced. It faces towards the level of sense, since what makes it rational to judge something about an object or a property depends upon how the object or property is thought about. But, since judgement also aims at truth, rationality is also partially dependent upon the relations of the judgement and its content to the external world. So rationality necessarily faces towards the level of reference too.

The argument for the Requirement then proceeds from the fact that good reasons for a judgement must be truth-conducive. A good reason for a judgement, even if it is not conclusive, must make it likely that the judgement is true; and this must be so for a priori reasons. That it must be so for a priori reasons can be made plausible from consideration of other examples of good reasons. (We will eventually give an argument for this general principle, at the start of Chapter 6.) It follows from these points that for a state to give a good reason for a judgement about the external world the state must have a content that is externally individuated. What it is for the thinker to be in the state (with its content) must be constituted in part at least by the thinker's relations to the external world. If a state were not so externally individuated then there would be no a priori or constitutive links between that state in itself and the condition of the external world. So the thinker's being in that state could not by itself, and considered as an a priori matter, make it more likely that a given content about the external world is true. But that is what is required for it to be a good reason for a judgement about the external world. This is the general argument for the Requirement.

However much we supplement an internally individuated state with others that are internally individuated we will never obtain a state that, a priori, gives prima facie reason for making a judgement about the external world. As an a priori matter, the internally individuated states, however complex they are, do not make anything about the external world more likely, and so cannot supply reasons for a judgement about the external world.

It may be said that an internally individuated state together with the context (maybe the normal context) of the thinker may together make rational a judgement about the external world. Some contents are, I agree, such that their judgement is made rational by the enjoyment of an internally individuated state in normal circumstances. But I would say that they are those contents that are classically conceived as predications of secondary qualities. A predication of the concept *red* of some object will fall under this case if it is given the treatment in terms of sensational properties that I offered in *Sense and Content*. Under that treatment the state of having a certain region of one's visual field instantiate the red′ property is not externally individuated. That we refer to the property as 'red′′' may be dependent upon its relations to red objects, in normal circumstances, but the property so picked out, as opposed to the means of picking it out, is not externally individuated. On the classical view, when 'red' is regarded as a predication of objects (as it is) there is some presupposition that there is some kind of constancy of ground, both across observers and over time in a given observer, in the production of experiences in which some region of the visual field is red′.

There is a sharp contrast with the spatial, temporal, and material properties and relations that are given in perceptions. What makes it the case that it is they that enter the representational content of perception has to do with the spatial, temporal, and material properties and relations that cause such perceptions when the perceiver is properly connected to the world. There is, in contrast with the classical view of secondary qualities, no substantive presupposition of constancy of ground in the causation of a certain appearance for these spatial, temporal, and material properties. If something is perceived as straight on two separate occasions the correctness conditions for that experience already require constancy of explanatory ground; namely, just the straightness of the object in question on those two occasions. Moreover, even in the case of secondary qualities of objects and events there is also a presupposed background of a spatial framework that it is very doubtful could be mastered unless the thinker were also capable of being in states with externally individuated contents.

The Requirement applies both to judgements of contents that give reasons for other judgements about the external world and to such reason-giving states as perceptions. In the case of an externally individuated perceptual state, that state can sometimes give a thinker reason to judge something about the external world without any reliance on premisses. In such cases the content judged contains an observational concept. The possession-condition for that concept will mention sensitivity to the occurrence of experiences with a certain representational content.

The framework of possession-conditions makes possible an argument from a different direction for the Requirement. In that framework, for each possession-condition there is a Determination Theory.[14] The Determination Theory specifies how the reference of the concept is determined from the possession-condition, together with the world. According to the framework this Determination Theory must fix the reference in such a way that when the thinker is judging a content in accordance with the possession-condition for the concept in question the judgement will, as an a priori matter, be likely to be true. But this requires that the reason-giving state mentioned in the possession-condition for an observational concept applicable to the external world must itself be externally individuated. Otherwise, once again, there would be no such a priori likelihood of the truth of the judged content when the thinker is judging in accordance with the possession-condition.

This second argument is not really an additional argument for the Requirement. It is a deployment of the same resources, in terms of the framework of possession-conditions, to the same conclusion. If reasons always depend upon their role in possession-conditions, and possession-conditions always individuate concepts in terms of reasons, one can move back and forth between arguments formulated in terms of reasons and arguments formulated in terms of possession-conditions. The two styles of approach are different perspectives on a single complex structured object, the network of constitutive relations between truth, a priori reasons, and judgements.

The possession-condition framework does, however, allow one to draw the following conclusion. If a judgement is about the external world, and by the above argument good reasons for it are externally individuated, and these reasons are mentioned in the possession-condition for the concept, then the concept is also externally individuated.

---

[14] See my *A Study of Concepts*, ch. 1, and the related arguments in Ch. 1, Sec. 2, of the present book.

Some writers draw a sharp contrast between a 'rational psychology' and a psychology that mentions mental states individuated by their relations to the environment. A vivid illustration is given by the remarks of Jerry Fodor in his influential paper 'Methodological Solipsism Considered as a Research Strategy for Cognitive Psychology'.[15] Fodor speaks of 'the two main traditions in the history of psychology: "Rational psychology" on the one hand, and "Naturalism" on the other' (p. 228). He goes on to characterize Naturalism as being the tradition concerned with organism–environment relations, and Rational psychology as entirely prescinding from them. If the Requirement I have been defending is correct this is a false contrast. For any content that is about the external world, a Rational psychology that appeals to states that can be reason-giving must also be one that mentions states that are environmentally individuated. This point applies, like all properly marshalled externalist arguments, to states picked out by *de dicto*, and not merely *de re*, characterizations. If we want to explain mental events and states under their content-involving descriptions, and to do so in a way that respects the rationality of a thinker's transitions to these states when the explained states are about the mind-independent world, the intentional contents of the explaining states must be individuated in part by their relations to the mind-independent world.

There is a parallel between the relation of making rational and the relation of computation between content-involving states, when the computation is regarded as content-involving.[16] Just as a mental state about the mind-independent world can be made rational only by another externally individuated state, so an externally individuated state can be computationally explained, under that description, only by another externally individuated state, or by a combination of such. An externally individuated state cannot be computed from states which are not externally individuated. The content-involving computation of one state from a prior state must involve either content-dependence on the prior state or extraction

---

[15] Reprinted in his collection *Representations: Philosophical Essays on the Foundations of Cognitive Science* (Brighton: Harvester Press, 1981). Fodor does describe his contrast as 'a mildly eccentric way of cutting the pie' (p. 228).

[16] There is further elaboration of such a conception of computational explanation in my paper 'Content, Computation and Externalism', *Mind and Language*, 9 (1994), 303–35.

of content from partially environmental states. Otherwise, the presence of the externally individuated content in the computed state would be a miracle, something that involves environmental relations coming from nowhere.

The conception of computation that explains percepts, beliefs, and desires must be a content-involving conception. A conception that is not content-involving would not have explained these propositional attitudes under their content-involving descriptions, but would explain at best something correlated with content.

Why does this parallel between rationalization and computation exist? In both cases we have the task of explaining something under a content-involving description. In both cases the relation is subject to constraints formulated in terms of the contents involved. For rationalization the relation requires (a priori) truth-conduciveness. For computation it requires a rule relating the contents; for correct computation it involves a correct rule. In both cases these constraints involve not just intentional content but also the level of reference.

In offering this explanation of the parallelism I decline the opportunity to say: 'Computation at the personal level is our only means to understanding what computational explanation is anywhere else; so computational explanation in psychology is simply conceived by analogy with personal-level explanation, and for that reason is subject to constraints analogous to those of personal-level rationality.' Contrary to the view expressed in this imagined quotation, I suggest that in engaging in conscious and personal-level computation an agent is trying to compute correctly, to respect the constraints on good computation. He is answerable to them, rather than their being extractable from the nature of his conscious activity. We cannot make sense of his mental activity except as that of one who has a goal of making correct computational transitions. Persons who compute and subpersonal and other systems that compute both make content-explained transitions that can be assessed as correct or incorrect. Both fall under a single notion of computation. The differences between them are to be explained as differences in respect of consciousness and intention in the whole process, rather than one of them being originally computation and the other only derivatively so.

4.4 Is the Explanatory Task an Illusion?

There are various approaches to perceptual entitlement that would declare the explanatory task—that of providing characterizations at Level (3)—to be either illusory or impossible (if not both). The explanatory task is that of explaining why certain methods, characterized in the generalizations at Level (2), really are entitling. The task is conceived as one which involves connecting use of those methods with the truth of the beliefs to which use of those methods leads. It follows that there are at least two ways in which the charge of illusion or impossibility may be supported. One way is to hold that there is no such notion of truth; that is, no notion of truth for which it is a genuine question whether those methods lead to true belief. The other way in which the charge may be levelled is to grant that there is such a notion of truth but to say that these generally characterized methods cannot be shown to be rational means of reaching the truth.

Some neo-Wittgensteinian views take the first tack. These views hold that experiences provide 'criteria' for observational statements. This thesis is held in combination with a criterial theory of meaning, together with a purely minimalist, 'redundancy' theory of truth. Such a position is outlined in some of Crispin Wright's early writings.[17] For such a neo-Wittgensteinian treatment there can be no real task of explaining why the fulfilment of a criterion is reason for believing the truth of the content for which it is a criterion. There is no notion of truth, on such a theory, for which this could be a real task. On the theory of meaning endorsed by the criterial approach the only conception we have of the truth of the observational sentence is one under which certain experiential conditions are criteria for its truth. Under this approach one gives the meaning of 'sentence s is true' simply by giving criteria for it. In the case in which s is an observational sentence the criteria for the truth of the sentence will be equivalent to the criteria for an observational sentence. For this view there is no intelligible notion of truth for which one can intelligibly ask whether the criteria are genuinely sufficient, or genuinely give good reasons for accepting the truth of the observational sentence in question.

---

[17] See e.g. his 'Strawson on Anti-Realism', repr. in his *Realism, Meaning and Truth* (Oxford: Blackwell, 1987), esp. at 75 ff.

It seems to me that it is a genuine question, in need of an answer, 'Why do these experiences give reason to think that the content in question is true?'. Scepticism ought to have been more easily dissolved were this not so. The question is one of a sort one can legitimately ask about any other entitling state and content that the state entitles one to judge. Even if the answer to this question about the perceptual case is one in which experiences of the kind in question play a role in individuating the content, that role must be linked to the truth-conditions of the content if the answer to the question is to be satisfying.

Neocriterial attempts to deny the existence of tasks at Level (3) in endorsing a conception of truth as explicable in terms of the fulfilment of criteria also commit themselves to a thoroughly anti-realistic view of truth. We have a realistic conception of truth under which a past-tense content can be true even though the announced criteria for it are not fulfilled, and might not even have been fulfilled had the matter been investigated earlier. Though a full development of the case would be a matter for a different book, it is arguable that the possibility of verification-transcendent truth is an inevitable concomitant of a proper characterization of the nature of our grasp of concepts of the spatio-temporal world.[18] If this is right, these attempts to dissolve the task at Level (3) would also dissolve our capacity for objective thought.

A different kind of theorist holds that we do indeed have a notion of truth which permits intelligible framing of questions at the third level, but holds also that we cannot give philosophical explanations at the third level of why generalizations at the second level hold. One prominent position of this sort is that of Humean naturalism as characterized by Peter Strawson in *Skepticism and Naturalism*.[19] Strawson endorses a view he attributes to Hume, and to Wittgenstein, 'the view that our "beliefs" in the existence of the body and, to speak roughly, in the reliability of induction are not grounded beliefs and at the same time are not open to serious doubt' (p. 19). 'To attempt to confront the professional sceptical doubt with argument in support of these beliefs, with rational justifications, is simply to show a total misunderstanding of the role they actually play in our belief

---

[18] See *Being Known*, ch. 3, sec. 2.
[19] *Skepticism and Naturalism: some varieties* (London: Methuen, 1985).

systems' (ibid). '[T]here is no such thing as *the reasons for which we hold these beliefs*' (p. 20). In short, 'one must refuse the challenge' (p. 25). He also observes that a theory commonly offered in justification of these beliefs, that their content provides the best explanation of our experiences, is not the ordinary person's reason for holding these beliefs. The more ambitious transcendental arguments in philosophy aimed to give reason for believing in the existence of material objects, or of other minds, from the starting point of the existence of self-conscious experiences. Under these late views of Strawson such ambitions should be abandoned. The most we could hope to establish is that if we have self-conscious experiences we must believe we have knowledge of material objects or other minds. Such arguments are certainly of philosophical value, but are manifestly less ambitious.

It is surely true that we do naturally believe in the existence of material bodies. That we naturally believe, without philosophical reasoning, what we are entitled to believe is not something the theorist of Level-(3) tasks is committed to denying.

On Strawson's other grounds for his sceptical naturalism it seems to me we need to start by distinguishing the entitling states from the principles which make them entitling. I suggest that some of what Strawson says about justifications is not true when taken to be about the entitling states, while if it is taken to concern the principles which make states entitling it is not an objection to the present approach.

The entitling states—the experiences of our senses—do give us reasons (non-inferential reasons) for believing in bodies. The answer of the ordinary person to the question 'Why do you believe there are material bodies?' is likely to be 'I see and feel them', and this is a pre-theoretical answer that accords with the theory of entitlement outlined here. The answer cites states that are entitling. The ordinary person will not or need not come up with any particular theory of why they are entitling. That could be an objection only if thinkers who are entitled to make certain transitions in thought also have to have some explicit account of why they are so entitled. This is not something we would accept when considering other topics. The idea that the thinker is entitled to make certain transitions but can be without a theory he can articulate of why they are transitions to which he is entitled seems to me a combination that we find when the non-philosophical thinker is making logical transitions, mathematical transitions, transitions involving the notion of probability, and indeed almost any transition whose legitimacy is grounded in the nature of notions of which he need not have a fully explicit grasp.

The theorist of Level-(3) characterizations need not at all be denying that the framework of material objects underlies 'all questions and all thinking'. I myself doubt that one can give an account of the capacity to think about experiences themselves without treating that ability as fundamentally dependent on the ability to think of non-mental things or events. It is also arguable that a conception of the representational content of one's perceptions as objective requires some grasp of a framework of non-mental objects and events.[20] These are just two of many ways in which the framework of material things and events underlies a domain of thought. Such framework theses seem to me to be entirely consistent with the existence of explanations of why certain states are entitling. They may not be consistent with certain bad attempts to carry through the Level-(3) task, attempts which suppose we have a conception of entitling experience entirely independent of our capacities to think about the external world. But we should not rule out a type of approach only because it has some bad versions, versions which contain extraneous elements that are in no way essential features of other answers to Level-(3) questions. Under this response to the later Strawson's arguments the prospects for the more ambitious forms of transcendental argument remain alive.

Other widely discussed approaches in epistemology do not explicitly refuse the sceptic's challenge, in the style of Strawsonian naturalism, but they still characterize normative notions in ways that seem to leave the challenge unaddressed. One such treatment is Goldman's, in his *Epistemology and Cognition*. He requires of a legitimate method only that it reliably produce truth in 'normal' worlds. More precisely: 'My proposal is that, according to our ordinary conception of justifiedness, a rule system is right in any world W just in case it has a sufficiently high truth ratio *in normal worlds*' (p. 107). 'Normal' here is used by Goldman in a semi-technical sense. Normal worlds in his sense 'are worlds consistent with our *general* beliefs about the actual

---

[20] See the final section of my 'Does Perception have a Non-Conceptual Content?'.

world' (p. 107). He mentions general beliefs about the sorts of objects, events, and changes that occur in the actual world. A little later, Goldman writes:

Imagine, the objection goes, that our *actual* world turns out to be an evil demon world. (Or imagine that we are actually brains in a vat being deceived by scheming scientists.) Intuitively, our beliefs would still be justified; yet the belief-forming processes being deployed are not reliable. Again the case is easy to handle. Its apparent strength rests on the assumption that the justificational status of the beliefs is determined by the reliability of their causal processes *in the actual world*. But this does not accord with our theory. Reliability is measured in normal worlds; and in this case, the actual world is an abnormal world! (p. 113).

Goldman is surely correct to classify worlds in which the thinker is a brain in a vat as not normal in his sense. But there seem to be legitimate questions. Why should I rely on a method which reliably yields true belief only in worlds in which my general beliefs are true? Can't I raise the question of whether those general beliefs themselves are justified? It seems to me that these are reasonable questions. Our ordinary notion of justification is not one for which the question of whether our general beliefs are justified is trivial. Whether our general beliefs about the sorts of things that there are in the world are justified beliefs is, it seems to me, a substantive normative question. It is substantive on our ordinary concept of justification. A more satisfying treatment must give the thinker some substantive reason, if only a defeasible one, for thinking that he is not the brain in a brain-in-a-vat world, a reason beyond the claim that that would be a world in which our general beliefs are not true. Otherwise, we will be back with sceptical conclusions. The appeal to the Complexity Reduction Principle aims to meet this need.

Complexity reduction is not an all-purpose answer to all sceptical problems. There is a huge variety of possible forms of scepticism. In fact, there is a distinctive variety of scepticism for each variety of entitlement, since each variety of entitlement may be questioned. One might be sceptical about judgements which go beyond those justified by experiences with instance-individuated contents; one might be sceptical about the capacities we exercise in abductive inferences; and so forth. The only cases in which complexity reduction is a candidate for addressing sceptical concerns in the way we have developed in this and the preceding chapter are those in which the entitling states are complex.

On the other hand, such cases do extend beyond those we have already discussed. To take one obvious case, autobiographical, personal memories have contents that are individuated by the perceptual experiences that give rise to them. Such memory states must be at least as complex as the perceptions in terms of which they are individuated. So they are candidates for the development of a complexity-reduction argument. If it can be shown that it is adaptive to have largely correct memories about one's past, such an argument has some prospects. There may also be other types of complexity involved in mental states with intentional content that equally permit the development of Level-(3) explanations. I have explored only a fragment of this territory.

CHAPTER 5
Induction

I will argue that the same principles of complexity reduction that we used to explain principles of perceptual entitlement in the preceding chapter can also be used to explain why the principles of inductive inference hold. In short, when we have a sound, non-conclusive inductive inference from a variety of Fs being G to the conclusion that all Fs are G this holds because the easiest way for the evidence to hold is one that also makes it the case that all Fs are G. My aim is to clarify and to elaborate this thesis and to do the same for some of its consequences.

The distinction between Levels (1), (2), and (3) on which we drew earlier applies equally to inductive inference. At Level (1) we have various examples of inductive transitions to which we are entitled. There is a sound inductive inference from instances of which we know to the generalization that all humans are mortal. At Level (2), as in other cases, we have generalizations about the conditions under which we are entitled to make particular inductive inferences. Some of these generalizations are about the conditions that must be met by our base of initial examples for the inductive inference to be justified. If our inference is from a range of known instances of the form *a is F and a is G*, inductive inference to *All Fs are G* is sound only if checking whether something is an F, or indeed whether it is G, does not affect whether it is G. Our initial base of examples must also be drawn from a wide variety of conditions. In our sample of humans an inductive inference to the conclusion *All humans are mortal* is justified only because our range of examples is not restricted to those who live in one particular climate, have a distinctive diet, or the like.

At Level (3) our task would be to explain why these generalizations about sound, non-conclusive inference hold. Some of the justly influential contributions to thought about induction can be seen as contributions to characterizing this third level—even if they are not always formulated in a way which makes it evident that they are such contributions. For example, in his famous discussion of these issues, Gilbert Harman wrote that 'other things being equal, we can infer a generalization only if it provides the most plausible way to explain our evidence'.[1] In an earlier article he wrote: 'All cases in which one appears to be using it [enumerative induction] may also be seen as cases in which one is making an inference to the best explanation'.[2] It would greatly understate the significance of Harman's point to treat his claims as confined to Level (2), as stating only the conditions under which an inductive entitlement exists. They are clearly pertinent to the explanation of the entitlement, even when it is formulated in a generalized form and is not confined to some specific inductive inference. If Harman is right it would be in the spirit of his position on this particular issue to say that the soundness of an inference from all observed Fs being Gs to the conclusion that all Fs are Gs is explained philosophically by the fact that it is a variety of inference to the best explanation; one in which, on Harman's view, the best explanation of all observed Fs being G is that all Fs are G. The theory I will be offering will also be at Level (3).

I say only that it would be 'in the spirit of his position on this particular issue' to take Harman as making claims about Level-(3) explanations because, at least in his book *Thought*, Harman accepts a psychologism about the notion of justification and inference.[3] If facts about entitlement can be explained at all, on a psychologistic view they can be at most facts about psychological states, rather than normative facts. On my account it is normative facts that Level-(3) explanations should explain. I am taking it, however, that Harman's contributions on inductive inference are of importance, and can be assessed, independently of his psychologism. Though I will be disagreeing with Harman on some significant points, the idea that explanation has some part to play in explaining why inductive inference is justified seems to me to be of permanent value, and needs to be incorporated into any account of these matters.

[1] *Thought*, 136.
[2] 'The Inference to the Best Explanation', *Philosophical Review*, 74 (1965), 88–95, at 90.
[3] See *Thought*, 18–19.

5.1 A Thesis and its Consequences

Suppose that in given circumstances a thinker is entitled to make the inconclusive inference from a set of singular premisses

> $Fa \; \& \; Ga$
> $Fb \; \& \; Gb$
> .
> .
> .
> $Fn \; \& \; Gn$

together with the premiss that $a, b, \ldots, n$ are all the observed Fs to the conclusion

> $All \; Fs \; are \; G.$

My thesis is that the explanation of the existence of this entitlement is that in the given circumstances it is reasonable to think that the easiest way for all of the singular propositions

> $Fa \; \& \; Ga$
> $Fb \; \& \; Gb$
> .
> .
> .
> $Fn \; \& \; Gn$

to hold in a case in which $a, b, \ldots, n$ are all the observed Fs is for some condition C to hold which explains why all Fs are G. One can rationally make such a leap to the universal quantification without knowing which condition C it is that will verify this existential quantification over conditions. Before much was known about why cells die, or even that there were cells, this was the state of affairs for peoples' knowledge that all humans are mortal.

Under this thesis if one can appreciate how it could easily come about that all the singular propositions $Fa \; \& \; Ga, \ldots, Fn \; \& \; Gn$ hold without there being any such explaining condition C one is not entitled to make the enumerative induction (and that is the reason one is not entitled to make it).

There are two phenomena exhibited by sound inductions that are explained by this thesis.

(a) The thesis explains why, other things equal, an induction is stronger when the initial sample is larger and is drawn from a variety of different background conditions. If the sample were narrow, or were drawn from a restricted variety of background conditions, it could easily fail to be the case that all Fs are G. Consider what has to be the case for the existence of some such explaining condition C to be the easiest way for all the propositions in the initial sample to hold. That is the easiest way only for a large sample drawn from a variety of conditions. For a narrow sample, or a sample drawn from restricted conditions, it would not be difficult for it to be a coincidence that all the propositions in the initial sample hold.

(b) The thesis explains why an entitlement to make an induction from instances lapses if one knows it to be purely a coincidence of any given F that it is also G. If one knows that whether an F thing is also G is determined by purely random processes then one cannot soundly make inductions from an initial sample of Fs that are G. The only way in which an accumulation of observed Fs that are G can make one become entitled to an inductive inference that all Fs are G is for that accumulation also to make it plausible that there is some condition C that explains why all Fs are G.

The explaining condition C will in some cases be a law or explanatory principle involving some property H such that it is a law that all Fs have H and a law that all things with H are G. The explanation of the mortality of all humans is that all humans are composed of cells of a certain kind and it is a law that all cells of that kind eventually decay which on a sufficiently large scale in one way or another results in death.

It is, however, important that there can be an explanatory condition C, and thereby sound enumerative induction, without there being a property H of the sort just described. Here are three examples.

(a) Consider the generalization that all surviving buildings from an ancient civilization in central America are made from stone. This generalization can be very well confirmed, by evidence from cities and settlements hundreds of miles apart, in very different climates. The requirements for a sound inductive inference can be fulfilled. The explaining condition C in this example will be this: Given the building materials available in this civilization, only those built from stone will survive the erosion and deterioration over the intervening centuries. This is an entirely satisfactory explanation; but it in no way explains why any particular building was given a stone structure. The explanation of that will be such factors as that its owner was rich enough to build in a stronger material than wood, and wanted a building that would last.

(b) Take the generalization that all the students ever attending a particular university now or in the past are from East Coast high schools. Suppose there is some explanation for this: say, that the university has an entrance requirement demanding proficiency in a certain language and that language is taught only in East Coast high schools. As we go through hundreds of students' records from over the years we can be entitled to make an enumerative inductive inference to the conclusion that all students at the university attended some or other East Coast high school. But the explaining condition does not account for the fact that some particular student at the university attended a given East Coast high school. That might have had to do with parental preference, or financial considerations, or virtually anything at all, consistently with the given explanation of why all students at the university in question are from East Coast high schools.

(c) Roger White, to whom I am indebted for pointing out to me the importance of not confusing an explanation of why all Fs are G with an explanation of why a particular F is G, mentioned the following example. If we have a large urn we may pull items out of it and discover that each item pulled out is green. There may be some explanation of this, as for instance that someone has decided to store only green items in the urn. But this explanation does not of course give an explanation of why some particular item in the urn is green. If one of the items is a blade of grass, it is the presence of chlorophyll in the blade of grass that will explain the greenness of that particular item in the urn.

How then does the approach that requires that it be reasonable to think there is some condition C which explains why all Fs are Gs differ from the treatment given by Harman? There are two differences.

First, it seems to me that there is an ambiguity in Harman's claim that 'we can infer a generalization only if it provides the most plausible way to explain our evidence'. We have to ask what it is whose explanation is in question in this requirement. There is an ambiguity in respect of the size of the scope of the operator 'explains that'. We can distinguish between

> explaining why all the observed Fs are Gs

where 'observed' falls within the scope of 'explaining that', so that the notion of observation enters what it is that is explained, and

> explaining, concerning each observed F, why it is G

Here the notion of observation is outside the scope of 'explaining', and does not enter what it is that is explained. We call the first displayed reading, in which 'explains' has wider scope, the 'wide-scope reading', and we call the second reading the 'narrow-scope reading'. Which of these two readings is the one we should use in construing Harman's account of the conditions for sound enumerative induction?

Under the wide-scope reading it seems to me correct to say that when the enumerative induction is sound the evidence—namely, that all observed Fs are Gs—is really explained by the fact that all Fs are G. Here we are explaining a partially psychological condition—that the Fs that are observed are really G—by the holding of a condition that (in at least this respect) is not psychological, that all Fs are G. Under this first reading, however, I do not think we have quite the right conditions for the soundness of an enumerative induction. For the explanatory claim we have just acknowledged will hold equally when the generalization that all Fs are Gs holds for entirely accidental reasons, and its holding may even be a result of objective randomness. Suppose one hundred spinnings of a roulette wheel are spinnings in which the ball lands on red, and suppose we observed the first fifty spinnings. The fact that all of the hundred spinnings ended with the ball landing on red is sufficient to explain why all the fifty observations of spinnings are ones in which the ball landed on red. But an inductive inference to the fifty-first spinning that it will end with the ball landing on red is unsound. The generalization does give the explanation of our evidence, but we are not entitled to the inductive inference if we know the wheel to be unbiased.

In classifying the example thus I am actually agreeing with some of Harman's other claims. He writes, in considering an inference to 'the next observed F will be G':

one must compare the hypothesis that the next [F] will be different from the preceding [F]s with the hypothesis that the next [F] will be similar to preceding [F]s. As long as the hypothesis that the next [F] will be similar is a better hypothesis in the light of all the evidence, the supposed induction is warranted. But if there is no reason to rule out a change, then the induction is unwarranted.[4]

There is no reason to rule out a change in the roulette example: there is no reason to rule out that the fifty-first spin will result in the ball landing on black. The induction would be unwarranted in this case; and so I conclude that this first reading, in which 'explains' has wide scope, does not give the correct conditions for warranted enumerative induction. We could make the same point for successive observations of some process such as radioactive decay, which is objectively random and is known by us to be so.

It may be said that this is unfair to Harman. At least in the case in which we do not know whether the roulette wheel is biased, or whether the physical process of decay is objectively random, we are in fact entitled to infer the generalization only if we are also entitled to believe that it is the best explanation of our evidence, in the sense of the wide-scope reading. I agree—but still I think Harman's account omits a crucial feature of our commitments in the case in which we are willing to make the inductive inference. There is a commitment to the existence of some condition C that explains why all the Fs are G. It is precisely the fact that this commitment is not fulfilled that explains our sense that in the case in which we make an inductive inference in a case in which a genuinely random, or unbiased, process just so happens to generate the result that all Fs are G we have been right merely as a matter of luck. Even though in such a case our evidence is explained by all Fs being G, in the sense of the wide-scope reading, we were committed in making the induction to more than that being the case. We were committed to the existence of an explanation of why all Fs are G.

Under the narrow-scope reading a different problem arises. Harman's claim that the generalization explains the evidence is, under this reading, taken to mean that the generalization explains of each particular observed F why it is G. Harman does hold that the generalization explains this, at least in some cases. He writes: 'That all

---

[4] 'The Inference to the Best Explanation', 91; I have changed Harman's 'A' and 'B' to 'F' and 'G' respectively.

emeralds are green does not cause a particular emerald to be green; but it can explain why that emerald is green'.[5] Harman's thesis as formulated using this narrow-scope reading faces two problems.

First, some generalizations to which we would be warranted in making an inductive inference do not even purport to provide explanations of why individual things are G. In our three examples (a)–(c) of a few paragraphs back the generalizations do not provide explanations of why a particular building in the ancient civilization was constructed from stone, or why a pupil attended a particular high school, or why a particular object is green.

Second, it is not at all clear to me that generalizations in any sense explain their instances. It is one thing for something's being a law to explain instances; but the explanation is always something more than the de facto generalization itself. Once again, a generalization can hold purely accidentally, or even randomly. It does not seem to me that such generalizations explain their instances. If they were counted as doing so Harman's account under this narrow-scope reading would give the wrong conditions for enumerative induction to be warranted; for it is not warranted in purely accidental or random cases.

It would, as far as I can see, be entirely within the spirit of Harman's general position to modify his account so as to require what I have suggested, that in a warranted induction to the conclusion that all Fs are G one incurs a commitment to the existence of some condition C that explains why all Fs are G.

In discussing these matters I have tried to respect the distinction between explaining a series of singular facts and explaining a universal quantification. We can distinguish a third explanandum, beyond the explananda in question in the wide- and narrow-scope readings we have already distinguished. Consider the following explanandum (OC), which is a conjunction of singular facts:

o_1 is an observation of a GF
o_2 is an observation of a GF
.
.
.
o_n is an observation of a GF

5 *Thought*, 131.

This conjunction of singular facts is explained by a conjunction of singular facts; namely, the conjunction of

x_1 is a GF
x_2 is a GF
.
.
.
x_n is a GF

where x_i is the object observed in observation o_i. It would indeed be explanatorily redundant to bring in the fact that all Fs are G in an attempt to explain the conjunction of singular facts (OC). The universal quantification that all Fs are G goes beyond the conjunction of all its singular instances, as Frank Ramsey famously observed. Even if the x_i are all the Fs there are, the universal quantification involves the holding not just of those singular facts but also the negative condition that there are no other Fs that are not G. (OC), as a conjunctive explanandum of singular facts, is to be sharply distinguished from the explanandum (OU):

All observations of Fs are observations of GFs.

(OU) is itself a fact involving universal quantification, something thereby involving a Ramseyan negative condition, and so cannot itself be fully explained simply by a conjunction of singular propositions. (OU) is properly explained by the universally quantified condition that all Fs are Gs. Noting this distinction, however, does nothing to restore the first reading of Harman's position as an account of inductive entitlement. For it remains that in the roulette case, for example, all observations of throws of the ball are observations of throws in which the ball comes to rest in a red compartment. One remains unentitled to inductive inference to the ball's landing in a red compartment on the next throw if one knows the roulette wheel to be genuinely unbiased.

As I said, it would not be contrary to the spirit of Harman's position to incorporate the condition I have suggested. There remains, however, a much deeper difference between Harman's treatment and the approach that offers Level-(3) explanations in terms of the easiest way in which the evidence could come about. This is the other major difference from Harman's treatment. The approach that appeals to easiness actually offers a Level-(3) explanation of abductive inference itself, and not just of inductive inference. It does not merely justify inductive inference by seeing it as a special case of abductive inference, but offers something that also explains the entitlement to abductive inference. An abductive inference is reasonable precisely in those cases in which the holding of the theory to which an abduction is made provides what it is rational to think is the easiest way for the evidence to have come about. The evidence is not a coincidence, does not result from highly special initial conditions, if the theory is correct.

Under this approach the fact that it is rational to believe that things have come about in easier rather than more difficult ways provides the Level-(3) explanation both of sound inductive principles and of sound abductive principles. Harman was right to link the soundness of inductive inference with that of inference to the best explanation (with the above qualification). But there is a common, deeper explanation of the soundness of both kinds of inference, an explanation which appeals to how difficult it would be for the evidence to hold in the absence of the explaining condition C to which both an induction and an abduction are committed.

Back in Chapter 4, Section 1(d), I distinguished between an objective rule and its subjective counterpart. In the present discussion of induction I have framed the questions as ones about the conditions under which a thinker is entitled to make an inductive inference. Those conditions advert to the rationality of thinking that there is an explaining condition C, and this is what we should expect when we are considering what is required for entitlement. The conditions which advert to the rationality of thinking that there is an explaining condition C should be seen as the subjective counterpart of an objective rule. The objective rule to which one is doing one's best to conform when one meets the subjective counterpart is this:

> Make an inductive inference to *All Fs are G* only if there is some condition C which explains why all the Fs are G.

5.2 Indispensability

Defeasible inductive inference seems to be indispensable under the present account. Suppose we have an inductive basis consisting in the set of singular propositions Fa & Ga, Fa & Gb, . . . , Fn & Gn, where we also have that $a, b, \ldots, n$ are all of the observed Fs. Let us suppose that all the conditions for an entitled use of induction are met: our sample is large, drawn from a wide variety of circumstances, there is no reason to think that the property G is instantiated as a result of random processes, and the like. Could we dispense with inductive inference, or defeasible inference in general, by simply relying on this additional premiss?

> The easiest way for Fa & $Ga, \ldots, Fn$ & Gn all to be true, where $a, b, \ldots, n$ are all of the observed Fs is for there to be some condition C whose holding explains why all Fs are Gs.

That would still not be sufficient to close the gap. We could not deductively infer from our evidential base together with the displayed proposition to the conclusion *All Fs are Gs*. For the simplest way of obtaining that conclusion deductively from a set of premisses including our inductive basis and the displayed proposition we would need also to have this further premiss: that it has come to be the case that Fa & $Ga, \ldots, Fn$ & Gn in the easiest way.

This further premiss is an empirical truth. It is not generally true without qualification that things come about in the easiest of empirically possible ways. Evidently they sometimes do not: coincidences do occur. Perhaps it is true, and perhaps it is reasonable to believe, that things do come about in the easiest way in the particular circumstances in which we are making the inductive inference in question. That would be sufficient to close the deductive gap. But it is hard to see how anyone could have reason for believing that premiss without relying on induction, or on other kinds of defeasible inference. It seems that any rationale for any inductive inference must rely on defeasible transitions at some point or other.

It is a highly plausible conjecture that this point holds for defeasible transitions in general. A conclusion reached by sound use of a defeasible form of entitlement can be reached by deductive means with additional premisses; but those additional premisses can be rationally accepted only by relying on some form of defeasible inference elsewhere. If this is true defeasible inference is indispensable. Some forms of defeasible transition may be reduced or defined in terms of others, and so may not be fundamental; but we cannot eliminate all forms of defeasible inference and still be able to make all the transitions that, rationally, we are entitled to make.

5.3 Induction, the Second Principle of Rationalism, and the A Priori

If thinkers are entitled to make sound inductions, and if induction is (non-conclusively) truth-conducive, then the second principle of rationalism, that we identified at the start of Chapter 2, must apply to it. That is, the rational truth-conduciveness of induction must have some philosophical explanation that appeals to the nature of the intentional contents and states involved when a thinker makes a sound inductive inference. What is that explanation?

Contrary to the views of some writers, it seems quite implausible to say that the soundness of inductive inference is required by the meaning of the universal quantification in *All Fs are G*, or by the meaning of 'the next F to be encountered'. A person can, both intuitively and on the present theory, intelligibly decline to make an inductive inference if he suspects that the evidence has not come about in the easiest of ways.

An implausible appeal to the meaning of 'all' or of 'the next F' is not, however, the only possible content or state-based source available to explain how the second principle of rationalism applies to inductive inference. Consider the principle that it is rational, other things equal, to judge that things come about in easier, rather than harder, ways. This principle seems to be a consequence of two basic principles: that judgement aims at truth, and that what can more easily be the case is more likely to be true. These principles concerns the nature of the states involved in sound inductive inference, and the properties involved in that nature. If the present approach is correct they explain why sound inductive inference is likely to be truth-conducive. Here, then, I am in agreement with Laurence BonJour, who holds that a priori principles can contain the notions of probability and likelihood.[6] The Level-(3) explanation of sound inductive inference

---

[6] See sect. 7.7, 'Toward an *A Priori* Justification of Induction', of his book *In Defense of Pure Reason* (Cambridge: Cambridge University Press, 1998). BonJour's a priori principles (I-1) and (I-2), which I accept, are also ones I would say are explained at Level (3) by facts about what can easily be the case.

offered here thus respects the general rationalist idea that the a priori status of any principle can be explained in terms of the identity of the states, contents, and concepts involved in that principle.

A sound inductive inference seems to be a priori: the thinker has an a priori, defeasible entitlement to make it. This is not to imply that in any case in which we are entitled to make an inductive inference to the conclusion that all Fs are G it holds conclusively and a priori that, given our evidence, there is some condition C that explains why all Fs are G. It is only to imply that it is a priori, given our evidence, that there is a defeasible entitlement to believe that there is some such explaining condition C. This defeasible a priori entitlement exists because we are entitled to believe that things have come about in easier, rather than harder, ways, and, given a wide range of evidence, the easiest way for it to have come about is for there to be some condition C which explains why all Fs are G. The Level-(3) explanation of why we are entitled to inductive inference is, on this view, also a priori—as it must be if it is to explain a priori status satisfactorily.

If the defeasible entitlement to inductive inference were not a priori in the way just outlined, rational inductive inference could never get started. The entitlement to inductive inference would in that case be a posteriori. But to conclude anything from the a posteriori success of inductive inferences in previous cases we would need an inductive principle, which would in turn need justification from experience. We seem to be started on an infinite regress.

Regressive arguments of this familiar kind have been used by some writers to promote either a scepticism, or a naturalism devoid of normative commitments about inductive inference (or both). The regressive arguments should rather be seen as strengthening the case for a conception of entitled inductive inference that involves a priori, albeit defeasible, status, and comes with some explanation of its rationality as a tool in the search for truth.

CHAPTER 6

A Priori Entitlement

6.1 The Third Principle of Rationalism

The third principle of rationalism that I offer is:

PRINCIPLE III: The Generalized Rationalist Thesis
All instances of the entitlement relation, both absolute and
relative, are fundamentally a priori.

Now there are certainly some instances of the entitlement relation
that are not, and could not be, a priori. I am entitled, in my present
state, to believe that Australian red wines are fruitier in taste than traditional French red wines. This entitlement is not a priori. It rests
squarely on my taste experiences of Australian and French wines. So
what could 'fundamentally a priori' mean when it occurs in the third
principle of rationalism?

In discussing these issues we have always to be careful to respect
the distinction between a thinker's beliefs and transitions on the
one hand and our theoretical classifications of them on the other.
A thinker's beliefs may or may not be a priori, may or may not be
ones he is entitled to form; but in any case these are our classifications, as theorists, of his, our subject's, attitudes. Our thinker need
not possess the concept of the a priori, and need not possess the
concept of entitlement. Yet still these notions may apply to his
beliefs and transitions. It follows that we cannot, if we want the
notion to have application at all, characterize an entitlement as fundamentally a priori if a statement saying such an entitlement exists
follows from the subject's beliefs of such-and-such a sort. Since the
subject may not even possess the concept of entitlement no interesting statements about it need follow from any of the subject's
own beliefs.

When someone makes a judgement his reasons for making it will involve various other attitudes and mental states, and he will also be making the judgement because it stands in a certain relation to those other attitudes and mental states. We can image attaching a label, analogous to writing a justification at a line of a proof, which states what the entitling principle is which permits the transition to this judgement (if it is one which is entitled). The hypothesis that all entitlements are fundamentally a priori can then be formulated as follows. In any such labelling of judgements either the entitling principle involves reliance on some kind of conscious experience (where the entitlement to such reliance is itself a priori) or else the entitling principle, whether conclusive or defeasible, is a priori. What is excluded is the case in which the entitlement is a posteriori but cannot be split up into reliance on experience and a transition from it to which there is a priori entitlement.

There is an equivalent but more formal characterization of the fundamentally a priori. A statement to the effect that a person in certain circumstances is entitled to form a belief with a given content is fundamentally a priori if that statement follows from and is explained by a set of statements about the person's mental states and his transitions from them each of which is either a statement about his conscious experiences and mental states or is a statement to the effect that the thinker is entitled to make a transition of a certain kind, where this entitlement to the transition is a priori.

Under this characterization an a posteriori entitlement, such as the one to form the judgement about the relative fruitiness of Australian and classical French wines, can be fundamentally a priori. My entitlement to form this judgement rests on a series of empirical, partially perceptual beliefs of the forms 'This wine tastes fruity and is Australian', 'This wine does not taste fruity and is French'. These are a posteriori beliefs. But the judgement about the fruitiness of the taste is a perceptual one, and I argued in Chapters 3 and 4 that the entitlement to make such transitions from experience to judgements, though defeasible, is a priori. The other entitlement from which the a posteriori entitlement to the judgement about the comparative fruitiness of Australian and classical French wines is derivative is straightforward induction, which I have also argued to have an a priori status. The only reason that the entitlement to my judgement about the relative fruitiness of Australian and classical French red wines is a posteriori is that it relies on the occurrence of my perceptual experiences of the taste of various red wines. All the instances of the entitlement relation on which this a posteriori entitlement rests can be analysed into purely a priori relations of entitlement.

It follows that the example of the wine is not a counterexample to the third rationalist principle, because the entitlement is wholly explicable in terms of instances of the entitlement relation that are a priori. The third principle of rationalism implies that any instance of the entitlement relation which is a posteriori can be analysed away in similar fashion. The a posteriori character of any such case is explicable by factors other than an irreducibly a posteriori instance of the entitlement relation.

In this sense truths about entitlement are fundamentally a priori. The way in which we have explained how this can be so, consistently with the existence of true a posteriori propositions about entitlement, like the statement about the wine, is parallel to strategies that are available in other domains. Consider the case of metaphysical necessity. There are, as the examples of Kripke and Kaplan have shown, clear examples of contents that are necessary a posteriori: familiar examples include the content that Hesperus is Phosphorus, and that water is H_2O. These a posteriori modal truths seem, however, always to be the consequence of truths each one of which is either modal and a priori, or is a posteriori but non-modal. Thus 'Necessarily, Hesperus is Phosphorus' is a consequence of two propositions: the necessity of identity, and the truth that Hesperus is Phosphorus. The former is a priori—in fact it is a theorem, as Ruth Marcus showed—and the latter is wholly non-modal. What we do not have are cases of the necessary a posteriori that are not explicable in this way, which are as we might say irreducibly necessary a posteriori. If there were such cases the epistemology of modality would be even more problematic than it actually is, and perhaps even insoluble. If this is all correct the sense in which truths about metaphysical necessity are fundamentally a priori is exactly the same as the sense in which truths about entitlement are fundamentally a priori.

So much by way of elucidation of what the third principle of rationalism is claiming. Is there any general reason for accepting the third principle of rationalism? One could be tempted to hold this Generalized Rationalist Thesis simply by extrapolation from examples. Logical and mathematical transitions to which one is entitled are a priori; and I made a case in the earlier chapters that defeasible perceptual and inductive entitlement is also a priori. Moreover, the Level-(3) explanations of such entitlements seem also to appeal to a priori principles. But such enumeration can at most make it inductively plausible that the Generalized Rationalist Thesis is true. An enumeration by itself offers little insight on the question of *why* the Generalized Rationalist Thesis should be true.

There are, however, two principled considerations that support this third principle of rationalism.

The first consideration is the nature of entitlement itself. Entitled judgement is rational judgement. Judgement in accordance with the entitlement relation in our wine example is rational only because the entitlement can be analysed into instances of the entitlement relation that are a priori (together with the occurrence of the entitling taste experiences). If an entitlement is not fundamentally a priori, but the very entitlement relation itself rests essentially on empirical information, how could judging in accordance with that relation be rational, if the thinker lacked the empirical information on which the relation rests? Such a judgement would be an irrational leap in the dark, a mere guess. If on the other hand the thinker has that empirical information then we have a case in which the entitlement is fundamentally a priori after all. The conditional that if the empirical condition in question holds then there is an entitlement will be fundamentally a priori. If it were not, there would still be a lack of rationality. That is the first general consideration in support of the third principle of rationalism. This consideration is at the level of instances of the entitlement relation. It does not presuppose anything about which generalizations concerning entitlement are correct, nor about the correct explanation of those generalizations.

The second general consideration in support of the third principle of rationalism comes from reflection on what it *is* for something to be a priori. A plausible philosophical theory of what makes a proposition or a transition a priori holds that its truth or truth-conduciveness can be explained philosophically from the nature of the contents and states involved in the judgement or the transition. Correlatively, what makes something an a priori way of coming to know a content can be explained philosophically in terms of the nature of the contents and states involved in the judgement or the transition. If this philosophical theory is correct the third principle of rationalism is a corollary of the first and second principles of rationalism.

This means that the correct philosophical explanation of the a priori is of even greater import for rationalism than it would otherwise have been. The nature of the correct explanation would already have been of significance, since 'a priori' is a crucial term of art in any characterization of rationalism, including the one I gave in Chapters 1 and 2. What any version of rationalism amounts to depends upon the correct elucidation of the a priori. But for the form of rationalism developed in the three principles of rationalism there is a much deeper significance. Under the theory that what explains a priori status is derivability of truth (or truth-preservation) of an a priori principle from the nature of the concepts, contents, and states involved we have some deeper unification of the three principles of rationalism. Rather than being arbitrarily pressed together, under that characterization of the a priori, the third principle follows from the first two, and each of the first two can be seen as part of an elaboration of rationality undergirding that characterization of the a priori.

We thus need to investigate the correct philosophical explanation of why some principles are a priori much more extensively, both for its own interest and to see whether this unification of the three principles of rationalism is possible. The characterization of the a priori that would unify the three principles is in effect yet another rationalist thesis. To avoid further proliferation of numerical terminology I will call that theory of the a priori the 'Rationalist Account of the A Priori'.

More specifically, for reasons I am about to explain, the theory can be described as the *moderate* explanatory rationalist account of the a priori. This moderate explanatory rationalism is a middle way between two more extreme positions.

6.2 Varieties of Rationalism, and the Middle Way

Any form of rationalism merits the name only if it holds that there are a priori ways of coming to know contents, and that the status of these ways as a priori depends upon grasp of the content in question. But the nature of this dependence, and more generally the kind of explanation of how it is that particular ways of coming to know have a priori status, can vary widely between different varieties of rationalism. Here I distinguish three broad varieties which lie along a spectrum. I argue on general grounds for the middle, intermediate variety.

At one extreme we have what we can call *faculty rationalism*. This view holds that there is a special faculty, not explicable in terms of other faculties, that enables us to recognize propositions as a priori. This faculty is supposed to put us in contact with the subject matter of the a priori propositions, and is sometimes conceived on a causal model, or by some kind of analogy with it. Such a conception is present in the philosophical writings of Kurt Gödel and (probably) Roger Penrose.[1] The idea of such a special faculty is evidently beset with problems. How such a faculty is meant to work; how it relates to understanding; how its existence is to be reconciled with everything else we know about the mind and causal mechanisms; and how it could deliver entitlements of the sort we actually have to a priori propositions and transitions remains wholly obscure.

Adherents of faculty rationalism often speak of rational intuition or rational insight. Although there is likely no special faculty which leads to a priori knowledge, the phenomena that have prompted faculty rationalists to speak of rational insight or rational intuition are real and philosophically challenging. Many phenomena in this area cry out for philosophical explanation. We have such phenomena as the a priori status of propositions stating colour incompatibilities ('No shade can be both a shade of red and a shade of green'). We have the ability to discover new a priori axioms for notions that do not follow from those previously accepted. We even have the phenomenon of rational acceptance of primitive axioms, where acceptance of those axioms is involved in grasping the notions they contain. Many philosophical positions have either neglected these phenomena or have offered wholly inadequate attempts at explanation. Sometimes a retreat to faculty rationalism expresses the attitude that postulation

---

[1] K. Gödel, 'What is Cantor's Continuum Problem', repr. in P. Benacerraf and H. Putnam (eds.), *Philosophy of Mathematics: Selected Readings,* (Cambridge: Cambridge University Press, 1983), esp. the sec. entitled 'Supplement to the Second Edition [1963]'; and the papers in *Kurt Gödel Collected Works, iii,* ed. Feferman, et al.; R. Penrose, *Shadows of the Mind: A Search for the Missing Science of Consciousness* (London: Viking, 1995).

of an I-know-not-what faculty is at least an acknowledgement that the phenomena exist, and need a better explanation.

At the opposite end of the spectrum from faculty rationalism, we have *minimalism*. To formulate minimalism in this area properly we need a distinction between composite and atomic ways of coming to know. One way of coming to know a logical truth is by working out a proof of it. The proof consists of a series of transitions each one of which involves a way of coming to know a certain kind of conclusion from a certain kind of premiss. The individual transitions at each line of the fully analysed proof involve an atomic way of coming to know, something which cannot be broken down further into other ways of coming to know. When you visually identify someone as a person who attended a course you gave some years ago, that can be broken down into constituent ways of coming to know. One constituent is your taking your perceptual experience at face value; another may be, for instance, your taking some memory image as of a student in your class at face value; and a third is your transition from the appearance of the face of the person currently perceived and that of the remembered/student to the conclusion that this is one and the same person. I will leave the distinction between atomic and composite methods at this relatively intuitive level for present purposes. It does need more elaboration, but this will be enough for a formulation of the core of the minimalist's position.

Minimalism is then the thesis that when an atomic way W is an a priori way of coming to know that p it is simply primitively written into the identity of one or more concepts in p that W is an a priori way of coming to know that p, or of coming to know contents of some kind under which p falls. That p can be known a priori in way W is, according to the minimalist, written into an account of understanding in the way that it is written into being a bachelor that bachelors are men, or, perhaps, written into being a chair that chairs have backs, or written into the relation of perception that a perceived object must causally affect the perceiver. It may be unobvious, and hard to discover, what is written into the identity of any given concept, but when one realizes that some property is so written in, it is just a mistake to think that there is any further question 'Why does that concept have that epistemic property?' which is in need of an answer. According to this minimalist position the fact that an atomic way W is an a priori way of coming to know that p is not consequential upon anything else. The minimalist will agree that composite ways of coming to know which are a priori can be explained as such by being built up from atomic ways which are ways of coming to know a priori; but for the status of atomic ways as a priori ways there is no further explanation to be given, beyond its being primitively constitutive of the identity of the concepts in the content known that they are so a priori. Perhaps the position would be better called 'conceptual minimalism', since the position employs talk of concepts without saying that such talk is a mere manner of speaking. There are more radical forms of minimalism. But this conceptual minimalism seems to be minimalist within the class of positions which take talk of concepts and meaning in the theory of thought and understanding at face value. What is crucial about conceptual minimalism is not that it regards the identity of concepts as in some cases given by the conditions for knowing certain contents, but that it regards the resource of what is primitively written into the identity of a concept as a full explanation of the relation between the a priori and the concepts featuring in the content of a priori knowledge. That certain concepts can be individuated by the conditions for knowing certain contents containing them was after all a thesis of my book *Being Known*. Conceptual minimalism is a stronger claim.

There is really a cluster of positions which can be called (conceptually) minimalist. One variant of minimalism holds that when a thinker comes to know via an atomic a priori way that p the thinker judges that p because of his grasp of the concepts in p. This statement is, according to this variant of minimalism, a genuinely explanatory true statement: understanding or grasp of the concepts in question explains the rational, a priori judgement that p. But that, according to this variant minimalist, is all that there is to be said on the matter.

The moderate rationalist, in the sense in which I will use that description, disagrees with all forms of minimalism. The first component of the moderate rationalist's view is that for any a priori way of coming to know a given content there is a substantive explanation of why it is an a priori way of coming to know that content, an explanation which involves the nature of the concepts in the given content. The moderate rationalist intends this claim to apply both to atomic and to composite ways of coming to know. For those who hold that concepts are individuated by the conditions for possessing them this first component of the moderate rationalist's claim unfolds into the thesis that for any a priori way of coming to know a given content there is an explanation of why it is an a priori way which has to do with the possession-conditions of the concepts in that content.

The moderate rationalist is, then, committed to the feasibility of a certain explanatory programme. The goal of her programme is to identify those features of concepts that explain why a given way of coming to know a particular content is an a priori way. If the moderate rationalist thinks that concepts are individuated in terms of the conditions for their possession, execution of that programme must involve appeals to explanatory properties of concept possession or understanding.

Of course I am not the only rationalist who would like to describe himself as 'moderate'. The very terminology of moderate rationalism is found in such recent writers as George Bealer and Laurence BonJour.[2] The characterization I am offering is an umbrella which covers rather different ways of implementing what seems to me the general theoretical idea of moderate rationalism. In particular, the present characterization remains neutral on the specific accounts of particular concepts, their possession, and how the nature of those concepts can contribute to the explanation of a priori status. I would disagree with the particular thesis that Bealer labels that of a moderate rationalist: '*most* of a person's non-inferential beliefs about the applicability of a concept to elementary hypothetical cases are true'.[3] But the details of that dispute do not matter for present purposes. What does matter is that even if we disagree with Bealer's thesis he still falls under the umbrella characterization of one who is attempting to found facts about the a priori in the nature of concepts, and their relation to the truth of certain contents containing them, whether or not he is right about the nature of those concepts.

BonJour comes under the same umbrella. He is not a faculty rationalist: he strongly emphasizes that it is 'anything but obvious' that the rational insight employed in attaining a priori knowledge involves

---

[2] G. Bealer, 'The Philosophical Limits of Scientific Essentialism', in *Philosophical Perspectives, i. Metaphysics*, J. Tomberlin (ed.), (Atascadero, Calif.: Ridgeview, 1987) and 'The Incoherence of Empiricism', in S. Wagner and R. Warner (eds.), *Naturalism: A Critical Appraisal* (Notre Dame: Notre Dame University Press, 1993); L. BonJour, *In Defense of Pure Reason*, esp. 16 ff.

[3] 'Philosophical Limits of Scientific Essentialism', 319.

'a distinct psychological faculty'. He holds that the faculty involved in attaining a priori knowledge 'is simply the ability to understand and think'.[4] The task is then to explain how understanding and thought generates a priori knowledge. If we identify having minimal understanding with possessing a concept, and concepts are individuated by their possession-conditions, this is precisely the moderate rationalist's task. While Bealer, BonJour, and I would disagree on many matters, we hold the core moderate-rationalist view that the existence of a priori ways of coming to know is to be explained by the nexus of relations between understanding, concepts, and truth, and without the postulation of further special-purpose faculties.

Much of the argument of earlier chapters of this book can be seen as attempting to carry through the moderate rationalist's explanatory programme in the case of a priori transitions used in forming perceptual judgements, in inductive entitlement, and so forth. But, to use a form of argument that is by now becoming familiar, that amounts at most to case-by-case confirmation of moderate rationalism. Are there any wholly general reasons for accepting moderate rationalism rather than either variety of minimalism?

I offer two arguments.

(i) We already have some theoretical conception of understanding and meaning. For some of us understanding consists in some form of grasp of truth-conditions; for others a notion of canonical conceptual role is said to be basic. These theoretical conceptions are never put forward as merely partial determinations of understanding. These conceptions are not ones under which meaning can be fully characterized only by specifying additionally, as a further and separate task, which ways of coming to know certain contents involving the meaning count as a priori ways of coming to know it. Once we have a conception of how meaning or content is determined, any links it has with the a priori have to be founded in that conception of how meaning or content is determined. If the links of meaning with the a priori cannot be so founded, one would not have fully explained meaning in terms of truth-conditions, or conceptual role, or whatever is the favoured notion. If meaning is already fixed as truth-conditions, or as canonical conceptual role, or whatever else is

⁴ In Defense of Pure Reason, 109.

favoured, to add links with the a priori as further primitive axioms for the notion of meaning is simply to concede that meaning is not fully characterized without those extra axioms.

It may help here to consider a parallel with Michael Dummett's writings on the justification of deduction. Dummett insisted, rightly in my view, that deductive relations must be philosophically explicable in terms of the meaning of the logical constants involved in those relations.[5] A theory of meaning must explain why those deductive relations hold. This is a point which can be accepted by realists and anti-realists alike. The same consideration applies to a priori ways in general, of which the deductive relations are but a special case. If some principle has an a priori status, its status as such must be explicable in terms of the meaning of the expressions occurring in that principle.

These considerations would have no force against the minimalist if the proper way of specifying grasp of a concept or a meaning were to specify which atomic ways of coming to know involving that concept or meaning are a priori ways which the thinker or understander must primitively appreciate as correct. Such a reconciliation is, however, not adequate to the phenomena of the a priori. Consider the Gödelian phenomenon of discovering new axioms correct for notions the thinker already possesses but which do not follow from principles already accepted, or again the apparently a priori principles of colour incompatibility. These are principles which are a priori, but thinkers apparently have to reflect and somehow work out on the basis of their understanding that they are correct, even though they do not follow logically from principles whose immediate acceptance is constitutive of possession of the concepts. Actually, even in cases in which immediate appreciation of an a priori principle is written into possession of the concept there is no easy reconciliation with a genuinely minimalist position. That acceptance of some principle is written into possession of some of the concepts it contains is one thing; it is another, and needs some theory, to explain why such a principle is true (or truth-preserving), as its a priori status implies.

(ii) This first point about meaning and understanding applies equally to the general concept of knowledge. We have some theoretical

---

[5] 'The Justification of Deduction', in *Truth and Other Enigmas* (London: Duckworth, 1978).

conception of what is involved in a way of coming to accept a content being a way of coming to know it. (The conception need not be reductive, of course.) If there are principles connecting understanding with those ways of coming to know which are a priori ways, the connecting principles cannot have the status of primitive stipulations or axioms of the sort envisaged by any kind of minimalism. The connecting principles must have their source in the nature of knowledge, as well as in the nature of understanding, and the consequent relations between the two.

Such are the initial, presumptive reasons in favour of developing a position which endorses the first component of a moderate rationalist's treatment of the a priori, the component which has a commitment to the possibility of explaining each case of a priori status by reference to features of understanding or concept possession. But this first component of moderate rationalism cannot exhaust the content of any rationalism which is entitled to the label 'moderate'. For all I have said so far, an explanation of a priori status might invoke a theory of understanding which is quite extreme. A Gödelian position, on which there is some faculty of rational intuition, allegedly analogous to perception, which puts a thinker in contact with concepts or meanings, could equally well endorse the existence of such explanations. In short, if the theory of understanding which proposes an explanation of the a priori status of a proposition is not itself moderate, the resulting position can hardly be a form of moderate rationalism either. So a second, obligatory, component of any rationalism which calls itself moderate must be the claim that the theory of understanding mentioned in its first component is not one which postulates causal or explanatory relations between properties of things in a third realm of concepts or meanings and says that those relations are involved in understanding.

6.3 Two Species of the A Priori

The general, overarching notion of the a priori that we have been using so far in fact covers two different more specific varieties of the a priori, of very different philosophical significance from each other.

The two species of the a priori can be introduced by first considering a much more general auxiliary notion. This more general notion in its most abstract form stretches far beyond the a priori. It is the notion of a judgement with a given intentional content being true in any circumstances in which it is reached in a given way. A judgement 'I'm in pain' that the thinker makes rationally because she consciously experiences pain falls under this general notion. In any circumstances in which a thinker comes to make the self-ascription of pain by rationally responding to her conscious experience of pain her self-ascription will be true. A judgement of a logical truth reached by accepting a proof of it equally falls under the same notion. I label this very general notion that of p's being *judgementally valid* with respect to a given way.

It is important that the judgemental validity of a content with respect to a given way turns only on the truth of the content in circumstances in which it is in fact judged (and reached in the given way). In assessing judgemental validity with respect to a given way we do not have to consider whether the content is true in circumstances in which it is not reached in that way. Nor do we have to consider whether the content has any kind of necessity.

Several famous concepts in philosophy are variants of this core notion of judgemental validity. Descartes was particularly interested in those contents with the following property: that there exists a way with respect to which they are judgementally valid, and which is indubitably so. Descartes's description of something that is 'necessarily true whenever it is put forward by me or conceived in my mind' is a variant, with additional restrictions, of the core idea of the judgementally valid.[6]

We can make use of this auxiliary notion of the judgementally valid in distinguishing the two species of the a priori that I want to separate. The first notion of the a priori to be distinguished is simply a restriction of the notion of judgemental validity. I say that

> p is *judgementally a priori* with respect to a way W just in case it is judgementally valid with respect to W, and the way W is an a priori way

The judgementally a priori includes some classical self-verifying cases. When the content 'I am thinking' is judged not as a report on the thinker's own recent conscious states but because the thinker

---

[6] Second Meditation, in *Philosophical Writings of Descartes, ii*, trans. J. Cottingham, R. Stoothof, and D. Murdoch (Cambridge: Cambridge University Press, 1984), 17.

appreciates, on the basis of his grasp of the concepts it contains, that it will be true in any circumstances in which he judges it, the content is judgementally a priori with respect to this way. The same applies to 'I hereby judge that water is H_2O'. The judgementally a priori will also include such traditionally acknowledged examples of the a priori as contents reached by mathematical proof.

Closely related to the judgementally a priori is a notion which is not itself a form of the a priori. Consider someone who makes the second-order self-ascriptive judgement 'I judge that $13 \times 5 = 65$', or makes the judgement 'I judge that if A and B then A'. Suppose this thinker comes to make these judgements by the procedure that Gareth Evans described. That is, to quote Evans's description, 'I get myself in a position to answer the question whether I believe that p by putting into operation whatever procedure I have for answering the question whether p'.[7] If, after applying this procedure, you reach the conclusion that p is the case, you are then willing to make the self-ascription 'I believe that p'; and otherwise not. So—to take the arithmetical case—suppose our thinker makes the self-ascription as follows. She first considers the first-order question of whether 13×5 is in fact 65. This will involve an arithmetical computation. In reaching the conclusion that $13 \times 5 = 65$ the thinker will not (or need not) be relying on a justification or an entitlement that involves the content or character of her conscious states. Employing the procedure described by Evans, our thinker then moves from her conclusion that $13 \times 5 = 65$ to the self-ascriptive judgement 'Yes, I believe that 13×5 is 65'. This self-ascriptive content is judgementally valid with respect to this method of coming to judge the self-ascriptive content.

The earlier stages of the way employed in reaching this self-ascription are a priori. The example can be such that only a priori premisses, and transitions, are used by the thinker in reaching the conclusion that $13 \times 5 = 65$. But is the whole method of coming to make the self-ascription also itself a priori? It is not. The transition the thinker makes from judging that $13 \times 5 = 65$ to judging that she judges that $13 \times 5 = 65$ is one to which the thinker is entitled only because she actually judges that $13 \times 5 = 65$. It is not like a case of

---

[7] *The Varieties of Reference* (Oxford: Oxford University Press, 1982), sect. 7. 4, p. 225.

perceiving a proof, in which the thinker has access to something which gives a rationale for the conclusion independently of the thinker's perception of the proof. In this self-ascriptive case the thinker's making the first-order judgement is part of the rationale for the self-ascription.

In Evans's procedure for self-ascription it seems, as Evans emphasizes, that the thinker does not engage in introspection in self-ascribing beliefs to herself. We can introduce the notion of a way of coming to judge a content being *non-introspective*, as follows. Such a way of coming to make a self-ascription is non-introspective in case (a) other than the final judgement reached in employing the way, the contents employed in using it are not about the thinker's own mental states or events; and (b) the means by which the thinker comes to accept these contents in employing the way do not involve checking on his own mental states or events. Evans's procedure, as used in self-ascribing the belief that $13 \times 5 = 65$, meets this condition for being a non-introspective way.

Here is another procedure which provides a non-introspective way of coming to make, in fact to know, a psychological self-ascription. One way of coming to judge, and to know, 'I see that there's a desk in front of me' is to investigate the world around one by looking, and make that self-ascription just in case one sees that there is a desk in front of one.

In neither the visual case nor the arithmetical case is the self-ascription reached by an a priori way. But in both cases the self-ascription is reached by a way that is non-introspective.

Other mental states besides acceptance, judgement, and perceptual states can be self-ascribed by ways which are non-introspective. Consider a self-ascription of an intention 'I intend to answer the objection in the next sentence'. A thinker may come to make the self-ascription in the following way. She goes through the procedure of deciding what to write next, and then makes the self-ascription of the intention if and only if she decides to answer the objection in the next sentence. This is the analogue for self-ascriptions of intention of Evans's procedure for the self-ascription of belief. The thinker's reasons for making her decision may have to do with such matters as what is a good reason for thinking what, and what layout of the argument will reflect this. In coming to make the self-ascription of the intention in this fashion the thinker will not be checking on her own mental states or events. The way in which the self-ascription is reached is non-introspective. The way is also not a priori. The thinker's entitlement to make the self-ascription of the intention depends upon her actually making the decision in question.

So much for illustration of the notion of the judgementally a priori, and its distinctness from what is judgementally valid in a non-introspective way. The second notion of the a priori of which I will be making extensive use I call the 'contentually a priori':

> *p* is *contentually a priori* with respect to a way W if W is an a priori way of coming to know *p* and W is also a way that ensures the following: the content *p* of the judgement it yields is true in the actual world, whichever world is labelled as the actual world, and is true regardless of whether that way W is used, and of whether the conditions of its use are met, in the world that is labelled as the actual world.[8]

Here the phrase 'whichever world is labelled as the actual world' is not meant to mean 'I don't care what the actual world is like'. 'Rather, *p* is true in the actual world, whichever is labelled as the actual world' here means: for any possible world, if it were actual, *p* would be true when evaluated with respect to it.

To say that something comes to be known in a way that ensures that it is true in the actual world, whichever is the actual world, is not to say this: that someone who comes to know something in this way thereby comes to know *that* it is true in the actual world, whichever is the actual world. The situation is quite parallel to the more straightforward case of the intuitive notion of an a priori way of coming to know some content. A person's entitlement can be a priori without her exercising, or even possessing, the concept of the a priori. The same point applies to the contentually a priori. A person can come to know something that is contentually a priori with respect to the way in which she comes to accept it without herself exercising or even possessing the concept of the contentually a priori. The fact, however, that there is a way of coming to accept a given content that does ensure that it is true in the actual world, whichever is the actual world, is something striking, and in need of philosophical explanation.

---

[8] This is a more refined version of the distinction drawn between 'the judgementally a priori' and 'the contentually a priori' in C. Peacocke, 'Implicit Conceptions, the A Priori, and the Identity of Concepts', in *Philosophical Issues*, 9 on 'Concepts', ed. Villaneuva, 121–41, at 136.

Being contentually a priori is a relation, between a content and a way. It will often be convenient to use an existential quantification of the relation. We say that something is contentually a priori *tout court* if there is some way with respect to which it is contentually a priori.

Those who are not made queasy by the whole idea of the a priori would count amongst the contentually a priori propositions the following: the known logical truths; known arithmetical truths; and propositions such as 'If I exist, and this place here exists, then I am here', 'No shade is both a shade of red and a shade of green', and 'If *p* then actually *p*'. As some of these examples illustrate, and as the writings of Kripke and Kaplan made clear, something can be contentually a priori without being metaphysically necessary.

In modal semantics Martin Davies and Lloyd Humberstone very helpfully introduced an operator 'Fixedly'. Its semantical clause states that 'Fixedly *p*' holds at a given world in a given model just in case it holds in that world in any model differing only in which world is labelled as the actual world.[9] All the contentually a priori propositions I just mentioned hold Fixedly Actually in the sense of Davies and Humberstone. That is, if we preface them with the pair of operators 'Fixedly' and 'Actually', in that order, the result is true.

Enthusiasts for philosophically significant formal semantics will also be struck by the affinity between the contentually a priori and David Kaplan's notion of validity in the logic of demonstratives; that is, the notion of truth with respect to every context in every structure.[10] The two notions are cousins. Kaplan is concerned with language rather than thought. For his semantical purposes Kaplan does not need to be concerned with ways of coming to know. But the property of being contentually a priori and the property of being valid in Kaplan's logic of demonstratives are not distant cousins. For a sentence type to be true in a given context, in Kaplan's treatment, it is not required that there exist an utterance of that sentence in that context. In Kaplan's words: 'to develop a logic of demonstratives it seems most natural to be able to evaluate several premises and a conclusion all in the same context. Thus the notion of φ *being true in c and A* does not require an utterance of φ'.[11]

---

[9] 'Two Notions of Necessity', *Philosophical Studies*, 38 (1980), 1–30, at 2.
[10] 'Demonstratives', in J. Almog, J. Perry, and H. Wettstein (eds.), *Themes from Kaplan* (New York: Oxford University Press, 1989), second definition on p. 547.   [11] Ibid. 546.

In Kaplan's development an expression type can be true with respect to a context without being uttered in that context. So, unlike 'I am here', 'I am uttering something' would not be valid in the logic of demonstratives (if the object language were extended to include 'utter'). Kaplan's notion of validity in the semantics of demonstratives is therefore not a variant of 'true whenever uttered'. It is closer to being a linguistic analogue of the contentually a priori than of the judgementally a priori. All the distinctive examples discussed by Kaplan of sentences which are valid in the logic of demonstratives are ones whose intentional contents are contentually a priori.

There is a sharp difference in extension between the judgementally a priori and the contentually a priori. Not everything that is judgementally a priori is contentually a priori. Simply considering the matter in the abstract one should expect this. For a content to be judgementally a priori it is required only that it be true in each world in which it comes, by a certain route, to be judged: whereas to be contentually a priori a content must be true in the actual world, whichever is the actual world, regardless of whether it is judged, or how it comes to be judged. (In the reverse direction, anything that is contentually a priori is judgementally a priori. If something is true in the actual world, whichever is the actual world, it will be true when evaluated with respect to any world in which it is judged. It also seems that if a way of coming to judge something yields a content which is true in the actual world, whichever is the actual world, it cannot be justificationally dependent on the content or kind of experience or conscious states a thinker enjoys.)

The examples bear out the expectation of a difference in extension. Some self-verifying judgements are judgementally a priori, but they do not have the property of being true in the actual world, whichever is the actual world. Worlds in which I am not thinking now, or not judging that water is H_2O, could have been actual.

The contentually a priori is also different in extension from being judgementally valid with respect to a non-introspective way. Worlds in which I never consider whether $13 \times 5 = 65$, or in which I consider the matter but make calculating errors, could have been actual.

Consider a way W which, when used, leads to judgement of a content that is judgementally a priori but not contentually a priori— that is, it leads to something which is *merely* judgementally a priori, as I will say. The explanation of why such a way W leads to a true judgement has to mention the fact that certain contents are actually accepted, or stand in other psychological relations, when the judgement is reached in that way. This applies to the explanation of the truth of such self-verifying judgements as 'I am thinking' and 'I (hereby) judge that water is H_2O'. The explanation of why their contents are true must mention the fact that the judgements are actually made.

A slightly different, but analogous, point holds for judgements reached by Evans's procedure for self-ascription. When employed in coming to judge 'I judge that $13 \times 5 = 65$' Evans's method yields knowledge only because in executing that procedure, and reaching this result, the subject also comes to accept that $13 \times 5 = 65$. The same applies to the procedure we mentioned for self-ascribing an intention. The procedure works only because it involves the formation of a certain attitude in its execution—in the example it was the decision to answer the objection in the next sentence.

All these cases contrast with acceptance of the first-order content '$13 \times 5 = 65$' on the basis of an arithmetical computation. The computational method is guaranteed to yield a result that is true in the actual world, whichever is the actual world, without reference to anything involving acceptance of the intermediate stages, or indeed anything psychological at all. That is why the first-order judgement of $13 \times 5 = 65$ meets the stronger condition of being contentually a priori.

The distinction between the contentually a priori and the judgementally a priori is significant in three respects.

First, the explanation of why a way of coming to accept a given content is judgementally a priori is, at least in the cases we have been considering, neither deep nor philosophically puzzling. All the judgementally a priori ways of coming to accept a content p that we have considered are ways that ensure that in any circumstances in which the judgement comes to be made in that way it is true. This is a full explanation of how a way can be judgementally a priori.

The same does not hold for ways that are contentually a priori. We need an explanation of why some experience-independent ways of coming to accept contents are ones that guarantee the truth of the judged content in the actual world, whichever is the actual world.

Correspondingly, if the true contents in a given domain are not merely judgementally a priori but are also contentually a priori, explaining why that is so presents a challenge to any philosophical theory of that domain.

The second reason the distinction between the judgementally a priori and the contentually a priori matters is that the existence of the contentually a priori provides a further difficulty for any form of faculty rationalism. Could we attempt to explain a priori knowledge of p by citing some kind of causal explanation of the belief that p by the holding of the fact that p? The existence of the contentually a priori gives us reasons of principle for thinking that no such approach can fully explain the phenomenon of a priori knowledge. The fact that the truth that p explains one's belief that p, and perhaps by some special causal route, involving some postulated special faculty, fails to imply a crucial feature of some cases of the a priori, which is that p will hold in the actual world, whichever world is the actual world. In short, any faculty conceived on a quasi-causal model, far from helping to explain the phenomena of rational intuition and a priori knowledge, is actually incompatible with the nature of the phenomena to be explained. Such a postulated faculty provides no explanation of the fact that a priori truths attained by means of it hold in the actual world, whichever world is the actual world.

Simply adding that p has that further property is to take for granted the contentually a priori, rather than giving an explanation of it. If it is specified that there is, in addition to the alleged causal interaction, some further feature of a way in which someone can come to believe p that ensures that p will hold whichever world is the actual world, this further feature is then doing all the work in explaining the a priori status of the proposition. When the feature is present, whatever it is, the appeal to causal explanation is then redundant.

These objections to attempts to use causal explanation by the fact that p in the explanation of a priori knowledge that p parallel the objections to attempts to use causal explanation by the fact that p in the epistemology of metaphysical necessity. Only what is actually the case—or, slightly better, only propositions whose truth is settled by what holds in the actual world—can enter causal explanations. The fact that p's holding causally explains certain other events can never be sufficient for it to be necessary that p, just as it can never be sufficient for p to hold in the actual world, however the actual world may be.

In both the a priori and the modal case we are well rid of any attempt at a causal epistemology. Attempts to develop the epistemology of the a priori or the modal in causal terms can only encourage the view that defenders of the a priori and of necessity must be committed to unacceptably non-naturalistic conceptions. One motivation for that charge is removed if our epistemology of these two notions is not causal.

The third respect in which the notion of the contentually a priori is significant is that in various ways it permits us to make something after all of Kant's idea that there is some intimate tie between the a priori and the necessary. He said of a priori judgements that they carry with them necessity. Necessity, he held, could never be gleaned from experience.[12] It is much too strong, as Kripke and Kaplan showed, to identify the a priori with the necessary, and some of Kant's formulations are certainly much too strong. Nonetheless, the spirit of Kant's idea that there is an intimate connection between the a priori and the necessary survives in the following ways.

(i) First, nothing in the Kripke-Kaplan examples establishes that necessity can be learned from perceptual experience. Experience is necessary to establish that Tully is Cicero. To move from that identity to the necessity, however, we need the principle of the necessity of identity. That principle is a priori, and is not learned from perceptual experience.

(ii) The second respect in which Kant's idea survives is that it is arguable that the source of metaphysical necessity is always fundamentally something which is contentually a priori. There are theories of the truth-conditions of modal statements according to which necessity is a matter of being true under all assignments which meet certain constraints on possibility, the so-called Principles of Possibility.[13] These Principles of Possibility include, for instance, the requirement that any genuine possibility involving a concept must respect the same rules for

---

[12] *Critique of Pure Reason*, B14; translating 'abgenommen' as 'gleaned', following Werner Pluhar's elegant suggestion in his translation (Indianapolis, Ind.: Hackett, 1996).
[13] *Being Known*, ch. 4.

assigning semantic values to concepts as govern that concept's semantic value in the actual world. These fundamental Principles of Possibility all seem to have an a priori status, more specifically a contentually a priori status. As we saw, the a posteriori necessities seem always to result from taking some fundamentally a priori necessity, like the necessity of identity, and then inferring from it, together with empirical but non-modal information ('Tully is Cicero') some modal proposition. We do not seem to find cases of the necessary a posteriori that cannot be explained in this fashion. This fact would be accounted for if modal truths are just those which can be explained from the contentually a priori Principles of Possibility.

(iii) For a proposition to hold Fixedly Actually is for it to exhibit a certain kind of necessity, as Davies and Humberstone rightly imply. This variety of necessity is much more closely connected with many cases of the a priori than is metaphysical necessity. None of the Kripke-Kaplan style examples cited above is a counterexample to the claim that what is contentually a priori is Fixedly Actually true. We can then formulate the claim, still Kantian in spirit, that perceptual experience alone cannot tell one that a proposition is true in the actual world whichever world is actual. This reformulated Kantian claim is highly plausible.

6.4 How Moderate Explanatory Rationalism Aims to Explain

Not every case of the a priori traces back exclusively to features of concepts—not even on the rationalist account of the a priori. The rationalist account of the a priori states that what makes a proposition or a transition a priori is that its truth or truth-conduciveness can be explained philosophically from the nature of the contents and states involved in the judgement or the transition. This characterization itself immediately allows for two ways in which a priori status may not trace back exclusively to the nature of concepts. The contents mentioned in the rationalist account of the a priori may be non-conceptual. We argued back in Chapters 3 and 4 that it is the nature of these non-conceptual states themselves that contributes to the explanation of basic perceptual entitlement.

The rationalist account of the a priori also alludes to the nature of the states involved in a transition. Sometimes the explanation of an entitlement depends as much upon the nature of these states as upon the nature of specific conceptual contents. The explanation we gave in the previous chapter of the entitlement to enumerative induction, and to abductive explanation, drew essentially upon the nature of belief as aiming at least at truth. It is this that mattered in the explanation of why it is on occasion rational to think that something has come about in an easier, or more likely, way, rather than in a less likely way.

Nonetheless, both historically and from the standpoint of recent discussions of the a priori, it is the a priori status of particular principles and transitions essentially involving certain conceptual contents that provides a broad range of central challenges for any positive philosophical theory of the a priori. Let us for the remainder of this section concentrate on those cases in which, intuitively, the identity of some particular concept is indispensable in characterizing the a priori principle or transition in question. With attention so restricted we can ask: How is the rationalist account of the a priori to be substantiated in detail?

For a truth-conditional theorist of intentional content, as for anyone else, the task is that of explaining why certain ways of coming to know a content are a priori. Any fully-developed truth-conditional theory of intentional content must be accompanied by an account of what it is to possess the concepts whose contributions to truth-conditions are given in the truth-conditional theory. Without prejudging anything as to its correct form, I will here use the word 'possession-condition' for a true statement of what it is, fundamentally, to possess a given concept. The theory of possession-conditions is the crucial resource on which truth-conditional theories need to draw in explaining why certain ways of coming to know are a priori ways.

The possession-condition for a concept may be given in terms of a certain role in inference; it may be given in part by certain canonical conditions for applying the concept, as in the case of observational concepts; it may be given by the role of the concept in some theory or range of theories; it may be given by the implicit conception a thinker must have if he is to possess the concept; it may be given by the concept's signficance for certain kinds of action; and so forth. There is an immense variety of possible forms of possession-conditions for a concept. But in so far as the notion of a concept is tied to that of cognitive significance, as it is here, possession-conditions of any kind whatever are required to explain facts about informativeness and potential informativeness. If a content composed from given concepts is informative, or is not informative, in given circumstances, the possession-conditions for those concepts must explain why it is informative in those circumstances, or must explain why it is not. Since for someone who is in pain but is also suffering from amnesia 'I am in pain' is not informative but 'René Descartes is in pain' is informative, his first-person concept and his concept *René Descartes* must be distinct. A good statement of the possession-conditions for these two concepts must explain why they differ in respect of informativeness in these circumstances.

There also has to be a theory connecting the account of possession-conditions for concepts with the level of reference, the semantic values for those concepts. Since judgement aims at truth, and truth depends on facts at the level of reference, not just the level of sense, we must explain why judging in accordance with the possession-conditions of concepts fulfils this goal. If sense together with the way the world is determines reference, and possession-conditions individuate senses, possession-conditions together with the way the world is must equally determine reference. More fundamentally (as Dummett has emphasized), if a sense is individuated by the condition for something to be its reference we must show how a possession-condition for a concept C fixes a condition for something to be the reference of C. I labelled the theory connecting possession-conditions and semantic values 'Determination Theory' in *A Study of Concepts*. There I proposed that the semantic value of a concept is that entity of the appropriate category which makes the transitions mentioned in its possession-condition always truth-preserving, and the outright principles so mentioned always true.

Suppose we conceive of concepts as individuated by possession-conditions and as having a Determination Theory which honours these internal links between the levels of sense and reference. The task for the truth-conditional theorist then becomes that of using these resources to coordinate and properly interrelate three apparently diverse things:

(1) a way of coming to know that p;
(2) the possession-conditions for the concepts in p; *and*
(3) the truth-value of the content p.

The aim is to do this in a way that explains the distinctive characteristics of the a priori we have already identified.

The core idea of one approach to the a priori coordinates these three elements in the following two claims.

> (a) An outright, non-defeasible, way of coming to know p is an a priori way if the possession-conditions for the concepts in p together with the Determination Theory jointly guarantee that use of that way leads to a true belief about whether p is the case. Similarly, a transition from one set of contents to a given content is an a priori transition if the possession-conditions for the contents involved together with the Determination Theory jointly guarantee that the transition is truth-preserving.
>
> (b) A content p is outright a priori if the possession-conditions for the concepts comprising p together with the Determination Theory jointly guarantee the truth of p.

The claims (a) and (b) constitute what back in 1993 I called the *metasemantic* theory of the a priori.[14] To illustrate with the most trivial case, consider the possession-condition for the concept of conjunction. On any theory, this possession-condition will entail that thinkers must find the transition from A and B to A compelling, and must do so without relying on any background information. A plausible Determination Theory will entail that semantic values are assigned to concepts in such a way as to make truth-preserving any transitions which, according to the possession-conditions for a concept, must be found compelling without further information. It is thus a consequence of the possession-condition for conjunction, together with the Determination Theory, that when A and B is true

---

[14] This was the name I gave to the theory when proposing it in 'How Are A Priori Truths Possible?'.

A is true. That, according to the metasemantic theory, is why the transition is a priori.

More generally, the metasemantic theory holds that at each line of a valid proof of an outright a priori proposition the transition involved is one whose truth-preserving character follows from the possession-conditions for the concepts involved together with the Determination Theory for those concepts.

How does the metasemantic theory explain why the use of a priori ways generates not merely true beliefs but knowledge? The theory of possession-conditions and the Determination Theory for the concepts comprising a given content p give an account of what has to be the case for the content p to be true. The semantic values fixed by the Determination Theory must, when combined to fix a truth-value in the way determined by the structure of the content p, determine the truth-value True or the truth-value False. The conditions under which they determine the truth-value True is a fundamental account of what it is, constitutively, for the content p to be true. According to the metasemantic theory, in using an a priori way of coming to judge that p a thinker is using a method which guarantees, as a result of the very nature of p and the way in which its truth-condition is determined, that the thinker judges that p only if it is the case that p. When the soundness of a method is thus internally related to what it is for the content to be true, it is hard to see what more could be required for knowledge. Such a constitutive grounding of the soundness of the method goes far beyond merely reliabilist conditions for knowledge.

In providing this connection with knowledge the metasemantic theory also meets the condition noted earlier, that the account of why a way or method is a priori should be a consequence of some more general thesis relating knowledge and understanding. We just gave an argument aiming to explain why ways whose soundness is underwritten by the possession-conditions and the Determination Theory will yield knowledge. The same applies equally in empirical cases. Take a case in which a thinker applies an observational concept to a perceptually given object, in accordance with the possession-condition for that observational concept. That is, the thinker's application of the concept to the object is an exercise of exactly that sensitivity to perceptual experience mentioned in the possession-condition for the concept. If the thinker is indeed perceiving properly, the natural Determination

Theory for observational concepts will imply that in such a case the semantic value of the observational concept will map the perceived object to the truth-value True. The truth of the thinker's judgement in this empirical case, when made in accordance with the possession-condition for the concept, is equally a consequence of an account of what it is for the content in question to be true. Again, the relation between the way of coming to judge and the account of what it is for the content to be true is so close that this is enough for knowledge. Once again, the relation goes far beyond reliability.

We noted that outright a priori ways of coming to know that p seem to be ways that ensure that p is true in the actual world, whichever is the actual world: that is, we have Fixedly Actually p. The metasemantic account can also explain this apparent datum. Possession-conditions hold Fixedly Actually. The statement of the possession-condition for a concept specifies what it is to be that concept. This is something which is invariant under which world is the actual world. The same holds for the principles of Determination Theory. The rule by which the semantic value of a concept depends on the way the world is, and on the nature of the concept's possession-condition, does not vary with which world is actual. Logical principles also hold Fixedly Actually.

Now consider the metasemantic theory. In one central kind of case in which a way of coming to know that p is a priori there is a derivation from the possession-conditions and the Determination Theory to the conclusion that the content p reached by use of that way is a true content. Since the premises of this derivation and its rules of inference all hold Fixedly Actually, it follows that p holds Fixedly Actually. This style of argument can also be carried over to the more general case in which we are concerned with model-theoretic consequence, rather than derivability.

The metasemantic theory does not have any special account of truth for a priori contents. On the contrary, it explains the a priori status of certain contents by considering the consequences of entirely general rules which determine the semantic values of concepts, the rules being exactly the same whether the concept is featuring in an empirical content or in an a priori content. It thus differs from all kinds of conventionalism about a priori contents (or special subsets of them). On the metasemantic account, a single possession-condition for each concept and a uniform Determination Theory explain the truth-conditions and epistemic character of contents of whatever stripe.

In the examples given so far we have not needed to appeal to mysterious mechanisms connecting thinkers who have a priori knowledge with a third realm of concepts. The metasemantic theory, properly developed, can thus be at the service of a moderate explanatory rationalism.

One legitimate concern about the metasemantic theory as so far presented is that it has so far been accompanied by an account of the possession of concepts which not only understates but omits almost altogether the role of reason in the formation of judgements involved in the possession of a concept. The possession-condition offered for the logical concept of conjunction mentions what the thinker finds primitively compelling. But rational judgement is not simply yielding to what one finds primitively compelling. The point has been well made by Bill Brewer.[15] Of judgements and transitions governed by reason Brewer writes: 'What drives one in genuine cases is precisely what one lacks if one has simply been drilled by the dictators of the International Academy of Logic, however benevolent they may be, to reason in ways for which one sees no evident rationale, no point or purpose' (pp. 242–3). Accounts of concepts that neglect rationality in this way are incorrect in themselves. They also hardly sit well with a broadly rationalist approach to our subject matter.

The point does not itself tell against the metasemantic account. It tells rather against the accounts of concepts which have been used in conjunction with the metasemantic account. Nonetheless, we need to know what the elements of a better model of concept possession would look like if we are to have any confidence that the metasemantic account will ever admit of application. It is also important that the need for a better form of account cannot be met simply by restricting the requirement that something be found primitively compelling to judgements which are properly written into the possession-conditions for the concepts in question. What we are missing is a requirement that the judgement or transition be rational from the thinker's own point of view. It does nothing towards meeting this need that a judgement or transition is one that is mentioned in a possession-condition.

---

[15] 'Compulsion by Reason', *Proceedings of the Aristotelian Society*, suppl. vol. 69 (1995), 237–53.

When a thinker makes a judgement rationally he makes it in part because it is a rational judgement. Rational judgement conforms to what logicians would call a fixed-point principle: It is a condition for a judgement to be rational that it be made in part because it is rational. None of the possession-conditions that mention only what the thinker finds primitively compelling exhibit, let alone elucidate, the rationality, from the thinker's own point of view, of the judgements and transitions they mention.

How can we elucidate the rationality of the thinker's judgements? One intuitive account is that in making a rational transition to a judgement that *p* a thinker must know what it is for it to be true that p, must appreciate that his grounds or reasons for the transition to the conclusion that *p* suffice for the truth of *p*, and must be making the judgement because of his appreciation that these grounds or reasons so suffice. In the case of non-conclusive grounds a similar requirement applies, but concerns the thinker's appreciation of his reasons as non-conclusive grounds for the content of his judgement.

A good theory of concepts has to elucidate this notion of knowing what it is for a given content to be true. For any given concept it has to show how its account of that concept contributes in a componential fashion to an account of a thinker's knowledge of what it is for a complete content containing that concept to be true.

In the light of this position, the possession-condition for conjunction seems like a potentially misleading case. It is potentially misleading because of its very simplicity. It is so simple that a very straightforward account of mastery of conjunction actually serves a purpose that would not be served so simply in other cases. It is highly plausible that there is no more to knowing what it is for a conjunction to be true than is given in a possession-condition based on primitive grasp of the introduction and elimination rules for conjunction. But it is not so plausible in other cases that there are conceptual roles specifiable in the A(C) form of *A Study of Concepts* which must be found primitively compelling for understanding. In such cases more needs to be said about what it is for the thinker to know what it is for contents containing the notion to be true. It also needs to be explained how the thinker can draw upon that knowledge in assessing a transition involving the concept as correct or as invalid.

The requirement of rationality from the thinker's own point of view goes far beyond Dummett's well-taken observation that the ability to respond correctly to circumstances with an utterance is not yet to realize that utterances in a language are 'purposive actions based upon a knowledge of their significance for others'.[16] An indicative utterance by one who understands the language is not only one whose significance for others is appreciated by the utterer. Rationality enters twice over here. An utterance, when made in accordance with the relevant norms, is also expressive of a judgement which itself has been rationally reached. This dovetails with the fact that in asserting something one thereby represents oneself as knowing it. The existence of such a norm of assertion means that one conforms to the norm only if the judgements expressed in making assertions are reached rationally.

Brewer's own suggestion is that this requirement of rationality is met in the case of perceptual beliefs. He argues, rightly in my view, that ordinary perception, in which objects and events are given as standing in certain relations to the perceiver, also rationalizes perceptual judgements in part because the subject appreciates that it is their standing in these relations that makes them perceptible to the subject.[17] If this is indeed the right account of how the requirement of rationality from the thinker's own point of view is met, it has consequences for the right way of conceiving of Level-(3) explanations. In particular, we cannot conceive of the Level-(3) explanations developed in Chapters 3 and 4 for taking perceptual experience at face value as part of the reasons which meet the demand of rationality from the subject's own point of view. In the Brewer-style account of why perceptual judgement is rational from the thinker's own point of view the judgement that objects stand in such-and-such relations to oneself involves taking perceptual experience at face value. This is not at all a defect in an elaboration of a species of rationality, and I will be discussing further what that species is. But the reliance on taking perceptual experience at face value does mean that such an account cannot itself explain the rationality of taking perceptual experience at face value. All this means is that the philosophical

---

[16] *The Logical Basis of Metaphysics* (Cambridge, Mass.: Harvard University Press, 1991), 95.

[17] 'Compulsion by Reason', 250–1, and at greater length in his *Perception and Reason* (Oxford: Oxford University Press, 1999).

enterprise of attempting to explain generalizations about entitlement is an attempt to elucidate various things that rationality from the thinker's own point of view takes for granted.

I suggest that the species of rationality involved in satisfaction of the requirement of rationality from the subject's own point of view is embedded rationality. By this I mean that the thinker is rational, from his own point of view, once he has taken at face value those states which he is entitled to take at face value. Such a notion of embedded rationality has several attractions. It invokes the kind of reasons that one ordinarily invokes when justification is required, as in the dialogue 'Why do you think that?'—'I see it to be so'. What one sees to be so also explains to one, as Brewer says, why it is that one can see it to be so.

In the case of logical transitions a thinker's knowledge of what it is for a content containing a given logical notion to be true can be identified, in the first instance, with his tacit knowledge of the contribution made to truth-conditions by the notion in question. This is tacit knowledge which is manifested in all sorts of ways, including the ability to evaluate propositions involving the notion in the light of information about the truth-value of contents on which it operates.[18] This makes room for the idea that the rationality from the thinker's own point of view of a logical transition consists in his appreciating in the right way that the truth of the premisses guarantees the truth of the conclusion, where the truth of the conclusion is conceived in accordance with the thinker's tacit knowledge of the contribution made to truth-conditions by its logical constituents. Under this approach even primitive axioms and inference rules can be rationally accepted. It also permits the appreciation of the validity of new axioms and rules that do not follow from those previously accepted.[19]

In respecting the norms of embedded rationality the thinker is also respecting those that are made available precisely because he is embedded in his world in a certain way, or is in states which are individuated by the ways they are embedded when the thinker is properly connected to the world. I argued in Chapters 3 and 4 that there is an entitlement to take the observational contents of experience at

---

[18] See 'Implicit Conceptions'.
[19] See 'Implicit Conceptions', and the later material in the present chapter.

face value because they are instance-individuated; that is, because they are individuated by the way they are embedded in the world in the circumstances of proper connection. The thinker who displays embedded rationality respects and builds on the norms made available by varieties of external individuation. Reason itself allows him to reach conclusions he could not otherwise attain if reason or content were purely a matter of internal individuation.

6.5 Tasks for the Metasemantic View

The moderate explanatory rationalist who adopts the metasemantic view faces a range of tasks. In any case in which something is known a priori outright it ought to be possible to identify the way in which it comes to be known a priori. It ought also to be possible to explain why that way of knowing is a priori on the basis of the possession-condition for the concepts that form the content in question. It is precisely because some extreme rationalists have not, on reflection, seen how to do this for certain a priori propositions that they have rejected a merely moderate explanatory rationalism. The moderate explanatory rationalist does, however, have more extensive resources in defending his position than may be apparent when one thinks only of the simpler and more familiar forms of possession-conditions. I indicate two such resources here, each relevant to examples that some have cited against other forms of moderate rationalism.

Not every a priori truth involving a concept follows from the principles that a thinker must find compelling in order to possess the concept. This was the burden of Gödel's effective point against Carnap—that we can, on the basis of our understanding, discover new axioms for concepts that do not follow from the principles we already accept.[20] The force of this point extends far beyond Carnapian conventionalist theories. The phenomena Gödel identified, concerning as they do the nature of understanding and the existence of new, understanding-based a priori principles, present a challenge to all theories of the a priori. The metasemantic account itself would be unable to explain the phenomenon if the only cases of the a priori it

[20] Carnap, *Logical Syntax of Language*; Gödel, 'Is Mathematics Syntax of Language?', in his *Collected Works*, iii, ed. S. Feferman, J. Dawson, jun., et al. (New York: Oxford University Press, 1995).

admitted were those that followed from principles whose acceptance by the thinker is already mentioned in the possession-conditions for the concepts in question. If that were the case the metasemantic theorist would have two options. Either he would have to deny the existence of the phenomenon, which would be quite implausible; or he would have to say that not all cases of understanding-based a priori propositions can be captured by appeal to possession-conditions, which is to abandon his version of the metasemantic theory.

The correct response to the phenomena is rather to acknowledge the existence of what I call implicit conceptions. In some cases possessing a concept involves having tacit knowledge of some condition for something to fall under the concept, a condition the thinker may not be able to articulate correctly. Cases of this phenomenon run from the most humble, such as our possession of a condition for something to be a chair (a condition which it is very easy to misarticulate), through understanding of moral and political concepts, which can have a rich, hidden structure, to the early use of mathematical and scientific concepts. That tacit knowledge that one condition rather than another underlies understanding is shown by the thinker's pattern of application of the concept in question. The tacit knowledge of the condition explains that pattern of application. Such implicit conceptions are also capable of explaining the phenomenon of understanding-based a priori knowledge of new principles that do not follow from those previously accepted. Consider an ordinary person's possession of the concept of a whole number. I would say that underlying this person's grasp of the concept is possession of an implicit conception with the content:

(1) 0 is a whole number;
(2) the successor of a whole number is a whole number;
(3) only what is determined to be a whole number on the basis of the preceding two conditions is a whole number.

Now consider the principle that any whole number has only finitely many predecessors. This principle cannot follow from what the ordinary thinker explicitly accepts. What he explicitly accepts has non-standard models, in which some objects within the extension of 'whole number' in those models do have infinitely many predecessors. But our ordinary thinker can reflect on his own practice, can think about which things are whole numbers and which are not. By an a priori abduction from cases he can come to the conclusion that the recursion displayed above, with its limiting clause, fixes what it is to be a whole number. This condition then rules out whole numbers with infinitely many predecessors. Because abduction from cases, and thinking of hypotheses that explain the cases, is a creative matter that not everyone who possesses the concept of natural number either can or will engage in, not everyone who has the concept of a whole number needs explicitly to accept that whole numbers do not have infinitely many predecessors. The ordinary thinker who uses the concept of a natural number need not even possess the concept of finiteness or of infinity.

Under this approach using implicit conceptions we explain the phenomenon of new principles consistently with the metasemantic theory. Unlike Gödel himself, we also remain within the bounds of a moderate rationalism.[21]

The other resource available to the metasemantic theory can be drawn upon in cases in which we are, intuitively, inclined to say that it is because we see the nature of some kind of entity—a set, a colour, a number, a shape—that we appreciate a priori that certain principles about that entity are correct. What, an opponent of moderate rationalism may ask, can this possibly have to do with concepts and understanding? Do we not rather have direct insight into the nature of these entities, an insight that enables us to appreciate a priori that certain principles hold of them?

The resourceful metasemantic theorist should agree that there is here a special class of examples of the a priori, but he should say that what distinguishes them is as follows. The conditions which individuate the entity in question (the set, colour, number, shape) actually enter the possession-condition for certain canonical concepts of these entities. As one could say, in these cases the concept is individuated by what individuates the object. The implicit conception detailed above which underlies mastery of the notion of a whole number already exemplifies this phenomenon. The content of that conception specifies what it

---

[21] For further discussion of implicit conceptions see 'Implicit Conceptions, Understanding and Rationality' and the comments and replies in that same volume. For further discussion of Gödel see my paper 'Explaining the A Priori: The Programme of Moderate Rationalism', in Boghossian and Peacocke (eds.), *New Essays on the A Priori*.

is to be a whole number. The phenomenon is not, however, restricted to implicit conceptions. There is a way of thinking of the colour green mastery of which involves sensitivity to the rough borders of which shades are shades of green, and which are not, when those shades are actually given in perception to the thinker. From this resource it is possible to explain why certain principles about the colour green, when so conceived, are a priori. I will argue that this resource permits an a priori derivation of the principle that no shade is a shade of both red and green.

Consider the colours red, green, blue, and the rest that are picked out by our ordinary colour concepts. Here I mean the colours themselves, not concepts of them, and not expressions for them. A colour's phenomenal properties are constitutive of it in at least the following respect. Take any particular finely discriminated colour shade s. This can be a shade as finely discriminated as Goodman would discriminate qualia: shade s is identical with shade r only if anything matching either matches both.[22] Here, as in Goodman, the range of 'anything' must be either universals or at least something going beyond the range of actual particulars. Fix also on a given colour—red, say. Then if s is a shade that is clearly within the colour red it is essentially and constitutively true of the colour red that s is clearly within it. (If s is a borderline case, that it is so is also essentially and constitutively true of the colour red.) The colour red is individuated by which shades fall within it, which fall outside it, and arguably by its pattern of borderline cases in respect of shades.

Since these phenomenal properties of the colour red are constitutive of it, they hold in all possible circumstances. It is a constraint on the genuine possibility of a world, or a world description, that it respect the constitutive properties of objects, including colours. Hence, whichever world is the actual world, these phenomenal properties will hold of the colour red. They hold both necessarily and Fixedly Actually. So far, these points all concern the level of reference, the level at which colours and shades themselves are located.

Now let us move to the level of concepts, sense, and thought. The possession-conditions for the concept *red* of the colour red are tied to these very conditions that individuate the colour red. Suppose

---

[22] See Goodman's criterion of identity for qualia in *The Structure of Appearance*, 3rd edn. (Dordrecht: Reidel, 1977).

a shade *s* is clearly a shade of red. If a thinker possesses the concept *red*, is taking his visual experience at face value, and if the experience represents an object as having shade *s*, then the thinker must be willing to judge 'That's red' of the presented object. We can relativize this to a part or region of the object; the point will still go through under such relativization. The thought 'That shade *s* [given in perception] is red' is not informative to the thinker who fully possesses the concept *red*.

Similarly, if a shade is clearly not a shade of red the thinker must in those given circumstances be willing to judge 'That's not red'.

Next take a given shade *s* that is a shade of red and is not a shade of green. By the same reasoning, applied both to the colour concept *red* and to the colour concept *green*, the thinker will be willing to judge, when taking perceptual experience at face value, when something is perceived as being shade *s*, 'That's red and not green'. The conditions for possessing the concepts *red* and *green* require the thinker to be willing to make this judgement; and it will be true.

It will also be relatively a priori that something with *that* shade (perceptually given) is red and not green. As before, what I mean here by the claim of relative a priority is that the thinker's entitlement to this belief does not rely on the content of her perceptual experiences, beyond that content needed for having the relevant concepts in the first place. There is a way of thinking of a particular shade that is made available only by perceiving that shade. Such experience is necessary to having any demonstrative thoughts about that shade, including for instance such thoughts as 'That shade is or is not displayed on my colour chart', which are equally properly classified as relatively a priori. Such relatively a priori judgements contrast with 'The book with that shade is closed', which is not relatively a priori. What matters is that no further feature of the experience, beyond experience of the shade itself, is needed for the thinker's entitlement to judge, knowledgeably, 'That shade is red'. That judgement will hold whichever world is the actual world. (It will also hold necessarily.)

Now we can go for something more general. A thinker can reflect on what she can correctly judge when presented with a given shade. She can appreciate that if it is correct to judge, on the basis of perception necessary for having the demonstrative concept, something of the form 'That shade is a shade of red' it will also be correct, on the same basis, to make the corresponding judgement 'That shade is not a shade of green'. Suppose, what is also plausible, that every case in which something is red, or is not red, or is green, or is not green, could either be known to be so on the basis of perception or else is a case in which something is counted as having one of these colour properties because it has the same physical properties which underlie the perception of colour in the perceptible cases. If a thinker can know all this she can come to know that no perceptible shade is both a shade of red and a shade of green. Since the basis of this reflection is the relation of shades to colours that are in fact constitutive of the colours thought about, the generalization holds whichever world is the actual world. It holds Fixedly Actually that any shade which is a shade of red is not a shade of green. No particular course of perceptual experience is required to attain this knowledge: it is a priori.

This description of how such knowledge is attainable is founded in the possession-conditions for the concepts *red* and *green*. Consider a concept whose possession-condition is not tied to rational responses to the shades which individuate the colour to which the concept refers. For such a concept it would not be possible for a thinker to appreciate such incompatibilities on a similar basis to that which we just outlined. Even if red is in fact the colour of the Chinese national flag, no merely understanding-based reflection could yield knowledge of the proposition that if a shade is of the same colour as that of the Chinese national flag then it is not a shade of green. Such knowledge would have to be founded on a the posteriori, and not purely understanding-based, information that the colour of the Chinese flag is red.

What is crucial to this argument is the close relation between the way the colour is individuated and the condition for grasping the concept *red* which refers to that colour. The relations to shades that contribute to the individuation of the colour are precisely those to which one who grasps the colour concept must be sensitive when making perceptually-based judgements involving the concept. In short, the colour concept is tied to the individuation of its reference. It is only because this is so that a priori reflection on what it would be correct to judge in various circumstances can yield knowledge of colour incompatibilities.[23]

The need to invoke the tie between the colour concepts and the individuation of their references also seems to me to be one lesson of reflection on the early Putnam's discussion of colour incompatibilities.[24] Putnam's argument merits a paper-length discussion of its own: but to illustrate the lesson I just mentioned I fix on the stage of his argument at which he writes 'And if it is true that no matter which shade of red and which shade of green we choose, nothing is both that shade of red and that shade of green, then it is true that "Nothing is both red and green" even if by "red" we mean not specific shades but broad classes of such shades' (p. 211).

I say this by itself is not enough to explain a priori status. If the broad colour red is in fact the colour allowed by the local school for its dress code it will equally be true that: no matter which shade of the colour allowed by the local school for its dress code and which shade of green we choose, nothing is both that shade of the colour allowed by the local school and that shade of green. But 'Nothing is both the colour allowed by the local school for its dress code and green' is not a priori. Putnam's principle needs some strengthening, some modal element, to get the stronger conclusion we need.[25] Putnam's principle is Fixedly Actually true, and the prefixing of a Fixedly Actually operator gives the stronger premiss. But then we have to ask: Why is the stronger premiss true? The answer I would give is that the concept *red* itself, unlike the concept *colour allowed by the local school for its dress code*, is tied to the individuation of the colour red. More specifically, this tie can be split up into several sublinks: the tie of *that shade* to a particular shade and what individuates it; the individuation of the colour in terms of its relations to the shades it includes; and the relation of the canonical broad colour concepts, *red, green,* and the rest, to the colours so individuated. So I think a fuller elaboration of this part of the early Putnam's position would need to draw on the resources I have been

[23] I emphasize that I haven't shown that a material object has, at each point on its surface, only one colour. That would require further argument. All I have argued for is the a priori status of the proposition 'Any shade which is definitely a shade of red is not definitely a shade of green'. This would not be contradicted by the possibility of reddish-green, asserted by C. Hardin in his *Color for Philosophers: Unweaving the Rainbow* (Indianapolis, Ind.: Hackett, 1988), 121–7.

[24] 'Reds, Greens and Logical Analysis', *Philosophical Review*, 65 (1956), 206–17, and 'Red and Green All Over Again: A Rejoinder to Arthur Pap', *Philosophical Review*, 66 (1957), 100–3.

[25] There is no modal element in his formalization of his argument later in the same paper.

offering, and crucially on the notion of a concept being tied to the individuation of what it picks out.

I also differ from Putnam on some other points, particularly over what counts as a rule of language. Putnam gives a postulate which he says 'formulates a feature of English usage pointed out in the informal discussion: Nothing can be classified as both a shade of red and a shade of green'. This seems to me a truth about the non-linguistic world, not one about English. Insofar as the world cannot be a certain way, that will have consequences for which English sentences cannot be true—but the source of such impossibilities seems to me to have nothing to do with language at all. In his rejoinder to Pap, Putnam says 'it seems plausible to take "Red and Green are different colours" ' as 'direct linguistic stipulation' (p. 102). I question this too. What is stipulated is which colour is the reference of the respective words; and then, given these referential stipulations, it's obvious with only a little thought (but not as a matter of any linguistic stipulation) that they are distinct. This is also what one would expect if understanding of colour words involves grasp of some class of paradigms and a closeness relation.

The explanation I have offered for a priori knowledge of colour incompatibilities, in being founded in the understanding-conditions for colour vocabulary, is one small step towards carrying through the moderate explanatory rationalist's programme. It is a small step even within the special domain of colour. The moderate rationalist will also have the ambition of explaining all the other apparently a priori principles about colour that so intrigued Wittgenstein at different stages of his life.[26]

While colour concepts have their own distinctive properties, they are far from unique in having the crucial property of being tied to the individuation of their references. This more general property can explain other examples of the a priori, in accordance with the moderate rationalist's programme, as in the next example.

Consider arithmetical relations such as 'n is the sum of m and k' and 'n is the product of m and k'. At the level of the arithmetical relation itself, what it is for a triple of natural numbers to stand in these relations is given by their standard recursive definitions. But to think of

---

[26] *Philosophical Remarks*, ed. R. Rhees (Oxford: Blackwell, 1975) and *Remarks on Colour* trans. L. McAlister and M. Schättle, ed. G. E. M. Anscombe. (Oxford: Blackwell, 1977).

these relations in the ways just given, as the sum relation and as the product relation respectively, is to have a fundamental method of calculating sums and products for which it is immediately obvious that it respects these recursions. So, for instance: the fundamental procedure for finding the sum of 7 and 5 involves counting up 5 steps from 7; and it is immediately obvious that this procedure respects the principle that 7 plus the successor of a number n is identical with the successor of the sum of 7 with n, i.e. that it respects the recursion for addition. A person may sometimes just see, or realize without conscious reasoning, that one number is the sum of two others; but if his judgement is queried he must fall back on methods of calculating the sum of which it is clear (without substantial arithmetical computation) that they respect the standard recursive definition of addition. These are the thinker's fundamental procedures.

Judgements about the sum of two numbers, made by counting correctly, and without other mistakes, in the way one does in ordinary arithmetical calculation, will be correct in the actual world. They will also be correct whatever the actual world is like, because they involve thinking of these relations in ways tied to their very individuation. So these ways of coming to know the sums of two numbers are a priori ways of coming to know. The position is in agreement with Kant that $7 + 5 = 12$ is a priori (though the reasons for this classification may not be the same). The a priori knowability of arithmetical sums is founded in the nature of the possession-conditions for the concepts it contains, for they are tied to the individuation of the very relations the concepts pick out. A similar argument can be given for the a priori knowability of arithmetical multiplications, in relation to methods of calculating them involving addition.

A parallel argument can also be given about the relation between the individuation of the natural numbers themselves and canonical concepts of them, if we regard conditions for application as partially or wholly individuative of the natural numbers. Once again, we first consider the natural numbers themselves, rather than concepts thereof. The number 0 is individuated by the condition that for there to be 0 Fs is for there to be nothing that is F. The number 1 is individuated by the condition that for there to be 1 F is for there to be something that is F and nothing else which is F. For any natural number which is the successor $s(n)$ of some natural number n, the number

$s(n)$ is individuated by its being such that, for any property F, for there to be $s(n)$ Fs is (as Frege would have said) for there to be an object u such that the number of Fs other than u is n. The individuation of any number n in terms of the condition for there to be n Fs holds in the actual world, however the actual world may be. In this case it is also necessary. This is still all at the level of reference, individuation, and metaphysics.

Then, at the level of thought, to have a canonical concept c of some natural number n is to have a fundamental procedure for determining whether there are c Fs for which it is immediately obvious that the procedure respects the condition for there to be n Fs which, the condition which is individuative of the number n. Counting is such a procedure. So the transition from the premises that the distinct objects x, y, and z are F, and exhaust the Fs, to the conclusion that there are 3 Fs, if the conclusion is reached by counting applied to x, y, and z, is an a priori transition. The transition is guaranteed to be true in the actual world, whichever is the actual world, because it is underwritten by what is individuative of the number 3.

This treatment of the case of numerical quantifiers can be combined with that of $7 + 5 = 12$. We can thereby argue that the a priori status of 'If there are 7 Fs and 5 Gs and nothing which is both F and G then there are 12 things which are either F or G' can also be traced back to the phenomenon of concepts being individuated by their relations to the objects, properties, and relations they pick out.

The metasemantic theory of the outright a priori may make it seem as if outright a priori status can have to do only with how we think of objects and properties, and nothing much to do with the nature of those objects and properties. But when we realize that sometimes senses or ways of thinking are individuated by their relations to the very nature of what they pick out it becomes clear that a priori truth can both be a phenomenon at the level of sense and also have something to do with the nature of the objects or properties thought about. There is no incompatibility between those two characteristics.

The characterization of what it is for a concept to be tied to the individuation of its reference may make it sound as if this approach to such cases is committed to taking the ontology at the level of reference as somehow explanatorily prior. But that is not so. All that is needed in these philosophical explanations of certain cases of the a priori is a *link* between the concept and the individuation of the reference. That link can still exist even for a theorist who regards, say, the ontology of natural numbers or other abstract objects as some kind of projection of certain kinds of discourse, or modes of thought. That is certainly not a view I would recommend; but such a theorist would still have access to the present treatment of some cases of the a priori.

It is worth considering the relation between a principle's having a priori status because its constituent concepts are tied to the individuation of the properties and relations it picks out and one of Frege's characterizations of a priority. In a famous passage Frege wrote:

It then depends on finding the proof and following it back up to the fundamental truths. If on this path one comes across only general logical laws and definitions one has an analytic truth . . . But if it is not possible to carry through the proof without using truths which are not of a general logical nature, but belong to a particular domain of knowledge, then the proposition is a synthetic one. For a truth to be a posteriori it is required that its proof should not go through without appeal to facts; that is, without appeal to unprovable truths lacking generality, and which contain assertions about particular objects. If on the contrary it is possible to carry through the proof wholly from general laws, which are neither capable of proof nor in need of it, then the truth is a priori.[27]

Few would want to argue that principles of colour exclusion are analytic in Frege's sense. But are such principles a priori by the characterization suggested by this passage? It is true that in this passage Frege is talking only about what makes a truth of mathematics an a priori truth. But no different criterion is suggested for other kinds of a priori truth; and his sufficient condition for being a posteriori is not confined to purely mathematical subject matter. Read strictly, Frege is here also offering only a sufficient condition for a truth to be a priori. (He may well also have believed it to be necessary. This is a complex and philosophically interesting question in Frege scholarship pursuit of which would take us too far off course.) In any case, let us ask: Is it possible to carry through proofs of principles of colour

---

[27] *The Foundations of Arithmetic*, sect. 3, my translation (with an improvement thanks to David Wiggins).

exclusion wholly from general laws which are neither capable of proof nor in need of it? As Tyler Burge remarked to me, we have to take note of Frege's differentiation between the 'general logical laws' mentioned in Frege's characterization of analyticity and the 'general laws', not necessarily logical, mentioned in Frege's condition for a priority. Our question is to be understood as concerning the latter general, and not necessarily logical, laws.

The argument I offered earlier to the conclusion that no shade is both a shade of red and a shade of green relied on two assertions which Frege would classify as 'lacking generality'. It relied on the possession-condition for the concept *red* of the colour red. That possession-condition is not, as far as I can tell, a consequence of completely general laws alone. The argument also relied on principles about what individuates the particular colour red. These too are specific to the colour red. There was a dependence on the possession-condition for the concept *red* in explaining the rationality (and relatively a priori character) of the transition from the experience of any given shade which is clearly a shade of red to 'That's a shade of red'. There was dependence on the individuation of the colour red in explaining why the argument is sound however the actual world turns out to be. There seems to be no satisfactory way to elaborate the soundness and a priori availability of this argument without appealing to truths about the particular colour red and the particular concept *red* (and, of course, their interrelations, which was the point of the preceding section).

It is true that I have relied upon a general philosophical theory of the way in which a relation between a concept and the individuation of the property or object it picks out can yield knowledge which is a priori. That general theory is formulated in terms which Frege would likely count as 'general laws'. But that general theory entails only conditionals of the form: If the relation between a property or object is of a certain specified kind then there will correspondingly exist a priori truths of a certain kind. To obtain specific truths which have an a priori status from the general theory we need information about specific concepts, properties, and objects which are of the specified kind.

On the position I have outlined in the cases of colour and natural numbers it is specifically a concept—that is, what is possessed in having understanding—which is tied to the conditions which individuate the object, property, or relation it picks out. But reflection on the quoted passage from Frege suggests that he may have been operating with a conception that recognizes three categories, of which, he seems to have held, only the first two may contain a priori truths. (a) There are the domain-independent logical laws. Arithmetical laws would reduce to these, in the presence of suitable definitions, were logicism to be correct. (b) There are general laws which are domain-specific, but which are neither capable of proof nor in need of it. Frege famously held that geometry is a priori.[28] If the condition in the displayed passage is intended as a necessary, as well as a sufficient, condition of being a priori, Frege is thereby committed to saying that the axioms of geometry fall in this second category (b) (and thereby of course he acquires many a problem). (c) There are truths which are both domain-specific and specific to certain entities within that domain. Again, if Frege is offering a necessary condition of being a priori then such truths as are in this category (c) will not be a priori.

It is from this last point that the moderate explanatory rationalist will dissent if he recognizes the consequences of the linking of certain concepts to the individuation of the properties or objects they pick out. That phenomenon generates a priori truths specific to particular concepts concerned with elements of a specific domain. The phenomenon is incompatible with simultaneous acceptance of the categorization (a) through (c) and of restriction of the a priori to the first two subcategories.

A rationalist may very reasonably want to distinguish between wholly general domain-unspecific principles and principles specific to particular subject matters. As far as I can see, however, there is no reason of principle to think that a priori knowledge must ultimately be explicable solely in terms of such general laws. There are even some reasons for doubting the coherence of such a position. For the same means by which one explains the possibility of a priori knowledge where it is not reducible to general laws also applies to general logical principles. What individuates a particular logical concept, whether one takes it to be a set of inferential rules or an underlying implicit conception which specifies a contribution to truth-conditions, is arguably equally tied to

---

[28] *The Foundations of Arithmetic*, sect. 87, 89.

the individuation of (for instance) a particular truth-function. If that is right, the a priori principles concerning specific objects or concepts come under the same general explanatory umbrella as the logical ones.

I also very briefly note the pertinence of the idea of something's being tied to the individuation of a property to the Kantian conception of pure intuition as an a priori means of establishing geometrical propositions. We can use some of the apparatus of this chapter to give a limited defence of Kant's conception. Suppose just for this paragraph that we do not count imagination as experience, so that acceptance of a proposition on the basis of the deliverances of pure intuition could in principle at least be an a priori way of coming to know it. Pure intuition can be conceived of as a faculty which supplies representations whose content depends only on the constitutive properties of geometric objects—lines, angles, and the rest. So one way of defending a neo-Kantian position about knowledge of pure geometry would be to note that in making geometrical judgements on the basis of the deliverances of pure intuition one is being sensitive only to the constitutive properties of geometric objects. Judgements made on the basis of a proper exercise of pure intuition are thus a priori ways of coming to know. The relation of the faculty of pure intuition to what individuates geometrical objects is an essential component of the explanation of why this is so. One could develop this position without any idealism, transcendental or otherwise, and without any commitment to the a priori applicability of Euclidean geometry. Nor is the position one which embraces what I earlier rejected; namely, causal explanations of a priori knowledge by the truths known. The reason why judgements of pure geometry based on pure intuition will hold whichever world is the actual world is not (of course) that there is causal access to the non-actual. It is rather that only the properties and relations constitutive of geometrical objects are employed by pure intuition in the first place, when that faculty is properly exercised.[29]

If we now step back from the data about particular a priori ways and propositions and ask what more generally we should want of a theory of the a priori there are two further natural demands. One natural demand is that the theory should explain why there should

---

[29] I believe the position outlined here is in the spirit of the remarks about the relation between geometry and a priori intuition by B. Longuenesse, *Kant and the Capacity to Judge* (Princeton, NJ: Princeton University Press, 1998), 290–1.

be a priori ways and truths at all. This condition is met by the metasemantic theory. In fact, the metasemantic theory predicts that for any concept at all there will be a priori principles involving it. This is so because any concept will have some possession-condition. By the account given in the metasemantic theory, that possession-condition and the Determination Theory applied to it will generate some a priori principles, and generate a priori ways of coming to know contents containing that concept. There will be at least one such way for each clause of the possession-condition.

The other natural demand is one that conventionalist theories of the a priori have conspicuously failed to meet. Some properties, considered as subject matter for a philosophical theory, have a distinctive characteristic. It is that any adequate theory of those properties must be self-applicable. For instance, a completely general account of truth must be self-applicable—for we want our account of truth to be true. Similarly, any fully general account of metaphysical necessity should be applicable to itself, if we are trying to provide an account of necessity which is not merely contingent.

A theory of the a priori is another case in point. Our philosophical theories of the a priori are not merely empirical. Any theory of the a priori must therefore be applicable to itself, if it is to be acceptable.

Carnapian and other conventionalist approaches do not meet this condition, unless we are prepared to take the extremely unintuitive position that adoption of a philosophical theory is itself a matter of convention, a matter of choice of a framework. On the metasemantic approach, however, the same explanation of the a priori status of philosophical knowledge can be offered as is given for the a priori status of our knowledge of arithmetic, logic, and the rest. The metasemantic theory of the a priori draws upon our understanding of what it is for something to be a concept. To possess the concept of a concept is to have some implicit conception of something individuated by a possession-condition. Our philosophical knowledge of the connection between the individuation of a concept and the existence of a priori ways of coming to know certain contents containing that concept results from an a priori abduction from a priori data about concepts. This abduction is not in its general structure and epistemic status any different from a priori abductions that allow us to reach new a priori principles in non-philosophical subject matters.

6.6. Does Naturalism Exclude the A Priori?

Is the existence of a priori propositions incompatible with a naturalistic world-view? The impression that there is such an incompatibility is often voiced in the literature by those sympathetic to broadly Quinean ideas. It is, however, surprisingly hard to formulate a credible version of naturalism and a plausible view of the a priori on which there is any incompatibility at all. A neo-Gödelian view that we are in some kind of causal contact with abstract objects, and that this is the source of some of our a priori knowledge, is certainly non-naturalistic. It postulates causal processes which cannot be embedded in our conception of the kinds of things with which minds can interact, which are always things or events in the spatial or temporal realm. But the moderate rationalism we outlined above fully embraces the a priori, and eschews mysterious causal interactions. A reasonable view of the a priori need not be non-naturalistic in the way in which any neo-Gödelian view is non-naturalistic.

Quine, rightly in my view, also objected to Carnap's 'internal'/'external' distinction, and insisted in effect that the notion of truth is uniform. Fundamentally the same notion of truth is applied to propositions of mathematics and logic as is applied to empirical sentences. But this doctrine of uniformity is equally endorsed in the metasemantic account of the a priori.

In *Theories and Things* Quine formulates a broad naturalistic doctrine. He characterizes naturalism as 'the recognition that it is within science itself, and not in some prior philosophy, that reality is to be identified and described'.[30] But it seems to me incoherent to suppose that the empirical ways of knowing employed in reaching empirical theories, including our theory of the layout of the observable world around us, could exhaust the ways of coming to know propositions. Any case of knowledge of an empirical theory exists only because some a priori entitlements also exist. Empirical knowledge is not merely inextricably entwined with the a priori. A better metaphor would be that the a priori provides the girders without which empirical entitlement would collapse.

---

[30] *Theories and Things* (Cambridge, Mass.: Harvard University Press, 1981), 21.

There are at least three ways in which any empirical theory involves the a priori. First, the methodology which is applied in reaching the theory has a fundamentally a priori status, even if the theory is empirical. The canons of confirmation, of inductive reasoning, and of abduction have an a priori status. Second, rational acceptance of any scientific theory rests ultimately upon some persons or other taking perceptual experience and memory at face value. The defeasible entitlement to do so also has an a priori status. Third, almost any theory beyond the rudimentary must include some kind of logic, which also has an a priori status. Though the matter is controversial, in my judgement no one has developed a thorough epistemological and semantical account on which the result of essentially empirical investigation could make it reasonable to revise one's logic. Beyond these three points, there are also more limited but very important respects, identified by Michael Friedman, in which not all elements of a mathematical physics face the tribunal of experience in the same way.[31]

One theorist who is much more explicit about why some naturalists have felt uncomfortable with the a priori is Hartry Field. He identifies empirical indefeasibility as the characteristic they find mysterious.[32] Field presents a radical treatment of the a priori, under which some propositions are said to be 'default reasonable', a technical term by which he means that they are reasonably believed without any justification at all (p. 119). According to Field, not all default-reasonable propositions are a priori: 'there is no obvious reason why propositions such as "People usually tell the truth" shouldn't count as default reasonable, and it would be odd to count such propositions a priori' (p. 120). Field has a non-factualist account of reasonableness: 'My proposal is that it [reasonableness] is an evaluative property, in a way incompatible with its being straightforwardly factual' (p. 127); 'reasonableness doesn't *consist in* anything: it is not a factual property' (ibid.).

Empirical indefeasibility, the phenomenon Field says is puzzling on a naturalistic worldview, seems to me to be explained by, and made less puzzling by, the metasemantic account. If *p* is guaranteed to be true in the actual world, however the actual world is, by the nature of

---

[31] Michael Friedman produced a series of papers on this theme in the period 1997–2001. See now his book *Dynamics of Reason* (Stanford, Calif.: CSLI Publications, 2001) and the references therein.

[32] 'Apriority as an Evaluative Notion', in Boghossian and Peacocke (eds.), *New Essays on the A Priori*.

the concepts in p, together with the rules for determining their semantic values and their mode of combination in p, then nothing we empirically discover will genuinely refute p. (There may always be misleading evidence, of course.) Why should this explanation be thought to be defective? One complaint might be that various rules and axioms, including the possession-conditions themselves, are used in the derivation that a certain content is guaranteed to be true. These rules and axioms must themselves be a priori if this explanation is to be fully successful. I agree. The rules of logic and the possession-conditions do seem to be themselves a priori. The metasemantic account is intuitively applicable to them too, as we noted. It must be so, if the metasemantic account is to cover all the ground.

It is not at all clear that there are default-reasonable propositions that are not a priori. In the case of Field's own example—'People normally tell the truth'—I would say that one is default-entitled to believe that a rational agent is telling the truth, and that relying on such a default entitlement is rational. But I would also say that it is an a priori entitlement, founded in the nature of rationality and interpretation.[33] The default entitlement is weaker than the 'usually' claim.

This parallels other cases of default entitlement. It is not outright a priori that experience is normally veridical; but one is entitled to take (at least the observational content of) experience at face value, in the absence of reasons for doubting it. This too is founded in the nature of the individuation of the content of perceptual states, if the argument of Chapters 2–4 is sound.

If all the examples that are thought to be propositions that are believed without any justification at all are ones to which there is a defeasible a priori entitlement, the question arises whether the non-factualist view is really offering any alternative to the moderate rationalist's account. Not just anything can be reasonably believed without any justification at all, and no empirical proposition can be reasonably believed without any justification at all. If default reasonableness turns out to coincide with a priori entitlement (outright or defeasible), that is something of which moderate rationalism can give an explanation. Non-factualism about reasonableness cannot.

---

[33] Along the lines of T. Burge's 'Acceptance Principle' in his 'Content Preservation'.

This has been a long chapter, and I pause to review the route we have taken. We started with the third principle of rationalism, which states that all instances of the entitlement relation are fundamentally a priori. Under the moderate rationalism developed in this chapter, the third principle is a corollary of the first two. The first two principles in effect ensure that the conditions for being a priori are fulfilled for an entitlement, under the moderate-rationalist account of the a priori.

We have noted that there is a variety of ways in which the possession-conditions for concepts and the identity-conditions for states can ensure that a transition is truth-preserving. Each way will result in a distinctive pattern of a priori principles. The treatment we gave of the a priori status of principles about colour is quite different from the treatment appropriate to account for the a priori status of logical principles.

To know the general form that must be taken by an account of possession of a concept is not to know in advance all the distinctive ways in which that form can be instantiated. There is much about particular principles with a priori status that remains ill understood—philosophy itself being only one amongst the disciplines that provide examples. Even if the moderate rationalist account is broadly correct there remains a broad scope for discoveries about new ways in which its abstract requirements can be met for novel subject matters.

CHAPTER 7

Moral Rationalism

Basic moral principles are known to us a priori. I will be arguing for this claim and discussing its ramifications for the epistemology, metaphysics, and the theory of understanding for moral language and thought.

The claim that basic moral principles are a priori was emphasized by Leibniz and, on some natural readings of the texts, endorsed by Kant.[1] Even a self-proclaimed empiricist like Locke sometimes veered towards endorsing this claim of a priori status.[2] Yet the character of this a priori status and its significance for the epistemology and metaphysics of moral claims have both been very largely lost in recent discussions of moral thought. I will be arguing that the nature of this a priori status is incompatible with subjectivist, judgement-dependent, and mind-dependent treatments of moral thought. Part of the task in establishing this incompatibility is to articulate more precisely the kind of a priori status that is in question here. It is easy to underestimate the problem for mind-dependent theories of moral thought if one starts by understating the sense in which basic moral principles are a priori.

If basic moral principles are a priori in a way that is incompatible with mind-dependent treatments, various tasks become pressing. One task is to develop a conception of the metaphysics and epistemology of morals, together with an integrated theory of understanding, that respects this status. Another is to address some of the motivations that

---

[1] Leibniz, *New Essays on Human Understanding*, esp. Bk. I, Ch. ii, pp. 91–4; Kant, *Groundwork of the Metaphysics of Morals*, at 4: 408 (pp.62–3) in *Practical Philosophy* trans. and ed. M. Gregor (Cambridge: Cambridge University Press, 1996). Rawls argues that only the procedure of the Categorical Imperative is a priori for Kant, and that moral principles are reached using it only in the presence of empirical information (see J. Rawls, *Lectures on the History of Moral Philosophy*, ed. B. Herman (Cambridge, Mass.: Harvard University Press, 2000), 247–52). If Rawls's reading is correct, it remains that one of the sources of true moral principles is fundamentally a priori.

[2] *An Essay Concerning Human Understanding*, Bk. IV, Ch. 4, sect. 7.

have made mind-dependent views of this territory so tempting. After attempting to make out the case against mind-dependent theories, I will try to outline some possible directions of development; and also to identify something I will call the 'Subjectivist Fallacy' which can make mind-dependent views of morality seem more attractive than they really are.

One could pursue these questions about the a priori status of basic moral principles as issues of interest in their own right in the subject of morality and its epistemology and metaphysics. But for the theses of the present book the case of moral thought is of interest as a test case for anyone sympathetic to the general programme of a moderate explanatory rationalism of the sort described in the preceding chapter. Moderate rationalism seeks to explain cases of a priori knowledge by appeal to the nature of the concepts that feature in contents that are known a priori. As we saw, for the moderate rationalist the explanations of a priori knowledge in various domains will not involve the postulation of causal interactions with non-physical or non-mental realms. That is what makes it more specifically a moderate rationalism. The explanations will also treat the a priori ways of coming to know as rational, as an exercise of reason. That is what makes the moderate position a form specifically of rationalism. What I have to say in this area can be seen as some first steps towards carrying through the moderate rationalist's programme in the special case of moral thought. Some of the considerations I offer will be of more general application, and may help in the development of a moderate rationalism in other areas.

7.1 The Claim of A Priori Status

Here is a first formulation of the claim of a priori status:

> Every moral principle that we know, or are entitled to accept, is either itself a priori or it is derivable from known a priori moral principles in conjunction with non-moral propositions which we know.

For an illustration of this Initial Thesis consider the moral proposition that national high-school examinations which assume that candidates have first-hand knowledge of vocabulary needed in snowy climates are unfair to those who live in southern states. That is not itself an a priori principle. No amount of a priori reflection would succeed in excogitating it. The moral proposition does, however, follow from two other truths: from the a priori principle that fair examinations will not include questions requiring background knowledge likely to be absent in one geographical group, together with the empirical, non-moral fact that it rarely snows in the southern states.

The Initial Thesis implies that for any moral proposition we are entitled to accept there is a similar division: into its a priori moral grounds on the one hand and its a posteriori non-moral grounds on the other. What the Initial Thesis excludes is the irreducibly a posteriori moral ground. The Initial Thesis is in the spirit of, indeed I would say a formulation of, Kant's claim that 'all moral philosophy is based entirely upon its pure part'.[3]

Why should we believe the Initial Thesis? All sorts of heavy-duty theories—theories of morality and of the a priori—might be offered in its support. I shall be touching on, and endorsing, some of them later. But the primary reason for accepting the Initial Thesis is not theoretical at all: it rests on the consideration of examples. Consider your belief that prima facie it is good if the institutions in a society are just; or your belief that prima facie it is wrong to cause avoidable suffering; or that prima facie legal trials should be governed by fair procedures. These beliefs of yours do not, and do not need to, rely on the contents of your perceptual experiences, or the character of the conscious states you happen to enjoy, in order for you rationally to hold them. Understanding of what justice is, of what suffering is, of what a trial and what fairness is makes these several beliefs rational without justificational reliance on empirical experience. Experience, as Kant said, may be necessary for the acquisition of these concepts, but that does not mean there cannot be propositions involving them that are a priori. Nor is it clear how empirical experience could rationally undermine these beliefs. Empirical information about extraordinary circumstances might convince us that it would be better on this occasion that a trial not be fair. That would not undermine the proposition that prima facie trials ought to be fair; and it is

---

[3] *Groundwork of the Metaphysic of Morals* at 4: 389, and I. Kant, *Practical Philosophy*, trans. and ed. M. Gregor (Cambridge: Cambridge University Press, 1996), 45.

not clear what could. Take any other moral principle that you are entitled to accept: I suggest that on examination it will always involve an a priori component, in the sense employed in the Initial Thesis.

The epistemic situation in the case of moral principles seems to me broadly similar to that concerning the status of logic and arithmetic. All sorts of heavy-duty theories—philosophical theories about logic, arithmetic, and the a priori—can be offered to support the view that logic and arithmetic are a priori. Those theories may or may not be convincing, but they could not be more convincing than the evidence they attempt to explain: such facts as that we are, apparently, justified in accepting that $2 + 2 = 4$, or that AvB follows from A, without justificational reliance on the content of our perceptual experiences, or other conscious states. In both the moral and the arithmetical and logical cases we must of course be prepared for the possibility that these appearances of a priori status are misleading. Anyone who defends the Initial Thesis must address all sorts of challenges. All I am emphasizing at this point is that there is strong prima facie support for the Initial Thesis from consideration of examples, in advance of any detailed philosophical theory of how or why the thesis holds.

The Initial Thesis is neutral on the question of whether every true moral principle could be known by us. People who disagree about that could both accept the Initial Thesis. The Initial Thesis concerns only the cases in which a principle is known, and says something about the existence of a priori ways of coming to know the principle.

This does not make the Initial Thesis a mere de facto claim about the moral principles we happen to know. The reasons for accepting the Initial Thesis go beyond what is provided by inspection of the particular moral principles we actually accept. I will be offering some general grounds for the Initial Thesis that are not dependent upon the particular moral principles we are currently entitled to accept. There is some plausibility in the further claim that the Initial Thesis, if true at all, is itself a priori. In any case, it has the status of a philosophical, not an empirical, claim.

For those who think that it is begging too many questions to formulate a thesis in a form that presupposes the possibility of moral knowledge we could frame a version, which may be more comfortable for those doubters, that mentions only entitlement to accept.

(I myself doubt that this really is weaker, but I mention it so that we can focus on the essential issues.) Any interesting version of the Initial Thesis must, however, make some use of some distinction between proper and improper acceptance of a moral principle. It could not be formulated in terms of mere acceptance.

The Initial Thesis is cagily formulated using 'we'. It will not be true of each individual thinker that every moral principle he is entitled to accept is either a priori or derivable from a priori moral principles and non-moral propositions he knows. Moral knowledge, like any other kind of knowledge, can be acquired by testimony. An empirical moral principle may be so acquired, and when it is, the acquirer himself need not know the a priori grounds of the empirical moral principle he learns through conversation. Nevertheless, someone must know or once have known them if the moral belief he acquires by testimony is to have the status of knowledge. The Initial Thesis is a thesis about actual epistemic grounds, in the epistemic community as a whole over time. The thesis goes far beyond claims about the mere possibility of grounds.

In the previous chapter we distinguished between the contentually a priori and the judgementally a priori. To remind ourselves: p is contentually a priori if there is an a priori way in which it can be known, a way which guarantees that p will be true in the actual world, whichever is the actual world (that it holds 'fixedly actually'); p is judgementally a priori if there is a way of coming to judge it that ensures that p is true in any world in which it comes to be judged in that way, and the way is also an a priori way. With this distinction in hand we can ask: Should the Initial Thesis be understood as concerned with the contentually a priori or with the judgmentally a priori? At first blush moral principles that are a priori do not seem to be merely judgementally a priori. They do not seem to be true only in worlds in which they come to be judged in a certain way. First blushes can be misleading, and have superficial causes, and I will return to the issue. For now I want to propose, consider, and defend the Initial Thesis in a sharpened and strengthened form, in which it concerns the contentually a priori. The Sharpened Thesis states:

> Every moral principle that we know, or that we are entitled to accept, is either contentually a priori or follows from contentually

a priori moral principles that are known in conjunction with non-moral propositions that we also know.

This needs argument and defence against a variety of challenges. I will try to provide some of what is needed a few paragraphs hence. First I offer some observations intended to bring out the nature of this Sharpened Thesis.

The Sharpened Thesis corresponds closely to parallel theses in two other areas in which knowable truth seems to be truth that is, at a fundamental level, contentually a priori.

The first of these areas is that of metaphysical necessity, whose partial parallels with the moral case I will consider at several points. As we observed at the start of Chapter 6, each truth that contains a metaphysical modality and that is also known to us seems to be either itself contentually a priori or it seems to follow from truths each of which is either a modal contentually a priori truth or is an a posteriori non-modal truth. It is necessary that Tully is Cicero. That modal truth is a posteriori. But it is a consequence of an a priori modal truth—the necessity of identity—together with the a posteriori but also non-modal truth that Tully is Cicero. More generally, a case can be made that every truth involving metaphysical necessity has its source in principles which are either necessary and a priori or non-modal and a posteriori.[4] What is excluded is an irreducibly a posteriori modal truth. The a priori modal principles that are fundamental under this conception of metaphysical necessity are plausibly contentually a priori, and not merely judgementally a priori.

The second case parallel to the Sharpened Thesis is that of evidential and confirmation relations. Many instances of evidential and confirmation relations are a posteriori. But it is arguable that each of them has an a priori component. A certain kind of rash confirms that an illness is meningitis. That is certainly a posteriori. But it rests on the a priori principle that a suitable range of instances gives non-conclusive support for a generalization, together with the truths about the presence of the rash in previous instances only in cases of meningitis, truths that are not themselves about the confirmation relation. What is excluded is an irreducibly a posteriori truth

---

[4] For a theory of necessity which offers an explanation of why this is so see *Being Known*, ch. 4, 'Necessity'.

essentially about confirmation. Again, the notion of the a priori on which these are plausible claims is that of the contentually a priori. If the earlier arguments of this book are correct, the principles of rationalism I formulated would provide some further explanation of why this is so. But one does not need that theory in order to accept the parallel between the evidential and confirmation relations on the one hand and the Initial Thesis on the other. One needs only the fundamentally contentually a priori status of evidential and confirmation relations, whatever the correct explanation of this phenomenon may be.

Since evidential and confirmation relations are normative relations, this second case does more than merely provide a parallel example. It further suggests a general hypothesis: that there is a significant range of normative kinds, such that each truth of that kind has an a priori component. This thought will be resurfacing at several points later on.

The Sharpened Thesis has a more general epistemological feature. There has in discussions of justification and the a priori long been circulating an argument to the effect that in any domain in which justifications and reasons exist some reason-giving relations must have an a priori status.[5] (Here the general hypothesis that all normative truths have an a priori component is resurfacing already.) It is hard to see how justification and the making of judgements for good reasons could ever get started if all reason-giving relations were a posteriori. My own view is that this traditional argument is sound, when it is properly framed. I endorsed essentially an argument in this spirit in Chapter 6, Section 1, in arguing for the third principle of rationalism—the Generalized Rationalist Thesis—to the effect that all instances of the entitlement relation are fundamentally a priori. There are all sorts of ways of mishandling this general idea, some of which have to do with certainty. One such way of mishandling the idea is the view that if anything is probable something must be certain.[6] But the idea that justification or entitlement could not get started unless some principles or relations are a priori can be developed without any commitment to the existence of such certainties.

---

[5] For an overview and defence see L. BonJour, *In Defense of Pure Reason*, 5 ff.

[6] A theme in C. I. Lewis's writings. See *Mind and the World Order: Outline of a Theory of Knowledge* (New York: Dover, 1956), for instance pp. 311–12.

If the reasoning of the traditional argument is sound, it applies as much in the domain of moral thought as it does in the area of empirical thought. Our Sharpened Thesis that all moral principles we are entitled to accept have a contentually a priori component dovetails with the traditional argument about justification. The Sharpened Thesis alludes to what must exist within the moral domain if the traditional argument is sound, and says that the a priori element that must be present in any kind of entitlement enters in the moral case at the level of the content of the moral principles themselves.

The Sharpened Thesis also has metaphysical ramifications, but I will first attempt to understand and explain its epistemic aspects.

7.2 The Claim Defended

A first objection to the claim of a priori status for basic moral principles may be that a thinker's impression, perhaps after some reflection, that a moral principle is correct is something that plays both a causal and a rational role in the thinker's acceptance of the moral principle. Why then is this impression not a conscious state whose role implies that basic moral principles are not a priori after all?

There must be something wrong with this objection, because such conscious states, playing a causal and a rational role, are present in clear cases of a priori status. A thinker may reflect rationally, and after her reflection be left with the impression that a principle is a logical law. The thinker's impression will be both causally and rationally operative in her acceptance of the principle as a law. It is rational, in the absence of reasons for doubt, to accept the outcome of such processes of reflective thinking. This can be an a priori way of coming to know the law.

What more specifically is wrong with the objection is that in the examples in question the impression is not a justification. The impression of correctness is itself a rational response to conditions that give grounds for thinking that (say) gratuitous infliction of pain is prima facie wrong, or give reasons for thinking that the logical law is valid. In the former case the fact that pain is subjectively awful provides such grounds; in the logical case the justifying condition for a reflective thinker must include the fact that the law is true under all relevant assignments, or can be derived from such laws. The thinker has an impression of correctness only because he appreciates these justifications. Since the impressions of correctness in these examples are not themselves justifications they cannot be used to support the claim that the thinker's operative justification in the moral or the logical cases is the character of one of his mental states.

This point is entirely consistent with the impression playing a causal role in the rational process leading up to the thinker's acceptance of the content. Of course the thinker would not have made the judgement in question if he had not had the impression that the content is correct. But that does not make the impression into a justification.

We can further emphasize the distance between impressions and justifications by considering their relations to correctness. For anything that is a justification for accepting a given content there must be an account of why that justification entitles the thinker to judge that the content is true—an account of the relation between justification and truth, in short. An explanation of how a judgement comes to be made that includes reference to an impression of correctness is not by itself an explanation of why that method of reaching the judgement is a correct method. For that we need an account that mentions that to which the impression is a rational response, when it is a rational response.

This treatment still sharply separates the a priori cases from those of perceptual knowledge. Suppose you come to have the perceptual knowledge 'That flower is yellow'. Your impression that this is a correct content is one to which you are entitled by the character of your perceptual experience; so the judgement is squarely a posteriori, indeed the paradigm case thereof. The explanation of why this is a correct way of reaching a judgement 'That flower is yellow' would certainly have to mention the perceptual experience, as a source of non-inferential information about the world. Your impression that the content 'That flower is yellow' is correct in these circumstances is parasitic on the justifying or entitling role of the mental state of perceptual experience, with its relation to correctness.

There are some kinds of example in which an impression is itself entitling. Propositional, non-autobiographical memory, of the sort likely instanced by your memory that the Bolshevik Revolution occurred in 1917, provides perhaps the clearest example. Here your impression is not a rational response to anything. Such impressions are entitling if we are entitled to take the deliverances of a memory faculty at face value. But the status of propositional memory that *p* as entitling depends on the thinker's entitlement to accept the information that *p* when he originally acquired it. At the time of acquisition what is entitling cannot be your memory impression. It may be an impression of correctness you have at the time of acquisition because some honest, knowledgeable interlocutor has informed you that *p*. This too can be entitling; but again, it seems that its status as such traces back eventually to the acquisition of an entitled belief that *p* where the entitlement does not consist solely in an impression of correctness.

In the logical case the reasons producing the impression that it is correct that a certain principle is a logical truth are reasons that are experience-independent and mind-independent. They consist in the existence of a proof that there is no falsifying assignment. As always, we must distinguish between the proof itself and access to the proof. Access to the proof must involve psychological matters; but that does not make what is accessed, the proof itself, into something mind-dependent.

Some theories treat the impression of the correctness of a moral principle as something which is not the appreciation of a reason which is explicable independently of the thinker's reactions on thinking about the principle, or its instances. There is a large subclass of such theories that treat moral properties as mind-dependent. Many different varieties of theory involve such mind-dependence. Mind-dependence is present in Christine Korsgaard's idea that the source of normativity is an agent's endorsement of 'a certain way she looks at herself, a description under which she finds her life worth living and her actions worth undertaking'.[7] It is present in judgement-dependent theories, in various forms of subjectivism, and in a range of dispositional theories, where the dispositions in question concern mental properties.[8]

---

[7] *The Sources of Normativity*, ed. O. O'Neill (Cambridge: Cambridge University Press, 1996), 249.

[8] For discussion of such approaches see C. Wright, *Truth and Objectivity* (Cambridge, Mass.: Harvard University Press, 1992), ch. 3, app. to ch. 3, and ch. 5; D. Wiggins, 'A Sensible Subjectivism?', in his *Needs, Values*, and *Truth* (Oxford: Blackwell, 1987); and the papers by D. Lewis, M. Johnston, and M. Smith in the symposium 'Dispositional Theories of Value', in *Proceedings of the Aristotelian Society*, suppl. vol. 63 (1989), 89–174.

Mind-dependence also seems to me to be present in Simon Blackburn's treatment of moral thought, even though he himself explicitly denies that his view involves mind-dependence.[9] Blackburn describes his view as a form of expressivism: In making moral judgements one expresses certain mental states, which, he holds, can be characterized as non-representational. Blackburn writes of an earlier paper of his: 'I said that the moral proposition was a "propositional reflection" of states that are first understood in other terms than that they represent anything, and that remains the core claim' (p. 77). A distinctive feature of Blackburn's position is that he allows that moral propositions can be assessed as true or false, and he appeals to a minimalism about truth in support of his position (p. 79).

It is, however, very hard to see how it can be denied that, under his approach, the conditions under which someone is correct in asserting a moral proposition have something to do with expressed mental states. To make this point is not to say that it is a consequence of Blackburn's position that someone making a moral claim is saying something about mental states. It is not a consequence. But it is equally not a consequence of a classical secondary-quality view of the property of being red that someone who says that an object is red is saying something about the experiences produced by that object. The classical secondary-quality view does, nevertheless, treat colour properties as mind-dependent. In neither the moral nor the colour case should the philosophical theory be put into the content of what the person is saying. It remains the case that, on both theories, the philosophically fundamental account of what it is for an utterance of a moral, or a colour, predication to be correct has to make reference to mental states.

For a theorist who holds that there is no such thing as a moral proposition the question of correctness would not even arise, and such a theorist might reasonably rebut the ascription to him of the view that the correctness of moral propositions is mind-dependent. But that is not Blackburn's position. I discuss Blackburn's detailed

---

[9] Blackburn has developed his view over many years. For a recent overview of his position see his *Ruling Passions: A Theory of Practical Reason* (Oxford: Oxford University Press, 1998). For a statement of his view that his quasi-realism does not commit him to mind-dependence see for instance his answer to question 2 (p. 311–12) of *Ruling Passions*. Page references appended to quotes from Blackburn are to this book. Blackburn no longer describes his view as 'projectivism', because that makes it sound as if projecting attitudes involves some kind of mistake (see p. 77).

reasons for rejecting the ascription to him of a mind-dependent treatment of morality later in this section.

I now want to raise the following general question, which arises for all mind-dependent theories of morality. Can theories which treat the correctness of moral propositions as mind-dependent explain the apparent fact that basic moral principles are contentually a priori?

To separate the issues clearly I first consider what the mind-dependent theorist can explain. Suppose we have some specific form of mind-dependent approach to moral norms. Suppose too that a thinker judges in ways acknowledged by that theory as suitably sensitive to the mind-dependent properties which he says are constitutive of moral norms. It will then hold according to that theory that the moral principles so reached will be true in any circumstances in which they are so reached. That is, under this mind-dependent theorist's conception, there is a way of reaching moral contents with respect to which they are judgementally valid.

It is hard to see how they could also be judgmentally a priori. Under a mind-dependent treatment the entitlement to make the moral judgements is constitutively dependent upon the instantiation of the mind-dependent properties to which the moral judgements are sensitive, when the thinker is judging knowledgably.

Can the mind-dependent theorist provide for non-introspective ways of coming to know moral propositions? It seems to me that he can allow for that. If statements of a certain kind are regarded as having mind-dependent truth-conditions, it does not follow that coming to know the truth of such a statement must (even in basic cases) involve checking on the thinker's own current mental states, or on anyone else's mental states. Statements about belief are certainly mind-dependent. Evans's procedure for self-ascription shows that a fundamental procedure for self-ascription may nevertheless involve looking outwards towards the world, not inwards to one's own mental states. Take the mental states to which, according to the mind-dependent theorist, a thinker must be sensitive if he is to be making moral judgements knowledgeably. If those mental states are not themselves about other mental states, the mind-dependent theorist can, it seems, consistently embrace the existence of non-introspective methods of coming to judge, knowledgeably, that certain moral propositions hold. Moral emotions, for example, are directed outwards to events, states of affairs, and other people, and are not at all well described as in general involving introspection of one's own mental states. While there are many good questions about whether the mind-dependent theorist can properly characterize the mental states in terms of which he wants to explain moral thought, I think we can still grant the conditional that if, within the terms of his own theory, he has access to those mental states we normally express in our moral thought he can legitimately claim that the ways of coming to know which he endorses are non-introspective.

Still, this is not to say that they are a priori. In particular, it does nothing to show that basic moral judgements are contentually a priori. Since I already argued that being contentually a priori implies being judgementally a priori, and suggested that under the mind-dependent view basic moral principles are not judgementally a priori, we already have an argument that the mind-dependent theorist cannot explain why basic moral principles are contentually a priori. But the arguments of particular theorists, such as those of Blackburn considered below, to the effect that there is no problem here for theories such as his own, mean that we have to consider the case of the contentually a priori separately.

The challenge to the mind-dependent theorist is to answer the following question. Must not his theory imply that were our morality-generating sentiments to be different what is actually wrong would no longer be so? If it does have that implication, he cannot explain the fact that basic moral principles are true in the actual world, whichever is the actual world, since it seems that they would not be true if the actual world were one in which we had different morality-generating attitudes. Can the mind-dependent theorist show that basic moral principles are true in the actual world whichever is the actual world?

The question has multiple readings. On a theory according to which psychological states are, in one way or another, the source of norms, in order to articulate this question more precisely we need to introduce some double indexing. We need to use the notion

> Proposition P, when evaluated from the standpoint of psychological states in w1, holds with respect to w2.

We can abbreviate this to P(w1, w2). It cannot be begging any questions against mind-dependent treatments to employ this doubly indexed notion. The first parameter makes explicit the dependence that the mind-dependent theorist himself needs to use in articulating his own theory. The second parameter is just assigned whatever world is the one with respect to which the proposition P is being evaluated. So in the case of a mind-dependent theory of morality in particular 'P(w1, w2)' means that proposition P, when assessed according to the moral standards said to result from thinker's psychological states in world w1, holds with respect to w2.

Here it helps to draw up some matrices, analogous to those introduced by Robert Stalnaker.[10] The mind-dependent theorist of moral thought is committed to holding that in each world there is some set of basic attitudes in terms of which moral truth, or entitlement to moral judgement, is elucidated philosophically and on which the correctness of moral claims depends. We can use the notation 'Atts$_i$' for such postulated basic attitudes as are held by thinkers in world i. Each matrix corresponds to a given moral statement S (as we can neutrally put it). In each column of the matrix we hold constant a parameter of the form Atts$_i$ for some fixed world i. The various entries in the column specify the truth-value of the statement S at a given world, with respect to the constant parameter Atts$_i$. So suppose that under the basic attitudes of world i an action of type A is prima facie good (in some given respect). We can suppose that this is a basic evaluation, and not subject to empirical variation, under the given standards. So in the column for Atts$_i$ every entry is a 'T' for true. But under the different attitudes of worlds j and k such an action type is not prima facie good; again we suppose that this is a basic evaluation. So the matrix for the statement 'Actions of type A are prima facie good' might be as follows:

	Atts$_i$	Atts$_j$	Atts$_k$
i	T	F	F
j	T	F	F
k	T	F	F

Our question was whether the mind-dependent theorist could explain the contentually a priori character of basic moral principles;

---

[10] *Context and Content* (Oxford: Oxford University Press, 1999), introd. and ch. 4, 'Assertion'.

that is, could explain the fact that they are true in the actual world, whichever is the actual world. There are clearly several possible readings of the phrase 'true in the actual world, whichever is the actual world' when we have double indexing.

We can distinguish three features which may be present independently of one another when a reading of this phrase is formulated in terms of the $P(w_1, w_2)$ notation. The three features correspond to positive answers to these three questions:

> Question (1): Is the first place, occupied by 'w_1' in '$P(w_1, w_2)$', universally quantified? In the matrix notation this is equivalent to the question: Are we considering a condition that universally quantifies over columns? In terms of the substantive philosophy this first question is asking: Are we considering variation in respect of the postulated basic attitudes?

> Question (2): Is the second place, occupied by 'w_2' in '$P(w_1, w_2)$', universally quantified? In matrix notation: Are we speaking of what holds in all entries in any given column? In terms of the substantive philosophy: Are we considering variation of possible worlds as points of evaluation, with respect to a given set of basic attitudes?

> Question (3): Are the variables or terms of the relation identified? That is, are we concerned with some condition about the instantiation of some monadic property involving the proposition P, of the form $\lambda w[\ldots P \ldots (w, w)]$? In matrix notation: Are we concerned with what holds along the diagonal?

Bearing these distinctions in mind, we can then distinguish at least the following readings of 'P is true in the actual world, whichever is the actual world'. (I prescind from relabellings of worlds as the actual world, so as not to distract attention from the central point):

> Reading (A): For any world w, $P(w, w)$.

This is equivalent to having the entry 'True' at each cell on the diagonal of the matrix that runs from top left to lower right. We can call this 'the diagonal reading'. It means this: Take any world, and the alleged basic morality-generating attitudes of that world, the proposition P will hold in that same world. On this reading we have both identification of variables and universal quantification of the monadic property $\lambda w[P(w, w)]$.

Reading (B): For any world w, $P(@, w)$.

Here there is no identification of variables, and universal quantification only with respect to the second place. This we can call the 'vertical reading', since it fixes on Atts$_@$, and for this reading to hold all the entries in the column Atts$_@$ must be 'True'.[11] It means this: Take our alleged morality-generating attitudes and hold them fixed: then P holds in every world, when evaluated with respect to those attitudes so held constant. There are variants of the diagonal and the vertical readings when one considers interactions with the labelling of a world as the actual world; but I will concentrate just on the diagonal reading (A) and the vertical reading (B).

In his quasi-realist writings Blackburn seeks to address the natural objection that even if our evaluative attitudes were different that would not make actions which we actually hold to be wrong into morally acceptable actions. Here is how he replies (I take a recent passage, which gives an answer that he has also developed in several other places):

According to me 'moral truths are mind-dependent' can *only* summarize a list like 'If there were no people (or people with different attitudes) then X . . .', where the dots are filled in with some moral claim about X. One can then only assess things on this list by contemplating the nearest possible world in which there are no people or people with different attitudes but X occurs. And then one gives a moral verdict on that situation.[12]

Here Blackburn is following broadly the structure of interpretation (B), the vertical reading. The 'moral verdict' of which he speaks is reached by employing our actual standards, which is why he holds that the objection fails.

In a similar spirit one might imagine a defender of Blackburn's position saying that on his position basic moral principles are indeed contentually a priori because we apply our actual basic moral standards,

---

[11] There will also be a generalized perpendicular reading, which asserts of an arbitrary world considered as actual what the preceding reading asserts only of the actual world. So the generalized perpendicular reading asserts:

(C) For any world w considered as actual (w/@), and for any world u, $P(w/@, u)$. One can also formally distinguish the cases $\forall w\, P(w,@)$ and $\forall w \forall u\, P(w, u)$.   [12] *Ruling Passions*, 311.

and if we do so then whichever world is the actual world the basic moral principles will be correct with respect to it.

Here I protest. On the quasi-realist's theory the acceptability of basic moral principles depends on some psychological attitudes. However this dependence is formulated, it must be possible in thought to consider which propositions are correct when we vary the standpoint of evaluation; that is, when we vary the first parameter, as in (A). Take a specific moral principle identified by its content, say 'Prima facie the infliction of avoidable pain is wrong'. Now consider the claim

> For any world w, prima facie the infliction of avoidable pain is wrong (w, w).

It seems to me that the quasi-realist, like other mind-dependent theorists, must say this is false. It is false at those entries in the diagonal for worlds in which we have different attitudes to the infliction of avoidable pain. The mind-dependent theorist has not, by his own lights, excluded those worlds. Unless the quasi-realist, or more generally any other mind-dependent theorist, has some way of showing that our basic evaluations could not have been different, I do not see how the mind-dependent theorist can avoid a commitment to denying this most recently displayed claim. In short, the objection to mind-dependent views concerns the diagonal reading, and the objection is that the mind-dependent theorist has not explained, by his lights, why there cannot be an entry 'False' somewhere on the diagonal. It cannot be an adequate answer to this objection that there are no 'False' entries on the vertical that corresponds to the actual world. Blackburn's defence cannot show that moral principles are contentually a priori in the sense of the diagonal reading: interpretation (A).

It may be helpful in clarifying the distinction between the diagonal and the vertical readings to fix on some very simple concepts where we would also want to invoke double indexing. It seems to be widely agreed that things would not stop being red if humans lost their colour vision and saw only in shades of grey. It is entirely consistent with this point to hold that which colours things have is in some way constitutively dependent upon how humans actually perceive them (in circumstances in which they have not lost their colour vision). If one does hold that further claim, the right way to formulate the dependence is not in terms of counterfactuals like 'If we were not to see things as red they would not be red', or any more sophisticated variants thereof. Such counterfactuals are evaluated from the standpoint of how humans perceive things in some central normal cases (that is, evaluated holding fixed the first parameter), and so cannot capture the intended dependence. But it is possible to formulate the proposed dependence all the same, either at a meta-level, or using some analogue of Davies and Humberstone's 'Fixedly Actually' operator. The best way of doing this would again depend on the resolution of various auxiliary issues, but one simple formulation of the suggested dependence is this:

> There is no physically individuated property Q such that it is fixedly actually the case that objects with Q are red.

In the spirit of our observation that everyone will accept that things would still be the same colours they actually are even if our vision were very different, this mind-dependent theorist will accept that

> For any world w, Q-objects are red (@, w)

in the case in which Q is in the actual world the underlying physical property of objects which are red. The crucial point, however, is that for an arbitrary physical property Q this imagined mind-dependent theorist will be committed to rejecting the claim that

> (DC) For any world w, Q-objects are red (w, w).

This is precisely parallel to the mind-dependent theorist of morality's commitment to rejecting the claim

> (DM) For any world w, prima facie the infliction of avoidable pain is wrong (w, w).

I am, then, committed to disagreeing with Blackburn's attitude to the seeming meta-level question of whether, on his view, moral truths are mind-dependent. He writes: 'But there is no such meta-level' (p. 311). We need only versions of the fixedly-actually operators to express what Blackburn implies cannot be expressed.

This discussion should also make clear the strict limits of the earlier concession to mind-dependent theorists that allowed them to regard moral principles as judgementally valid. That concession can be granted only on the understanding that the first parameter, the attitudes that according to them are the source of moral truth, is held fixed.

We might pick out a moral principle not by its content but by some definite description that relates it to those who accept it. The mind-dependent theorist does have access to some principle such as the following: In any world a basic principle that is morally endorsed in that world will be one that holds in that world. This is identifying a moral principle by description, rather than by its content. Now a given matrix of the sort I have introduced corresponds to a statement identified by its content, by a that-clause. So the principle to which I have just agreed the mind-dependent theorist does have access is not a principle that ensures that in a *given* matrix all the entries along the diagonal are 'True'. Rather, what it ensures is something concerning a set of many different matrices. It ensures that for a given world w if P is a statement endorsed by the basic morality-generating attitudes in w then the entry in the matrix in the column labelled 'Att$_w$' for the row for w will be 'True'. This does not ensure what is required by the status of a given proposition as contentually a priori; namely, possession of the entry 'True' along the diagonal of a single given matrix. Rather, it gives only something weaker. It gives a diagonal of 'True' entries in three dimensions, if you will, across a series of different two-dimensional matrices.

My position, in contrast to all mind-dependent views of moral principles, is that there is no sense in which moral principles fail to be contentually a priori. I hold this to be an epistemic and metaphysical truth. It is not itself a moral truth. The trouble for mind-dependent theorists is caused by variation with respect to the first parameter in P(w1, w2). If any form of mind-dependent theory of moral judgement is correct, that parameter must be articulable, at least at the level of philosophical reflection. My own view is that a proper appreciation of the contentually a priori status of moral principles ought to lead us to believe that any such parameter or argument place is otiose. The moderate rationalist about morality who is also tempted to some form of subjectivism about colour will say that while basic moral principles are contentually a priori, so that—if the relativization is insisted upon—(DM) is true, in the case of colour the characteristic consequence of one form of subjectivism holds, in that (DC) is false.

It is not in fact my view that our basic moral prima facie principles could intelligibly have been utterly different, in ways which have no connection with rationales for the principles we in fact accept. That possibility was being entertained in the preceding part of the argument only for *ad hominem* purposes. My claim is that the mind-dependent theorists do not have the resources to rule out such variation, and so cannot explain why basic moral principles are contentually a priori.

There is of course no general incompatibility between a domain of truths being mind-dependent and the existence, within that domain, of contentually a priori truths linking the properties ascribed in that domain. Principles of colour incompatibility are contentually a priori. This is not merely consistent with truths about the colour of particular physical objects being significantly mind-dependent. In my judgement, the explanation of their status as contentually a priori has to draw upon the special relation of colour concepts to colour experience. That was a feature of the explanation of the a priori status of certain principles of colour incompatibility that I offered in Chapter 6, Section 5. The crucial difference between colour incompatibilities under this treatment and Blackburn's treatment of moral principles is that in the latter case there is a parameter in the formulation of the mind-dependent view, namely the alleged morality-determining attitudes, which is not subject to a priori constraints within that theory itself. There is no such parameter determining truth from such free-floating attitudes in the treatment of colour incompatibilities. If we combine that treatment with mind-dependence of colour attributions, in the manner of the theorist envisaged above, the difference between the colour case and that of morality remains sharp. The diagonal claim (DC) remains false in the colour case. But for anyone who believes that basic moral principles are contentually a priori the whole notion of morality-generating attitudes has no application, and there will be no world, considered as actual, with respect to which it is not prima facie wrong to cause avoidable pain.

In this discussion I have focused on the formulations developed by Blackburn, which are admirable for their explicitness. But the points I have been making seem to apply to any subjectivist or mind-dependent theory that tries to avoid these problems by using an

'Actually' operator. Subjectivist and mind-dependent theorists are naturally tempted to appeal to our actual subjective states, or judgements, and to say that modal propositions about the moral should be evaluated always with reference to those actual states or judgements.[13] Contrary to the views of many writers in this area, I myself think that a proper deployment of the formal modal apparatus all things considered tells against mind-dependent approaches to morality in a way in which it does not tell against mind-dependent approaches to statements about colours.[14]

There are links and affinities between the Sharpened Thesis and G. E. Moore's justly famous paper 'The Conception of Intrinsic Value'.[15] Moore was very opposed to the idea that the goodness of something could be a matter of its extrinsic, rather than its intrinsic, properties. He was equally opposed whether the extrinsic properties in question were conceived of as mind-dependent or were conceived of as mind-independent. But in the special case in which mind-dependent qualities were offered as an analysis of goodness he wrote of 'the fact that, on any "subjective" interpretation, the very same kind of thing which, under some circumstances, is better than another, would, under others, be worse—which constitutes, so far as I can see, the fundamental objection to all "subjective" interpretations' (p. 283). This formulation is of course ineffective against the subjectivist who uses 'Actually' operators; but it would be a very superficial understanding of Moore which took this as a reason for saying that his 'fundamental objection' fails. On Moore's view, as he stated it in italics, 'To say that a kind of value is "intrinsic" means merely that the question whether a thing possesses it, and in what degree it possesses it, depends solely on the intrinsic nature of the thing in question' (p. 286). There is clearly still dependence of value on a thinker's

---

[13] For such use of an 'actually' operator in defending a subjectivist theory see Wiggins, 'A Sensible Subjectivism', p. 206. Wright, in *Truth and Objectivity*, describes the use of an 'actually' operator as 'an attractive strategy' (p. 114), but goes on to caution that 'no proposition whose necessity is owing entirely to actualisations can be known *a priori*' (p. 116).

[14] Wiggins cites Davies and Humberstone, 'Two Notions of Necessity', 22–5, in support of his use of an 'actually' operator to meet the objections to subjectivism. D. Lewis gives a very clear acknowledgment of the problem for a subjectivist theory: 'The trick of rigidifying seems more to hinder the expression of our worry than to make it go away. It can still be expressed' ('Dispositional Theories of Value', 132 ff.).

[15] In his *Philosophical Papers* (London: Routledge and Kegan Paul, 1922), 253–75, but now most accessible in the revised edition of *Principia Ethica*, ed. T. Baldwin (Cambridge: Cambridge University Press, 1993), 280–98. Page references in the main text above are to this more recent volume.

mental states if the subjectivist formulates his theory using 'Actually' operators. The right way to demonstrate this dependence is to appeal not to metaphysical possibilities but to the failure of this subjectivist's conditions to hold Fixedly Actually. There is still dependence of the sort to which Moore objects if the dependence is on thinkers' actual attitudes or other subjective states.

With this understanding of Moore's intentions, there is an intuitive argument from Moore's thesis that moral values are intrinsic to the Sharpened Thesis.[16] We can argue by contraposition. If the Sharpened Thesis were false then there would be moral principles, and so statements of value, that could be known only by empirical investigation of the actual world. It is hard to see how those values, thus knowable only empirically, would be intrinsic in the sense that mattered to Moore.[17]

If we step back to reflect on the argument I have given so far it is apparent that it does not depend on features that are unique to morality. The argument I have offered so far can be developed in corresponding form to reject any mind-dependent treatment of any domain in which there are principles that are contentually a priori, and in which the mind-dependent treatment involves a parameter of allegedly truth-determining attitudes that are not constrained by the theory to have any particular contents or relations to other states. The argument could, for instance, be marshalled against certain mind-dependent treatments of metaphysical necessity (if further arguments against such treatments were thought to be needed). All the arguments against mind-dependent treatments in the moral case would carry through *pari passu* for the modal case, applied now to the allegedly 'necessity-determining attitudes'. One could even imagine a G. E. Moore-like philosopher writing a paper called 'The Conception of Intrinsic Necessity' in which the author insists that whether a proposition is necessary depends only upon the nature of its various

---

[16] Moore writes about values more generally, including aesthetic value. Obviously the Sharpened Thesis, restricted as it is to moral values, could have consequences at most for moral values.

[17] The converse implication holds only under the additional supposition that any extrinsic property is not knowable a priori. This supposition would not be true for arithmetic. It is not an intrinsic property of the number 4, but it is knowable contentually a priori, that it is the minimum number needed to colour an arbitrary map on the plane without adjacent regions having the same colour. The notions in play at this stage of the discussion would thus need some refinement for this converse implication to be established. I conjecture that such refinement is possible.

constituents, and does not depend on any thing external to those constituents, whether it be mental or non-mental.

7.3 Explaining the A Priori Status of Morality: A Schema

The claim that basic moral principles are contentually a priori does not by itself imply the view that they can be derived from the law of non-contradiction. The laws of modal logic, and other basic principles of metaphysical necessity, are also a priori. But they are not literally derivable from the law of non-contradiction alone. Otherwise modal logic would be a part of first-order logic, which it is not. Kant himself of course believed in a connection between what you can will without contradiction and the correctness of a principle. But his *Groundwork* also contains another idea, a more general idea which does not in its basic formulation mention non-contradiction. This more general idea contains the seeds of an explanation of the a priori status of moral principles. Kant writes:

the ground of obligation here must not be sought in the nature of the human being or in the circumstances of the world in which he is placed, but a priori simply in concepts of pure reason[18]

This claim of Kant's is a consequence of the highly plausible principle that ways of coming to know a given proposition that are a priori ways have their source in the nature of one or more concepts or contents in the given proposition. This principle is part of moderate explanatory rationalism. If moral principles are a priori, and a priori ways of coming to know a proposition trace back to the nature of the concepts it contains, it follows that some ways of coming to know a moral principle have to do with the nature of moral concepts. Our task is to say how this is so.

I have already mentioned the modal case twice, and it will continue to help us to consider the partial parallel between modal and moral concepts. As I said, modal truth seems to be fundamentally contentually a priori, like basic moral principles. Elsewhere I argued

---

[18] *Groundwork* 4: 389 and Kant, *Practical Philosophy*, trans. and ed. Gregor, 45.

that our understanding of modal truth is best explained by our having an implicit conception whose content is given by a set of principles that collectively determine which world descriptions represent genuine possibilities.[19] Those principles I called the 'Principles of Possibility'. The Principles of Possibility, whose details do not matter for present purposes, include principles entailing that genuine possibilities respect what is constitutive of the identity of the concepts, objects, properties, and relations they concern. What matters in considering a partial parallel with the moral case is the model of understanding, epistemology, and metaphysics instantiated by this principle-based approach. Under the principle-based approach, to understand modal operators is to evaluate modal claims as true or false in accordance with these principles. The principles are at most tacitly known to an ordinary thinker when she evaluates modal claims. It takes philosophical thought to work out what those principles are.

The principle-based approach to modality has two features that we equally need to provide for in the moral case.

First, it gives an account of how a way of coming to know, even one employed by a non-philosophical thinker, can be a way that ensures that what is known is true in the actual world, whichever is the actual world. In evaluating modal claims the thinker draws on the content of tacit knowledge of the Principles of Possibility. These Principles state what it is, constitutively, for a description to represent a genuine possibility. The Principles are themselves true in the actual world, whichever is the actual world—they hold Fixedly Actually. Standard logical inferences will preserve Fixedly Actual truth. Truths about what is constitutive of particular concepts, objects, properties, and relations are equally plausibly truths that hold Fixedly Actually. If our thinker draws only on information which holds Fixedly Actually, by rules which preserve that property, when she evaluates modal truths then the modal truth she comes to know thereby will hold Fixedly Actually. This is a way of coming to know a modal truth that ensures that what is known will hold in the actual world, whichever is the actual world.

In attempting to use this general method of evaluating modal claims a thinker is not thereby infallible. Infallibility in such cases

---

[19] *Being Known*, ch. 4.

never exists. A thinker may make mistakes about what is constitutive of the identity of a concept, object, property, or relation; she may also make inferential mistakes. When, however, there are no such mistakes in a thinker's use of this general method in reaching a modal belief the method ensures that the modal content judged is true in the actual world, whichever is the actual world. Since the existence of such ways of coming to know contentually a priori modal propositions relies on an account of understanding modal notions, and does not involve causal interaction with a modal realm, the principle-based account is a species of moderate rationalism for the modal case.

The other feature of the principle-based approach to modality that we also need to provide for in the moral case is some analogue of its straightforward means for integrating the modal epistemology and modal metaphysics that steers between the extremes of mind-dependence on the one hand and an epistemology that requires causal contact with a modal realm on the other. If the Principles of Possibility state what it is for something to be a genuine possibility, and those Principles are properly applied in reaching modal beliefs, we already have an explanation of how modal knowledge is possible. Such a middle course, avoiding both mind-dependence and inter-actionism, is just what we need in the case of morality too.

The moral analogue of the principle-based treatment of modality is a treatment under which to possess moral concepts involves having an implicit conception whose content is operative when one assesses moral propositions. Full grasp of a given moral concept, if such a thing is ever possible, would involve possession of an implicit conception whose content formulates what it is, constitutively, for something to fall under that moral concept. The general idea of a principle-based treatment is in itself neutral on what the contents of the implicit conceptions are. Many different first-order moral views could avail themselves of a principle-based treatment in attempting to address epistemological and metaphysical issues about the status of morality. So equally could many different philosophical views about what unifies the principles that form the content of the implicit conceptions. I will not be taking on the task of addressing particular first-order moral views here, nor the question of what unifies them. My aim is rather to consider what resources a principle-based treatment makes available to a variety of conceptions when they turn to address epistemological and metaphysical issues.

The implicit conceptions possessed by a moral thinker will be complex and structured. They will concern values, ideals, their relative importance, and something about their underlying sources. Even from a description as brief as that there are two apparent differences from the modal case. One of the most important differences is the need for some kind of 'prima facie' or '*pro tanto*' operator in the moral case, which, in my view, has no analogue in the modal case. It is plausible that one will need to employ, in any principle-based account of moral truth and moral epistemology, principles of the form 'Prima facie given that an action is F it is good in such-and-such a respect'. The same applies to evaluations of states of affairs. The presence of a prima facie operator has many repercussions, including some for the issue of determinacy. There is nothing in such structures to rule out the possibility that some type of action may be prima facie good in certain respects, prima facie bad in others, and there be nothing further in the principles to settle outright whether it is good or bad.

A second difference from the modal case concerns completeness. There is some plausibility that we can give a very general characterization of what is required for a description to represent a genuine possibility. It is arguable that if a description respects what is constitutive of concepts, objects, properties, and relations, it represents a genuine possibility. Though we are certainly ignorant for many concepts and objects of what it is that is constitutive of them, such ignorance concerns whether the conditions for certain possibilities are met, and is not about what it is for something to be possible. It is not apparent that anything analogous has to hold in the case of moral thought. Even our implicit conceptions may be incomplete, may need further articulation from reflection on examples and other principles.

A thinker may have an implicit conception with a correct content involving a given concept but nevertheless make mistakes when asked to formulate general propositions involving that concept. This is a familiar phenomenon of implicit conceptions in other domains, evidenced by the frequent inability of thinkers to, say, define 'chair' correctly, or to state explicitly the rules of grammar they are following. Indeed, even the simple example I have been using needs qualification. The infliction of avoidable pain is not prima facie wrong in the case in which the pain still exists, but is not experienced as hurting, as can be the case for one who has taken morphine. The infliction of pain is prima facie wrong only when it is a form of suffering, and is wrong for the same reason as it is wrong to cause, say, avoidable depression or severe anxiety in a person. Reflection on the ways in which we can correct our initial impressions of wrongness or rightness will make the principle-based theorist say that not all cases are like those which Prichard described as immediate apprehension, in which 'insight into the nature of the subject directly leads us to recognize its possession of the predicate'.[20]

A thinker who judges that some type of action is wrong may be more or less articulate in his ability to say why it is so. At the least articulate level the thinker may just make some clear intuitive judgement that it is wrong, without being at all confident in any particular explanation of why it is wrong. At one step up from this the thinker may be able to give a ground: 'because it would be a betrayal', 'because it hurts him and the hurting is avoidable'. At another step up the thinker may be able to say why these are grounds. Higher levels of justification involve abductions from a priori examples and other apparently a priori principles—at this level of description the methodology is the same as that found in other domains in which truth is fundamentally a priori. The possibilities of error are the same as in other a priori domains.

A principle-based approach can share each of the features that made the parallel to the modal case tempting. Even if a thinker's implicit conception of some moral property is incomplete the content of that conception can still be a correct partial statement of what it is, constitutively, for something to fall under that concept. They will, for instance, be a correct partial statement of what determines the semantic value of a concept like *is prima facie wrong*. When they are so, and when the information is properly drawn upon in the evaluation of contents containing that concept, the contents thus reached will be true. And, as in the modal case, since the rule determining the semantic value of a concept applies whichever world is the actual

---

[20] 'Does Moral Philosophy Rest on a Mistake?', repr. in *Moral Obligation, and Duty and Interest: Essays and Lectures by H. A. Prichard*, ed. J.O. Urmson (Oxford: Oxford University Press, 1968), at 8.

world, propositions thus reached will be reached in a way that guarantees that what is known in that way will also hold in the actual world, whichever is the actual world.

The fact that implicit conceptions are involved in the evaluation of moral propositions does not by itself suffice to account for the contentually a priori status of basic moral principles. There is no contradiction in the idea of an implicit conception having an a posteriori content. In fact, an implicit conception with the content that the word 'chair' in one's own language applies to things having certain properties is an implicit conception with an empirical content. What matters for a priori status is rather that the given way of coming to know is guaranteed to be correct by the way in which the semantic values of the relevant concepts are fixed. Implicit conceptions whose contents either consist of principles that state what it is for something to be wrong, for instance, or consist of consequences thereof meet this further condition. Without this further condition we would not have an explanation of the contentually a priori status of basic moral principles. The same applies to the modal case.

This integration of the metaphysics of the moral—what it is to fall under certain normative concepts—with an epistemology steers the same middle course as the principle-based account of modality. It involves neither a mind-dependent account of moral truth nor a causal epistemology for the contentually a priori principles. It does not follow that moral properties may not be involved in other causal explanations, not having to do with knowledge of a priori principles. We will turn to those issues in the next chapter.

The point that fundamental principles help to determine the semantic value of concepts like *is prima facie wrong* is important in separating any principle-based conception from mind-dependent treatments of moral thought. Mind-dependent theorists can fairly insist that on their views a certain set of moral principles is correct, and can equally insist that some principles are more fundamental than others. That does not imply that mind-dependent theorists can simply take over the apparatus of the principle-based view. The objection remains outstanding against the mind-dependent theories that they cannot explain the contentually a priori status of basic moral principles. To try to meet the objection by saying that the principles themselves determine the semantic value of moral concepts, regardless of what attitudes minds take to them, would be to abandon any claim of mind-dependence. A principle-based conception is a very different animal from any mind-dependent view.

7.4 The Subjectivist Fallacy

The Subjectivist Fallacy is the fallacy of moving from a premiss stating that certain mental states are sufficient, or stating that certain mental states are necessary, for a given content to be true to the conclusion that the truth of the content consists, at least in part, in something subjective or mental. I say that this is a fallacy even in the case in which the premiss stating that certain mental states are sufficient, or are necessary, holds true a priori. To say that it is a fallacy is not of course to say that the conclusion is not true; only that it cannot be supported just from these premisses.

The Subjectivist Fallacy is a fallacy because it may be possible to explain why the mental states are necessary or sufficient for the truth of the target content by exhibiting this necessity or sufficiency as a consequence of a more fundamental account of what is involved in the truth of the target content, a more fundamental account that does not mention mental states at all. The fact that there is in a certain sense no gap between certain mental conditions obtaining and the holding of the target content may have a non-subjectivist explanation.

Here is an example of the Subjectivist Fallacy, an example which would be recognized as such on all but the most extreme views of the nature of meaning and rule-following. The case involves a hypothetical position on the understanding of arithmetical relations. We can imagine a theorist who starts from this true premiss:

> Within the accessible numbers it is sufficient for $n + m$ to equal k that a thinker who reaches his judgement about what $n + m$ equals in accordance with certain recursive procedures will judge that $n + m = k$.

From this truth our imagined theorist moves to the conclusion:

> Equations involving addition have partially mind-dependent truth-conditions concerning what a certain kind of thinker would judge.

Almost everyone will agree that this hypothetical theorist's mistake lies in not realizing the judgements of his hypothetical calculating subject are correct only because they respect the recursive equations for addition. The fact that there is (and is a priori) a necessary and sufficient condition, framed in terms of the judgements of a hypothetical thinker, for the holding of the addition relation on the accessible numbers is just a by-product of something more fundamental. This more fundamental condition is the non-psychological truth-condition for equations involving addition determined by the recursive characterization of the addition relation.

How does this bear on constructivism in ethics? Constructivists need not be mind-dependent theorists. Constructivists too can agree that the displayed transition about addition moves from a true premiss to a false conclusion, provided their constructivism is of a non-psychological variety. Their constructivism will be of a non-psychological variety only if the 'can' in the phrase 'can be constructed' which features in a statement of constructivism is not explained in psychological terms. It is also a necessary condition of the constructivism being non-psychological that the particular rules or recursions it mentions are not mentioned there by virtue of their meeting some mind-dependent condition. Some versions of constructivism meet these conditions. Hence constructivists need not be mind-dependent theorists.

A second example of the Subjectivist Fallacy moves from truths about concept possession to a general subjectivism about truth. The premiss of this second illustration of the Subjectivist Fallacy is available to anyone who accepts two points about concept possession. The first point is that in the possession-condition for a concept, reference is made to what the thinker must be willing to judge in certain circumstances. If such reference is thought to be required only in certain cases then the premiss of this illustration will correspondingly be available only in that restricted class of cases. The second point needed for the availability of the example concerns the theory of concepts and the theory of the way in which their reference is determined. These two theories must, one way or another, jointly have the consequence that the judgements a thinker is required to make in given circumstances, if he is to be credited with possession of the concept, are ones which are true in those same circumstances. (On some theories this second point is secured by the account of how semantic values are assigned to concepts.) In any case, if these two points are accepted, perhaps just for a restricted range of concepts φ, then a premiss of the following form will be correct:

> If the thinker judges in the given circumstances that something is φ, then it is φ.

Does it follow that something's being φ, at least in the specified circumstances, is a mind-dependent, subjective matter? It certainly does not. The possession-condition framed in terms of willingness to judge may determine a property an object has to have if it is to fall under the concept φ, a property that may, for all that has been said so far, be wholly mind-independent. In the case in which the concept is one of a logical constant the property determined may be (or determine) a certain truth-function. In any case in which such a property is determined the truth of the premiss will be explicable from a non-subjective account of the truth of contents of the form 'a is φ'. The same point applies when the property determined is one that would classically be recognized as a primary quality.

The more general fallacy described in the second illustration actually has the first illustration, about elementary addition, as a special case. It is the special case in which the concept is that of addition, and the possession-condition for the concept requires computational practices which obviously respect the recursion which defines addition.

One element in Wittgenstein's rule-following considerations—perhaps not the only element, but an important and extensive element—is that justification comes to an end, and that in an account of understanding at a certain point we have to speak of an ability to go on in the right way. This is captured in possession-conditions that speak of what the thinker finds primitively compelling, without proceeding through inferential justifications for applying the concept in question. I have argued that we can recognize the Subjectivist Fallacy as a fallacy whilst employing such possession-conditions for concepts. If that is correct, it follows that there is nothing in this element of the rule-following considerations to exclude the more rationalist conception of moral thought that I was suggesting earlier.[21] Only on much more radical views of rule-following, for instance the view that the correctness of a judgement is not fundamentally the result of two components, the way the world is and the nature of the concepts employed, would such general conclusions of mind-dependence be acceptable.

The crucial step in the Subjectivist Fallacy as I have described it is acceptance of an incorrect criterion for the mind-dependence of a given property. Hence it is possible to make what seems to me the same mistake as is made in the Subjectivist Fallacy without actually being a subjectivist. Even a theorist who rejects subjectivism about a given domain may still be using a questionable account of mind-dependence of a given property. The theorist may even be relying on that account in his rejection of subjectivism.

The writings of Crispin Wright and Mark Johnston contain examples of criteria for mind-dependence that seem to me open to question in this way. In his well-known discussion of the Euthyphro Contrast, Wright introduces the notion of a 'provisional equation', which is something having the form of a conditional whose consequent is itself a biconditional, i.e. the form $A \supset (B \equiv C)$. A provisional equation is something of the form 'If CS then (it would be the case that p if and only if S would judge that p)'.[22] A substantial provisional equation, says Wright, has an antecedent CS in which 'a concrete conception is conveyed of what it actually does take' for the subject to be operating under conditions in which her opinion is true.[23] Wright endorses this conditional: 'if a discourse sustains substantially formulated true provisional equations which can be known a priori to be true, then that makes the beginnings of a case for regarding the discourse as dealing in states of affairs whose details are conceptually dependent upon our best opinions'.[24] Similarly Mark Johnston in addressing the question 'How then are we to demarcate the response-dependent concepts?' offers the answer that if a concept C is one interdependent with or dependent upon the

---

[21] For an expression of sympathy with certain Wittgensteinian views in support of a treatment of moral thought that is very distant from the present rationalist view see B. Williams, 'Philosophy as a Humanistic Discipline', *Philosophy*, 75 (2000), 477–96.

[22] *Truth and Objectivity*, 119. I have altered only Wright's notation for propositions.

[23] Ibid. 112.   [24] Ibid. 119–20.

responses of subjects 'then something of the following form will hold *a priori*':

> x is C iff: In K, Ss are disposed to produce x-directed response R (or x is such as to produce R in Ss under conditions K).[25]

This biconditional will be fulfilled in our first, arithmetical, example when we take the concept C to be the property of (say) being the sum of 7 and 5, the condition K to be the condition of exercising properly functioning memory and perceptual systems, and the response to be that of making a certain judgement expressing the outcome of the subject's computation in accordance with certain rules. A corresponding point could be made about Wright's criterion. In both Johnston's and Wright's proposals the test proposed for mind-dependence is too easily met by propositions whose truth is not mind-dependent. Nothing can be validly concluded from the existence of such a priori conditionals or biconditionals in a given domain about the mind-dependence of that domain.

There is nothing inimical in these illustrations and arguments to the idea that some contents do have mind-dependent truth-conditions. They do when their truth-conditions concern a property whose nature—what it is, constitutively, to have the property—is to be explained in terms of properties of the mind. The burden of the preceding remarks is that this constitutive condition cannot be reduced to something involving a priori equivalence with conditions concerning certain mental states.

The Subjectivist Fallacy is an instance of a more general fallacy concerning the nature of properties. The more general fallacy is that of moving from the a priori truth of a biconditional of the form

$$F(x) \quad \text{iff} \quad A(x)$$

to the conclusion that being A is what *makes* something F. I call this the 'Biconditional Fallacy'. Just as in the subjectivist case, it is a fallacy because the correct account of what makes something F may have a consequence that it is a priori that something is F iff it is A; but the constitutive account may not mention properties or notions of the sort mentioned in the condition $A(x)$. One of the tasks facing

---

[25] 'Dispositional Theories of Value', 145.

those who want to develop discourse ethics, for example, is to show that it can be done without committing this fallacy. Jürgen Habermas formulates the central claim of discourse ethics as follows: 'Only those norms can claim to be valid that meet (or could meet) with the approval of all affected in their capacity as participants in a practical discourse'.[26] Let us suppose that the theorist of discourse ethics makes a good case that this condition is a priori true. Nothing would follow about what makes something a valid norm. The approval, in the appropriate practical discourse, of those affected might be a consequence of more fundamental principles about norms that have this approval as a consequence. Consistently with the principle Habermas formulated being a priori, practical discourse might not be mentioned in an account of what is fundamentally constitutive of the notion of a valid norm. It is that further claim about fundamental constitution that discourse ethics would have to establish if it is to speak to the nature of morality.

I conclude this chapter with a more general reflection on the theoretical options available to us. When one reads the literature on judgement-dependent and other mind-dependent approaches to ethics and other subject matters the impression is often conveyed that when we do have an a priori biconditional linking some property with thinkers' mental states there are only two options. Either we read the psychological material of the right-hand side as providing what is constitutive of the left-hand side's holding, or else we must accept some form of 'detectivism', with the overtones of 'detection' involving a causal epistemology for the states of affairs detected.[27] To think that these are the only two possibilities is to overlook broadly rationalist approaches that are neither mind-dependent nor committed to the possibility of causal interaction. It is as if the only two possibilities in the philosophy of arithmetic, or the philosophy of modality, were either subjectivism or a commitment to causal interaction. I suggest that a good rationalist treatment of mathematics, modality, and morality involves neither of those two positions, but presents a genuinely distinct third way.

---

[26] *Moral Consciousness and Communicative Action*, trans. C. Lenhardt and S. Weber Nicholsen (Cambridge, Mass.: MIT Press, 1990), 93.

[27] See Wright, *Truth and Objectivity*, app. to ch. 3, on the Euthyphro Contrast.

CHAPTER 8

Moral Rationalism, Realism, and the Emotions

8.1 Is Moral Rationalism Consistent with Moral Realism?

Can a moral rationalist be a moral realist? And, if this is a different question, can a moral rationalist hold that moral properties are sometimes involved in causal explanations?

These questions are made pressing by various conflicting cross currents. On the one hand moral rationalism can appear to be a reasonable middle position. I have presented moral rationalism both as avoiding an extreme view on which there is causal explanation of moral beliefs by moral facts, via some faculty sensitive to those facts, and as equally avoiding a subjectivism or mind-dependence about moral claims. Yet on the other hand there are considerations that may seem to imply that there is no such middle ground for moral rationalism to occupy. As Nicholas Sturgeon famously observed, it certainly seems that the injustice of some social structure can causally explain its overthrow.[1] If this can be true, is there any obstacle to the causal explanation by moral truths of moral beliefs? If there is not, maybe moral rationalism is misconceived; maybe we need an entirely different model for the grasp of moral notions.

Cutting across the direction of these concerns are further issues about the relation between moral rationalism and moral realism. Some of the extant characterizations of the varieties of realism in the moral domain are either so strict as to apply only to the interactionist-faculty

---

[1] N. Sturgeon, 'Moral Explanations', in *Morality, Reason and Truth: New Essays on the Foundations of Ethics*, D. Copp and D. Zimmerman (eds.), (Totowa, NJ: Rowman and Allanheld, 1985), esp. 63 ff.

view rejected by a reasonable moral rationalism or so weak as to apply also to mind-dependent views. Can we even identify a middle sense in which a moral rationalist can be a moral realist? And does any such sense allow for the genuine cases of explanation by moral truths?

Moral rationalism as I have characterized it is not a single position but is rather a family of positions. To be a moral rationalist is to hold the following theses. (i) For any moral proposition that is known there is an a priori way of coming to know it. More particularly, there is a way of coming to know the moral proposition that ensures that it is true in the actual world, whichever world is labelled as the actual world. That is, the proposition is contentually a priori. (ii) The ability to know moral propositions in a way that is a priori traces back to the nature of understanding—to what is involved in grasping the moral concepts. (iii) The notion of truth that is applied to moral propositions is uniform with that applied to other propositions in any other domain. Though truths in different domains will have different characteristics, those differences will trace back to differences between those domains, rather than to any fragmentation in the notion of truth itself.

A Kantian position that sees the origin of the correctness of a moral claim in the Categorical Imperative could be developed in a way that makes it a moral-rationalist theory. So equally could a theory which sees all moral principles as furthering some end, provided this theory holds that this end is an a priori goal of morality.

Any moral-rationalist theory will identify a set of designated principles that fix a corresponding account of moral truth. For a moral proposition to be true is for it to be a consequence of this set of designated principles (in combination, if need be, with nonmoral information). Some of these principles will be prima facie principles, stating that actions or states of affairs of such-and-such kind are prima facie good, or prima facie wrong; others will state principles for ranking values when they conflict; and so forth. The designated principles, taken together, may sometimes count an action in given circumstances as outright wrong, or outright right. But this need not always be so. Such a structure in its abstract form already provides for the possibility of some indeterminacy. Some actions may be prima facie wrong in some respects prima facie right in others, and the ranking principles may not settle that they are outright wrong or outright right.

Amongst ways of coming to judge a given content some can be classified as *constitutively sound*. A way of coming to judge that a particular thing is F is constitutively sound if it draws on information about what makes something F, and applies that information correctly. In finding out the numerical product of 12 and 13 by first taking the product of 12 and 12 and then adding another 12 one uses a constitutively sound method. The method is correct because what it is for a number to be n times the successor of x is for it to be the sum of n times x with x.

Information may be deployed by a thinker even though it is only tacitly known. Ordinary speakers of English find great difficulty in giving a correct definition of 'chair', but have no difficulty in applying the concept it expresses to examples. They can be drawing on information about what makes something a chair without being able to articulate what that information is, and so may still be applying a constitutively sound method. Similarly, on the principle-based account of modality I offered in *Being Known*, thinkers are regarded as drawing on information about what makes something necessary when they evaluate modal claims. When they do this properly, they too are employing a constitutively sound way.

The moral rationalist should elaborate his position by observing that under his approach there are constitutively sound ways of coming to judge that something has a moral property. They are precisely the ways that draw on information given in the contentually a priori principles which state the conditions under which actions have moral properties. We can say that a theory of truth taken together with a theory of understanding for a given domain 'recognizes constitutive ways' if taken together they imply that there are constitutively sound ways of coming to judge contents about that domain.

Not only the moral rationalist but also the mind-dependent theorist can insist that on his theory there are constitutively sound ways of coming to judge that something has a moral property. They are the ways that are sensitive to the particular mental properties he cites in his account of the foundations of moral truth.

One distinctive feature of the moral rationalist's position is that he holds a species of mind-independence about moral truth. His theory of mind-independent truth in morality, when taken together with his theory of understanding, still recognizes constitutive ways. The significance of the existence of this position in logical space is that it shows that one can consistently reject mind-dependence of moral truths, and also hold that there are constitutively sound ways of coming to judge moral contents, without at all being committed to a model of moral knowledge that involves use of a faculty whose states are causally explained by the moral facts themselves. I shall describe such a position as a 'moderate realism with the constitutive property'.

It can be helpful to locate the position of a moderate realism that recognizes constitutive ways in relation to Christine Korsgaard's well-known distinction between procedural and substantive moral realism.[2] In *The Sources of Normativity* she writes: 'Procedural moral realism is the view that there are answers to moral questions' (p. 35). Moderate realism is stronger than a treatment which endorses merely procedural moral realism. As Korsgaard notes, even views that treat morality as the projection of human sentiments are committed to procedural realism.

Does this mean that a moderate realism that recognizes constitutive ways is a variety of substantive moral realism in Korsgaard's sense? Substantive moral realism Korsgaard first characterizes as the view that 'there are answers to moral questions *because* there are moral facts or truths' (p. 35). Later she speaks of the substantive realist as holding that there are normative truths which we notice (p. 44). She also rejects substantive realism because it is not the purpose of normative principles to explain or describe phenomena, including the existence of moral beliefs (p. 46). Of Gilbert Harman's argument that we do not need to invoke moral facts to explain moral beliefs or actions she says: 'A more carefully formulated version of this argument has some force against substantive moral realism' (p. 45).[3]

It seems, then, that on Korsgaard's conception the substantive moral realist is committed to holding that moral facts causally explain our acceptance of moral principles. Our moderate realism need not be a substantive realism in that sense. In fact, further below I will be arguing that a causal epistemology is incompatible with the

---

[2] *The Sources of Normativity*, ed. O'Neill, 35–48.
[3] Gilbert Harman's argument is in chapter 1 of his book *The Nature of Morality: An Introduction to Ethics* (New York: Oxford University Press, 1977).

contentually a priori status of basic moral principles. In short, the moral rationalist's position amounts to more than procedural moral realism, but it is not substantive moral realism in Korsgaard's sense either. It is a third position.

In general, the middle ground between procedural moral realism and substantive moral realism tends to be ignored or overlooked by adherents whose own position lies at one of these two extremes. The substantive moral realist will think he has support for his position if he can show that more is needed than mere procedural realism. The merely procedural realist on the other hand will think he has support if rejection of his position involves commitment to a substantive moral realism that involves an epistemology of causal interaction with moral facts even for the holding of basic moral principles. Both attitudes are mistaken if there is a middle ground occupied by moderate realism that recognizes constitutive ways. Rejection of either one of these extremes should not move one to the other extreme.

We can illustrate the significance of the middle position for discussions of realism by considering Crispin Wright's discussion of these matters in his book *Truth and Objectivity*. One of Wright's concerns is the question of what realism about a discourse involves, beyond acknowledgment of a minimal truth-predicate applied to sentences in that discourse. By a minimal truth-predicate he means one for which there are appropriate standards for warranted assertion, so that the discourse has a certain discipline. Wright conjectures that a necessary condition for any defensible form of realism about a given area of discourse is that it conforms to what in that book he calls 'Cognitive Command':

A discourse exhibits Cognitive Command if and only if it is a priori that differences of opinion within it can be satisfactorily explained only in terms of 'divergent input', that is, the disputants' working on the basis of different information . . . or 'unsuitable conditions' . . . or 'malfunction' . . . [4]

A more liberal variant of the criterion of Cognitive Command requires only that there be such explanations of differences of opinion for certain propositions, or certain subclasses of proposition,

---

[4] *Truth and Objectivity*, 92–3. The material replaced here by ' . . . ' consists of elaborations of the conditions listed. For the conjecture see p. 175 and earlier passages. Later in his discussion vagueness also enters as a possible explanation of difference of opinion consistent with Cognitive Command.

within the relevant domain. Wright also says that if Cognitive Command holds for a given discourse, that is 'consonant' with the view that we 'interact in a cognitive-representational manner with matters that are independent of us' (p. 175). The chapter in Wright's *Truth and Objectivity* entitled 'Realism and the Best Explanation of Belief' argues that our knowledge of moral propositions should not be regarded as involving any such interaction with moral states of affairs, and that any phenomena which may seem to support such interaction can in fact be perfectly well explained by supposing that moral discourse has merely a minimal truth-predicate applicable to it.

Can Cognitive Command hold for a given domain without our beliefs in that area being causally explained by the truth of those beliefs? The model of causal influence by the states of affairs thought about is not the only way in which a discourse can exhibit Cognitive Command. That should already be clear from the case of elementary arithmetic. The properties of the numbers do not causally explain our arithmetical beliefs. Those beliefs are explained by the results of computations we carry out. Nevertheless, Cognitive Command still holds: if two thinkers diverge in their opinion about an equation of elementary arithmetic they either have divergent initial information or are working in unsuitable conditions of such a sort as to produce errors of calculation. Early in his book Wright correctly remarks that we may want a characterization of realism which applies even when propositions in a given domain are decidable (p. 9). Such a characterization would naturally apply to arithmetic but not, for instance, to discourse about what is funny. There seems to be no problem in the arithmetical case in combining realism and Cognitive Command whilst simultaneously rejecting causal explanation of beliefs by the holding of their contents.

The question then naturally arises of why, in the moral case, at least the more liberal variant of Cognitive Command could not be fulfilled without any commitment to causal explanation of moral beliefs by moral states of affairs. I would argue that we have just this combination in the case of metaphysical necessity too. Suppose, as I suggested in earlier efforts, that to understand an operator for metaphysical necessity is to have tacit knowledge of a set of principles determining which descriptions represent genuine possibilities, and which do not. If two thinkers have such understanding, and so have the same tacit knowledge, differences in modal opinion will be explicable by such matters as divergent initial information (to which the tacit knowledge is applied), unsuitable conditions (for tacit inference from the principles), or some independently certifiable malfunction. The case would not be like differences in beliefs about what is funny, which need have no such explanations.

All this is wholly consistent with our epistemology of the modal being acausal. The idea that the possibility of a state of affairs causally explains belief in its possibility is a problematic one, and one that need not be involved in a principle-based conception of modality that implies the holding of Cognitive Command for modal discourse.

In the moral case, if understanding consists in tacit knowledge of a set of principles involving moral concepts, a similar point holds. There certainly seem to be some moral propositions, such as the proposition that prima facie a just set of institutions is better than an unjust set, disagreement over which is explicable only by divergent information, unsuitable conditions, or malfunction.[5] Agreement on moral propositions by thinkers who are equally informed, properly functioning, and so forth can be explained not by the fact that they are causally responsive to the same moral state of affairs, but simply by the fact that they are, either consciously or tacitly, applying the same set of principles, constitutive of possibility, in reaching judgements about what is right or wrong. In short, sometimes the 'discipline' of a minimally truth-apt discourse, even when there is no issue of causal interaction with a subject matter, may itself have a source that ensures that Cognitive Command will hold in that discourse.

In the philosophy of mathematics Hartry Field has labelled as 'Benaceraff's challenge' the challenge of explaining why nearly all instances of the schema 'If mathematicians accept 'p', then p' are true, when 'p' is replaced by a sentence of mathematics.[6] Benaceraff's challenge can be raised for any domain in which such schemata are true, and it always deserves an answer—it is just easier to answer for some

---

[5] It is not plausible that this holds for all moral disagreement. Morality itself provides for the possibility that two thinkers who fully grasp modal notions, who have the same initial information, and are not malfunctioning (etc.) disagree over whether, for instance, gambling or drinking alcohol is wrong. Morality provides for differing ideals, and differing weightings of accepted ideals.

[6] Introduction to Field's *Realism, Mathematics, and Modality* (Oxford: Blackwell, 1989) 26; the paper by P. Benaceraff in which the challenge is formulated is 'Mathematical Truth', *Journal of Philosophy*, 70 (1973), 661–79.

domains than others. It has not, historically, proved easy for the philosophy of modality and for the philosophy of morality to meet Benaceraff's challenge. No doubt both our modal and our moral beliefs are more error-prone than the mathematical beliefs of mathematicians. But it is plausible that the elements of a large core of our modal and moral beliefs are correct. In both the moral and the modal case this needs explanation. Part of the significance of acknowledging an acausal way in which Cognitive Command can hold is the bearing of such ways on meeting Benaceraff-style challenges in these other areas. If the model of tacit knowledge of a set of principles which are constitutive of modal notion and of moral notions is a correct theory of understanding, and entailment by the content of those principles is a correct account of truth in those two areas, then this approach can contribute to solving the Benaceraff challenge in these two domains.

If we do not regard our moral beliefs as explained by moral states of affairs what description can we give of development and refinement in moral thought over time? Wright discusses a minimalist view of truth in morals, under which it is held merely that there is a disciplined practice of warranted assertibility which in this case, according to Wright, draws on a certain moral sensibility. Of this view Wright says:

the refinement of which our moral sensibilities are capable can only be a matter of the approaching of a certain equilibrium as appraised by the exercise of those very sensibilities. There will be no defensible analogue of the scientific realist's thought that the real progress of science is measured by the extent to which our theories represent a reality whose nature owes nothing to our natures or the standards that inform our conception of responsible discourse about it. It will not be possible to regard the disciplined formation of a moral view as a seriously representational mode of function, or as a mode of activity in which we respond to states of affairs which, precisely because they are at the service of explanations of other things, can be put to serious work in explaining the course assumed by those responses (p. 200).

Now the view of moral thought I have been presenting is not a version of the variety of minimalism which is Wright's target here, precisely because I have endorsed a form of Cognitive Command that is not founded in a causal conception of the relations between moral thought and its subject matter. All the same, the question arises: Do Wright's remarks about his targeted form of minimalism apply equally to the middle-position moral rationalism I have been advocating? The challenge of accounting for the development of moral thought in a way that is not committed to causal interaction applies as much to moral rationalism as it does to the targeted form of minimalism about truth in morals.

Here the parallel with modality is one that is helpful—though modality is just one of several subject matters for which corresponding points could be made. Modal truths do not have what Wright calls a 'wide cosmological role' (p. 196); that is, they are not involved in the causal explanation of matters other than modal beliefs (and arguably they are not causally implicated in the explanation of those beliefs either). Yet there has over the centuries been development and refinement in modal thought, and this is not plausibly regarded as appraisal by some form of modal sensibility. I would say that the massive improvement in modal thought in the past century—the development of modal logic, modal semantics, and the clarification of many modal distinctions—comes from making explicit certain features of the implicit conceptions that we possess and exercise in ordinary modal thought. Progress consists in better articulation of the principles of which we have tacit knowledge, and in a better theoretical unification of them. One would say the same in discussing progress in many other a priori domains—our understanding of the natural numbers, or of logical notions. At least part of moral progress consists of the same kind of improvement of understanding that the rationalist will say is in principle possible in any domain in which knowledge is fundamentally a priori. None of this requires broad causal roles for the states of affairs in question. The explicit articulation of what was previously merely tacitly known can bring about substantive development in moral thought. In seeing what unifies cases one has previously classified together at an intuitive level one may see that one's previous restriction of rights or privileges to a certain group cannot be justified on the basis of the principles that unify one's previous classifications. Making explicit various principles and rationales is also the essential first step in formulating explanatory theories which can account for the holding of those principles. In short, some moral progress has the same structure and epistemology as progress in other a priori domains that are first grasped only intuitively, and whose principles are only later made explicit.

Not all cases of moral development fit this rationalist model. Other examples of progress in moral thought may, of course, simply be improvements in non-moral beliefs on which other moral judgements and practices rest. Much improvement in the treatment of children, or of the mentally ill, can be attributed to improved knowledge of their psychology. These improvements evidently do not require causal interaction between moral subject matter and the rest of the world. Our modal beliefs about what is really possible can equally be improved by improved non-modal knowledge about the constitution of things. This is entirely consistent with a non-causal epistemology of the modal.

8.2 Moral Rationalism and Explanation: The Eirenic Combination

The Eirenic Combination for which I will be arguing holds the following two theses:

(i) Causal explanation of a priori moral beliefs by moral facts is excluded by the a priori status of those beliefs; but

(ii) this is compatible with the moral properties mentioned in the a priori principles playing a significant part in empirical explanations, which they sometimes do.

The danger of attempting peacemaking is that one satisfies nobody. The Eirenic Combination is going to be found unsatisfactory by those who hold that we need causal explanation by moral facts even in the a priori cases. It will equally be found unsatisfactory by those who think that explanation by moral facts never really exists, other than as a way of speaking. I will attempt to answer such sceptics, and will present the Eirenic Combination as a plausible, and curiously neglected, position in the moral case. It is a position wholly consistent with moral rationalism.

The first half of the Eirenic Combination is entailed by claims for which I have already argued. I argued that some moral claims do not rest on empirical information. They plausibly include such principles as that the avoidable infliction of pain is prima facie wrong, or that each person has an equal claim to consideration in assessing courses of action. These claims do not seem merely to be true in any world in which they are accepted. Rather, they seem to be true whichever world is the actual world. This does not seem to be true of just one or two non-empirical moral claims but of an open-ended class. That is, it seems that something about the way in which we come to judge non-empirical moral propositions, when we are assessing them for ourselves, ensures that they are true in the actual world, whichever is the actual world. I will take this as a prima facie datum in need of explanation.

In the spirit, and in some cases the letter, of the general treatment of the a priori in the preceding chapter, I suggest two general principles, applicable to any domain, about the property of being contentually a priori.

(1) The first principle, which we extracted in our discussion of Gödel back in Chapter 6, states that causation of the belief that p by its being the case that p, however tightly the path of the causal chain through various states and events is circumscribed, is never by itself sufficient for a way of coming to know that p to be a contentually a priori way of coming to know it. The argument for this principle is simple and general. Suppose someone's belief that p is causally explained by its being the case that p. That alone does not ensure that whichever is the actual world p will be true in the actual world. If a belief reached in this causal way has the property of being true in the actual world, whatever is the actual world, that must be because the causing condition also has this same property. But nothing in the method as described ensures that it does.

Maybe there is something additional in the method that ensures that it can be applied only to contentually a priori propositions. If so, that feature of the method needs to be identified, and the existence of this feature means that more is involved in the method than simply a causal sensitivity to whether p is the case. The original point holds, that causal sensitivity to whether p is the case is not by itself sufficient for that method or way to be a contentually a priori way of coming to know that p.

(2) The second principle is closely related to the first, and has the same underlying rationale. It states that to know that whichever is

the actual world, p is true in the actual world it is not sufficient to have one's belief that p caused by the truth that p. That could (at most) give one knowledge that p actually holds, not that it holds whichever is the actual world. And if the thinker does have a way of coming to know that whichever is the actual world p holds in it, causation may well then be irrelevant to the epistemic status of the thinker's belief that p. If the thinker has an entitlement to accept that p holds in the actual world, whichever is the actual world, causation seems to drop out of the epistemology of such propositions altogether.

In the case in which the causation by the fact that p is meant to proceed via an experience as of it's being the case that p these principles are rejecting a conception of the a priori which is of the type to which Wittgenstein was also objecting in the *Tractatus*. 'No part of our experience', wrote Wittgenstein, 'is at the same time a priori. Whatever we see could be other than it is' (5. 634).

The two principles (1) and (2) are as general as the arguments for them. They are independent of any particular subject matter. For an illustration of an epistemology which does not respect these principles I take Russell's 1913 treatment of self-evidence in his now famous manuscript *Theory of Knowledge*.

Russell's idea was that a self-evident judgement is one in which the thinker perceives the fact that the judgement corresponds to the truth.[7] Russell was aiming at an account of self-evidence on which self-evidence entails truth. Whatever the other problems of his account it does have that entailment, on the natural understanding of Russell's phrase 'x perceives the fact that p' as entailing the truth of p.

Russell's account of self-evidence is, however, quite inadequate to domains in which the basic principles are contentually a priori (which will include logic and mathematics). Self-evidence in Russell's sense does not imply that if p is self-evident then whichever is the actual world p will be true in it. So to find something self-evident in Russell's sense is not a way of coming to know that it is contentually a priori. Russell does write that 'self-evident judgements are by nature incapable of falsehood' (p. 166). Here there is more than a whiff of a modal fallacy. What is true is that (necessarily

---

[7] *Theory of Knowledge: The 1913 Manuscript*, ed. E. Eames (London: Routledge, 1984) Ch. VI, esp. pp. 164–6.

and a priori): if p is self-evident in Russell's sense, p is true. It does not follow from this that p is incapable of falsehood. A fortiori, Russell's account also fails to supply the resources for explaining how one can know that something is true in the actual world, whichever is the actual world.

It seems to me that any attempt at a perceptual account of the epistemology of a domain in which truth is a priori will have problems precisely analogous to Russell's. The point applies as much to morality as it does to logic, mathematics, and modality. On a principle-based account of moral understanding, understanding of moral discourse consists in tacit knowledge of a set of principles that are constitutive for determining the extension of moral predicates, or are a priori consequences of what is so constitutive. Moral knowledge is obtained by proper application of this tacit knowledge. This account of knowledge of those moral principles which are a priori does not at all require that the moral fact that p causally explain the moral belief that p.

So much by way of summary consideration of reasons that support the first half of the Eirenic Combination. What of the second half, which states that the moral properties identified in moral principles may nevertheless function in empirical explanations? Might one not naturally wonder whether there is any need to admit such cases at all, once we have an underlying conception of moral thought that conforms to the first half of the Eirenic Combination? Some have certainly adopted that position. But to soften the reader a little towards the Eirenic Combination in the moral case I want to consider a partially parallel territory for which the analogue of the Eirenic Combination has some attractions.

The partially parallel territory concerns the application of the abstract objects of mathematics to the concrete world. Here too we have a domain in which truth is fundamentally a priori combined with explanation in the empirical world that essentially involves mathematical properties and conditions.

(a) The Mathematical Case as Eirenic, and Generality of Explanation

In the case of arithmetic the Peano laws are a priori. So too are the principles linking numbers with applications, when they are used to classify concepts or properties. It is a priori that there are 3 Fs iff there are objects x, y, and z distinct from one another, which are each F, and such that anything that is F is either x, y, or z.

Similarly, the laws of the real numbers are also a priori. Though a full defence would need much independent discussion, I would argue that the conditions for applying the real numbers in measuring magnitudes are also a priori. The real numbers can be connected with their role in measuring magnitudes by taking literally the idea that the magnitudes—the sizes, masses, and so forth—of objects are real quantities with causes and effects. Some approaches to the issue of applying the real numbers, inspired by the achievements of the formal theory of measurement, proceed by linking the reals with underlying non-numerical relations, such as sameness of mass or distance, that involve neither numbers nor magnitudes.[8] One challenge for this approach is to account for various modal truths about measurement. It is not necessary for something to be 5 grams in weight that it bears a certain relation to the object that is the standard gram in Paris, since in some possible circumstances that object does not weigh one gram. This style of approach is debarred from answering this objection by appealing to the actual weight of the standard object. The phrase 'the actual weight of the standard object' must refer under this theory to its actual assignment of a number as its weight, in which case the real numbers have not been eliminated at this level of application in the explanation of modalities. It is highly intuitive to take 'the actual weight' as referring to an actual magnitudes—the object's weight— and an approach that includes these in its ontology can accommodate these modal facts. This is not the place to develop that style of approach in detail. All that matters for the moment is its possibility. Under this approach the condition for something to have a certain real-valued number as its weight, or height, and so forth can be given in a way that makes it a priori.

These a priori laws and conditions of application for the natural numbers and for the reals are the first part of the Eirenic Combination for the case of abstract objects. The second part is supported by such examples as the following, each of which seems to be a true

---

[8] For an illumating approach of this kind see H. Field, 'Can We Dispense With Space-Time?', in his *Realism, Mathematics and Modality*, esp. 186 ff.

explanatory statement about the world beyond that of abstract objects. In each case, the explaining conditions involves numbers:

> (i) Squadron A gained a decisive victory over squadron B in the fixed battle because it outnumbered the enemy by a ratio of more than 3 to 1.
>
> (ii) The fact that the pendulum has a certain period T is explained by that number bearing a certain relation to the square root of its length.

How close is the parallel between the moral and the mathematical cases? One strategy for claiming there is a relevant difference is to say that all the displayed explanatory conditions have equivalents which do not mention numbers, and it is these non-numerical equivalents that really do the explaining. On this view we make statements of the sorts displayed when there is a non-numerical equivalent which really does the explanation. So the case of numbers does not, on this view, at the most fundamental level conform to the second part of the Eirenic Combination.

I reply that even when the condition applying numbers in the non-numerical world does have an equivalent that does not mention numbers the non-numerical equivalent does not have the same explanatory powers as the original condition involving numbers. The explaining condition in the statement (i) about the decisive victory is equivalent to an infinite disjunction of conjunctions of the following form, where the numerical quantifiers are expanded to eliminate reference to the natural numbers, and contain only logical vocabulary, identity, and quantifiers over non-numbers:

> *Either:* There is 1 member in squadron A, and 3 in B, or 4, or 5 . . .
> *Or:* There are 2 members in A, and 6 in B, or 7, or 8 . . .
> *Or:* There are 3 members in A, and 9 in B, or 10, or 11 . . .
> *Or:* Etc. . . .

This is much less explanatory than the original mixed explaining condition in (i). On the objector's view, only one of these disjuncts is going to be really explanatory, since the other disjuncts are false. But the particular disjunct the objector says is explanatory will not hold in a case in which the squadrons have sizes other than their actual sizes. The explanation offered in (i) is, however, general, and applies whatever the size of the squadrons. If (i) is true, it is the same explanation which applies, whatever the size of the squadron. But the objector who insists that just one disjunct of his number-free equivalent is explanatory is not offering the same explanation in all such cases. His proposed explanation lacks generality. It does not project to new cases.

The same is true of example (ii). Sameness and generality of explanation is a crucial feature of cases which display the Eirenic Combination. The mathematical parallel suggests that it is not true that whenever we have a version of the Eirenic Combination holding in some domain only the supervened-upon conditions are genuinely explanatory.

(b) *Explaining Relational Facts*

We can broaden our perspective and consider explanation in other areas. The principle that only supervened-upon relations causally explain would rule out distinctive explanations in chemistry, genetics, psychology, and economics. In my judgement, it is no accident that the notion of sameness of explanation, and the generality of a higher-level explanation across cases, is crucial in defending the significance of the higher-level explanations in these cases. We need to consider the nature of explanation by conditions involving moral properties against the background of a more general conception of higher-level explanation.

We can sometimes explain relational facts—facts to the effect that certain objects stand in a certain relation. The fact that someone perceives a given object can contribute to the explanation of various facts about his relation to the object perceived. If an adult is watching over a young child, in order to be able to intervene to help or prevent harm, the adult will maintain a spatial relation to the child which allows him to see what the child is doing, and at a distance from which quick intervention is possible. Equally, perception can contribute to an explanation of his keeping his distance from a perceived object he takes to be dangerous.[9]

---

[9] For more on the need to explain relational facts, and what it involves, see my 'Externalist Explanation', *Proceedings of the Aristotelian Society*, 93 (1993), 203–30.

Mere truth of the subject's belief about the object will not explain such an agent's reliably maintaining a certain kind of relation to the object in question. Mere truth of the agent's beliefs would be compatible with its truth being accidental or a matter of luck: whereas in these cases the maintenance of the relations is not accidental, and is projectible to (nearby) counterfactual circumstances. Bringing the agent's continuing perception of the object to which the spatial relations are maintained into the explanation, and thereby his knowledge of where the object is, can close this explanatory gap in a satisfying fashion.

In the moral case Wright and Korsgaard suggest that many of the cases in which it has been held that moral truths enter empirical explanations are really merely cases in which it is only various thinkers' moral beliefs that do the explaining;[10] or only the non-moral properties on which moral qualities supervene. The question arises of whether this conception is capable of explaining the relations which hold between thinkers and persons, events, and states of affairs that have moral properties. Consider Sturgeon's example again: The fact that some institution, such as chattel slavery, is very unjust can explain its overthrow. Is mere belief in the great injustice sufficient to explain the relational facts? Beliefs can be enough to explain actions, but one of the explananda here is this: that there is repeated opposition towards, leading to overthrow of, institutions that really are very unjust. This is not an accidental correlation: it projects to new cases, and to (nearby) counterfactual cases. It is because certain institutions are very unjust that they are overthrown, and the stage at which the detailed explanation of this fact goes through the psychological states of persons involves not just the belief, but the knowledge, that these institutions are very unjust.[11]

The injustice of chattel slavery supervenes upon various non-moral properties and relations of persons subjected to this arrangement. These non-moral properties may vary across different examples of the institution. But there is an important respect in which this variation

---

[10] *Truth and Objectivity*, 195–6; *Sources of Normativity*, 45 ff.

[11] On explanations by knowledge see in particular T. Williamson, *Knowledge and Its Limits* (Oxford: Oxford University Press, 2000), ch. 1. Many of the points here about explanation by moral facts complement the illuminating discussion in P. Railton's paper 'Moral Realism', repr. in S. Darwall, A. Gibbard, and P. Railton (eds.), *Moral Discourse and Practice: Some Philosophical Approaches* (New York: Oxford University Press, 1997), see esp. 150–3.

across cases is irrelevant to the explanation of the overthrow of the institution. The explanation simply involves the great injustice, and its appreciation. This is the same explanation across different cases of slavery. It is the same explanation, just as it was the same explanation of why one squadron defeats another across different cases with different particular numbers in each squadron; and as it was the same explanation across different substances with different microstructures in Putnam's example of the explanation of why a square peg will not fit into a round hole.

These points do not give moral properties a very wide cosmological role. Wright emphasizes the range of phenomena that can be explained by the wetness of the rocks, and there is nothing in these points to suggest that moral properties can explain as wide a range of phenomena as the property of being wet.

(c) *Minimal Truth and Width of Cosmological Role*

What is the relation between breadth of cosmological role for properties in some domain and the availability of something stronger than Wright's minimal truth for that domain? Wright is surely correct that Cognitive Command for a discourse is a stronger property than that of the existence of minimal truth within that domain. It is, however, consistent with that fact that what makes possible the holding of Cognitive Command in a given domain of discourse is the very same thing as what makes available minimal truth in that particular domain. That is, we cannot always regard the facts on which Cognitive Command is founded as something entirely additional to, and not implicit in, what makes minimal truth possible in the domain in question.

When we have a notion of minimal truth for a domain—that is, a notion of warranted assertibility—we need to ask: What account of understanding for the sentences in question makes such warranted assertibility possible? In some cases understanding itself requires a causal sensitivity on the part of the thinker to the instantiation of some property or relation which has a range of causal powers far beyond that of causing beliefs about the instantiation of the property. Understanding of basic terms for spatial and temporal properties and relations plausibly has this property. In general, for these cases what in *Being Known* I called the 'model of constitutive causal sensitivity' applies to such understanding. Warranted assertibility for discourse involving such properties will necessarily already involve thinkers' being sensitive to the instantiation of a property with a wide causal role. Cognitive Command will then be a consequence of this account of understanding.

It is different for the moral and the modal cases, where such constitutive causal sensitivity is not at all plausibly written into an account of understanding. On plausible principle-based accounts of understanding of these notions, a moral property cannot be instantiated without some non-moral supervenience base being instantiated. Similarly, to use the terminology of *Being Known*, a modal property cannot be instantiated without some condition on admissibility holding. So one would expect that in any case in which a moral property causally explains something some non-moral supervenience base will in one way or another be implicated in the explanation too (even if, as we have emphasized, it will not always be the full explanation). This limitation comes from the nature of truth for the moral domain, when such truth is related to a principle-based account of understanding. By contrast, in cases where causal sensitivity to instances of properties and relations themselves is built into an account of understanding there is no analogous and relevant supervenience claim extractible from the account of understanding itself. Spatial and temporal properties and relations do not supervene on non-spatial and non-temporal properties and relations. Nor do accounts of grasp of these notions imply that they do.

The phenomenon can be illustrated in a simpler case. Any theory of understanding of existential quantification will contain the principle that an understander must be willing to infer such a quantification from an arbitrary instance. Correspondingly, in the theory of truth and reference the quantification cannot be true without there being some particular object of which the predicate in the quantification is true.

Because this is so, whenever something is empirically explained on a single occasion by the holding of an existential quantification it seems that some singular instance is equally implicated in the explanation. The fact that there is someone on the porch may causally explain the sounding of the burglar alarm. But that explanatory statement could not be true without it also holding of the particular person who is on the porch that the alarm sounds because he is there. When we are concerned with a range of events—for example, in explaining why the dog in the house runs up to the front door— the general, projectible explanation may be that there is someone on the porch. But even this can be true only because on each particular occasion some particular person's being there explains the dog's reaction. The fundamental account of truth for propositions of a given kind, whether they be existential quantifications, moral propositions, or propositions about space and time, constrains how they may feature in explanations.

(d) *Moral Rationalism and Cornell Realism*

What then is the relation of the variety of moral rationalism defended here to what is sometimes called 'Cornell realism'? For specificity, and because of its extensive comparisons with other areas, I will consider Richard Boyd's paper 'How To Be a Moral Realist'.[12] I suggest that there is no incompatibility between many of the principles of Boyd's moral realism and the moral rationalism endorsed here.

Initially Boyd characterizes moral realism as making three claims: that moral statements are the sorts of statements that can be true or false; that this truth or falsity is largely independent of our moral opinions and theories; and that ordinary canons of moral reasoning (together with those of scientific and everyday factual reasoning) constitute 'under many circumstances at least' a reliable method of attaining moral knowledge (p. 105). So far this is all consistent with moral rationalism. But Boyd also describes his aim as that of showing that moral beliefs and methods 'are much more like our current conception of scientific beliefs and methods (more "objective", "external", "empirical", "intersubjective", for example) than we now think' (p. 107). Part of this at least has the appearance of incompatibility with moral rationalism. If moral methods are empirical is that not inconsistent with basic moral principles being contentually a priori?

It is not at all clear on closer consideration that there is any inconsistency. Boyd's position is, in outline, that 'actions, policies, character

---

[12] Reprinted in Darwall, Gibbard, and Railton (eds.), *Moral Discourse and Practice*.

traits, etc.' are good to the extent to which they foster human goods; human goods are homeostatically clustered; and human goods satisfy important human needs (p. 122). One might dispute some of these claims, but the major issue here is not one about the content of these theses. It is a more general structural point. All Boyd's points seem consistent with the following division into the a priori and the empirical:

> It is a priori that goods satisfy human needs.
> It is a posteriori what these needs are.

A moral rationalist can be content with a division of this general kind, and acknowledge too that what the needs of humans are can be causally fixed, and may be a matter of the homeostatic mechanisms Boyd describes.

I would add also that some of the phenomena Boyd mentions, those of the operation of reflective equilibrium, and of the discovery of hidden essences, can also be found in fundamentally a priori domains. In modal, mathematical, and logical theory we equally have to attain an equilibrium between initial intuition and general theory. The need for such an equilibrium seems to be a feature of any domain in which rational thought is possible. Similarly, the discovery of an essence need not always be a purely empirical matter. The essence of being a continuous function, or being the limit of a series, was hidden from great thinkers for many decades; but its discovery was still an a priori matter.

8.3 The Emotions and Moral Rationalism

The emotions, and especially the moral emotions, play an enormous part in the course of our ordinary, first-level moral thought about what is right and what is wrong. The course of our ordinary moral thought would not be as it actually is if we were not susceptible to such emotions as moral indignation, compassion, guilt, admiration, and sympathy. Moral emotions can make us change or reconsider our moral views. They can help us to formulate new principles. They can even lead to the formation of new, morally significant concepts. Few would be willing to say that it would be either more rational or better if our moral thought were not influenced by such emotions. Is this extensive role of the moral emotions compatible with moral rationalism?

The challenge for the moral rationalist can be divided into three parts, identified by these three questions:

(1) Does the role of the emotions in moral thought support the position that moral truth is, after all, in some way mind-dependent?
(2) Does the role of the emotions in moral thought undermine the position that the most fundamental moral principles are a priori?
(3) If the answer to the first two questions is negative, how is the moral rationalist to account for the role of the emotions in moral thought?

Some of the philosophical literature on the emotions is concerned with the analysis and philosophical understanding of various particular emotions. Though there is a great deal to be learned from such an approach, questions (1)–(3) are unavoidably general in nature. They can be addressed properly only by attempting at least the beginnings of a general theory of the role of the emotions in thought. To make any such general theory plausible we need to draw upon some account of the emotions in general.

Conscious emotions have affect and representational content. The distinctive affect of an emotion for its experiencer is pleasant or unpleasant, and the affect—or at least its cause—influences the character of the subject's thoughts and moods. Affect, which remains very ill understood, is crucial not only for explaining what makes something an emotion. It is important also for understanding the expression of emotions, and for a philosophical account of aesthetic phenomena, including the appreciation of literature, drama, and music.

Almost all emotions also have contents which are assessable as true or false. In experiencing fear when near the edge of a cliff it seems to me that I am in danger of falling. In experiencing joy at the success of a friend it seems to me that it is good that he should succeed. In experiencing moral indignation at an injustice it seems to me that some event or condition is unfair. These representational contents of the emotions are not merely intentional contents. They are contents which, by virtue of his having the emotion, seem to the experiencer of the emotion to be correct.

The representational content of an emotion seems always to involve an evaluative notion. The simple examples already used involve the notions *danger*, *goodness*, and *unfairness*. A subclass of the emotions are more specifically moral emotions. It is not sufficient for an emotion to be a moral emotion that it has a moral concept in its representational content. Malicious delight that an adversary has not been fairly treated has the moral concept of fairness in its representational content, but that does not make such delight a moral emotion. What, additionally, is required for an emotion to be a moral emotion is that the positive or negative emotion, such as the delight or the indignation, be delight or indignation at a state of affairs that is (or is thought by the person having the emotion to be) morally good or morally bad respectively. The delight or the indignation must also be explained by the thinker's moral thought. When you admire some selfless action your admiration is a moral emotion because you take it to be morally good for the agent to act so selflessly.

Like the representational content of perception, the representational content of an emotion is belief-independent in the sense Evans noted.[13] I can experience fear even when I know I am perfectly safe, protected from a fall by thick glass or a steel grating. Conversely, I can believe I am in danger of falling without having a fear of heights at all. Hume already noticed this independence of emotion from belief. A particularly clear statement of the independence is found more recently in Robert Roberts, and is prefigured in William Alston.[14]

We can make sense of the idea of representational content also in the case of unconscious emotions. The phenomena of unconscious anger and of unconscious envy, for instance, are all too familiar in everyday life. It is part of making sense of actions as explained by an agent's unconscious anger to see those actions as best explained by an unconscious state that represents to the subject that, for example, someone has harmed him in some way.

A persistent trend contrary to the thesis of the belief-independence of the emotions holds that emotions are judgements of one sort or another. The view has most recently been defended by Martha

---

[13] *The Varieties of Reference*, 123–4.
[14] Robert C. Roberts, 'What an Emotion Is: A Sketch', *Philosophical Review*, 97 (1988), 183–209; William Alston, 'Emotion and Feeling', in P. Edwards (ed.), *The Encyclopedia of Philosophy*, ii (New York: Macmillan, 1967), 479–86.

Nussbaum.[15] Nussbaum writes that 'emotions are forms of evaluative judgement that ascribe to certain things and persons outside a person's own control great importance for the person's own flourishing'(p. 22).

Nussbaum argues extensively that the emotions have intentional content. This point will be enthusiastically endorsed by the theorist of belief-independent emotions, since belief-independent states like perception equally have intentional content. Acknowledgement that the emotions have intentional content is entirely consistent with their not being judgements.

How does Nussbaum respond to the arguments in support of the belief-independent character of the emotions? Of the case in which someone experiences fear without judging that the relevant situation is dangerous Nussbaum writes that this is a case of the subject having contradictory beliefs (p. 35). But in the case in which the subject discounts or overrules an emotion there need not be anything which suggests that the subject is accepting the content of the emotion as correct.

Nussbaum considers examples of contradictory beliefs in which the subject is inclined, for instance, to answer questions unreflectively in accordance with a belief that is overruled by other judgements. That is a possible case, but it need not be like that in the case of the emotion overruled by judgement. We may consider the (very) partial parallel with the belief-independent content of perception. One's knowledge that the painting of a violin is a perfect *trompe l'oeil* may completely overrule the content of one's perception. The perceptual experience of this person still has the representational content that there is a violin on the wall—it is a perfect *trompe l'oeil*, after all. But this need not be a person with contradictory beliefs. This subject need not have the slightest inclination to reach for the wall when seeking for a violin on which to play. To be subject to a perceptual illusion is not to have contradictory beliefs. The same holds for emotions whose representational content the thinker rejects.

In one of her extended examples Nussbaum considers the emotions she herself experienced on learning that her mother was fatally

---

[15] *Upheavals of Thought: The Intelligence of Emotions* (Cambridge: Cambridge University Press, 2001). There is much with which I agree in Nussbaum's book, and which can be defended independently of the thesis that emotions are judgements.

ill, and when rushing back across the Atlantic to be with her. In considering the relation of 'appearance' to emotion, she rightly says that there was an appearance that her mother was lost to her, an appearance she came 'to embrace . . . as the way things are' (p. 40) when she saw her mother's body in the hospital. On the view I am defending, the belief-independent 'appearance' involved in an emotion is not at all to be identified with a tentative assessment based on incomplete evidence. The representational content involved in grief is something like this: 'My mother was a tremendously valuable person who is now lost to us.' The content 'My mother is dead' will have been the content of various fears, wonderings, and suspicions on the flight back; but that is not the content that I am taking to be the full representational content of the emotion. The full content contains the evaluative material (as Nussbaum would also agree). Grief represents that content as correct. Yet grief remains distinct from judgement of that content. Someone can judge that a tremendously valuable person is lost to us without experiencing grief, not even unconscious grief. Depression or preoccupation with other matters can lead to this state of affairs.

It is an important point, on which Nussbaum rightly insists, that an emotion can be 'justified or unjustified, reasonable or unreasonable' (p. 46). I suggest that an emotion is unreasonable when it is unreasonable for its subject to accept as true the representational content of the emotion. So a fear of open spaces, or of fountain pens, would be unreasonable given our ordinary background beliefs. The fears could become reasonable in the presence of extraordinary background beliefs, for example that there are snipers around, or that fountain pens here may contain explosives. This account of what it is for an emotion to be unreasonable does not imply that emotions are judgements. (My account does also suggest a puzzle, to which I will return.)

There are several other reasons that emotions could not be judgements. One is that judging something to be the case is a mental action, something the subject *does*. Other examples of mental actions include forming an intention, calculating, and, in some cases, imagining something. Experiencing an emotion is not something the subject does at all. The subject is, at least at the time of the experience, passive in this respect. This is another respect in which emotions resemble perceptions. The only sense in which one has control over what one perceives is by changing one's relation to the world, so that what happens to one in experience is different. Similarly, there are all sorts of things one can do to affect what emotions one experiences in various circumstances. Once one is in those circumstances, however, experiencing an emotion is no more an exercise of agency than is having a visual experience. In this respect the position I am offering is at one with the spirit, if not the letter, of one of Hume's statements: 'In short, a passion must be accompany'd with some false judgement, in order to its being unreasonable; and even then 'tis not the passion, properly speaking, which is unreasonable, but the judgement' (*Treatise*, bk. II, pt. III, sect. 3).[16] Hume explicitly conceives of 'passions' as contentless: 'When I am angry, I am actually possest with the passion, and in that emotion have no more reference to any other object, than when I am thirsty, or sick, or more than five foot high' (II. III. 3 (p.266)). We cannot follow him in that. But if we replace 'judgement' with 'representational content' in the earlier quote from Hume the resulting position is more plausible.

The fact that the emotions have representational content has an immediate bearing on our opening question, of whether the role of the emotions in moral thought offers any support at all for the position that moral truth is mind-dependent—our Question (1) at the start of this section. Suppose a thinker forms a moral judgement by taking the representational content of a moral emotion at face value. That is entirely consistent with the truth of the content judged not being a mind-dependent matter at all. We make judgements, indeed obtain knowledge, of the spatial properties and relations of objects, and the temporal properties and relations of events, by taking the representational content of perception at face value. It can hardly follow that spatial and temporal properties are mind-dependent. The mind-dependence of the experience with the representational content leaves it completely open whether the correctness of the representational content of the experience is a mind-dependent matter. It neither rules it in nor does it rule it out.

The most pressing issue that now arises in addressing our three questions is this: How, if at all, do moral emotions entitle thinkers to

---

[16] D. Hume, *A Treatise of Human Nature*, ed. D. Norton and M. Norton (Oxford: Oxford University Press, 2000), 267. The spirit rather than the letter not only because of the points to follow but because we approach closer to the truth if 'false' in Hume's statement is replaced with 'unreasonable'.

take their representational contents as correct, and if they do so what is the philosophical explanation of why this entitlement exists? And what are the repercussions of the answer to this question for claims of mind-dependence? To address these issues I suggest that we have to press rather deeper into the way in which emotions have representational content.

8.4 Entitlement, the Emotions, and Two Relations to a Representational Content

In volume II of his *Remarks on the Philosophy of Psychology* Wittgenstein writes that one of the things that distinguishes emotions from sensory experiences (*Empfindungen*) is that the emotions teach us nothing about the external world ('sie unterrichten uns nicht über die Aussenwelt').[17] He adds that this is a grammatical remark, which is likely a theory-laden way of saying that he is identifying a constitutive feature of the emotions. But what feature is it? Wittgenstein's claim about one of the distinctions between sensory experience and the emotions sounds plausible, but it is a challenge to articulate it more precisely. In particular, if we think that Wittgenstein is saying something true we cannot regard him as saying that emotions do not have a representational content concerning the external world. I have been arguing precisely that they do have such a content.

As a first step, but only the first step, to capturing what Wittgenstein may have had in mind, I suggest what I call the No Addition Thesis. The No Addition Thesis states that

> For any emotion which is not irrational its representational content is one that is in principle inferable from other information (or misinformation) possessed by the person who has the emotion.

To illustrate the No Addition Thesis, take your fear that there will be an anthrax attack on the mail reaching your office. This fear is not irrational if there have been attacks on relevantly similar offices. The content that there is a danger of such an attack on your office is

---

[17] *Remarks on the Philosophy of Psychology, ii*, trans. C. Luckhardt and M. Aue, ed. G. von Wright and H. Nyman (Oxford: Blackwell, 1980), sect. 148; my translation.

inferable from other information you have. If it is not, then your fear is irrational. Failure of the representational content of one of your emotions to be inferable from what you already accept is one way in which an emotion can be irrational. (It is not the only way: another is for the degree of affect to be disproportionate to the emotion's representational content.)

The No Addition Thesis is an initial gloss on Wittgenstein's observation that the emotions teach us nothing about the external world. If the No Addition Thesis is correct then for emotions which are not irrational the content of the emotion is in some sense not telling us anything new. In this respect the emotions contrast sharply with perception and with memory. Perceptions and memories are not irrational, and they certainly give us new information which could not, in many cases, be inferred from what we already accept.

The No Addition Thesis is only a first step towards elucidating the point that Wittgenstein noticed, and for two reasons. First, we need an explanation of why the emotions are so different from perception and memory in respect of whether a No Addition Thesis holds for them. What is the source of this difference?

Second, the phenomenological difference Wittgenstein noticed is not confined to emotions which are not irrational. Subjectively, even an irrational emotion is not one which seems to be teaching us about the external world. So we need a deeper account of the distinction, one which explains the No Addition Thesis and which also speaks to the phenomenology of all emotions.

While both perceptions and emotions have representational contents, they stand in different kinds of relation to those contents. A perception presents the world as being a certain way; the phenomenology of a perception is presentational. An emotion, by contrast, is experienced as a reaction to some perceived or represented state of affairs. Its phenomenology is that of a reaction; more specifically, a reaction of affect. The response itself involves a state with representational content, but the content is an element of a state which is experienced as being a reactive state of affect. To capture this difference between perception and emotion we may speak of perception as having a presentational relation to its representational content and emotion as having a reactive-affective relation to its representational content.

This gives a respect in which emotions do not teach us anything new about the external world, a respect which involves their phenomenology. When a representational content is experienced as the content of an affective, reactive state, the experience is not one in which the world is presented as being a certain way. This phenomenological difference applies whether the emotion is rational or irrational.

This difference between perception and emotion makes the question of how the moral emotions can entitle us to make moral judgements all the more pressing. The cases in which it is rational to take representational content at face value in coming to make a judgement are all ones in which that content is presentationally given in the state, rather than given in a reactive-affective manner. What could entitle us to take the reactive-affective representational content of an emotion at face value?

One possible stance would be that moral concepts are individuated by their capacity to feature in the content of certain emotions. Under this view, although it would be agreed that there is a distinction between representational content that is given presentationally and representational content that is reactive-affective, nonetheless there is a system of relations between the emotions and moral concepts that parallels that system of relations between perceptual experiences and observational concepts. This description of the stance specifies a general kind of view. Different members of the kind will vary in what account they give of the individuating relations that are said to hold between moral concepts and the emotions. I call the general stance 'the stance of emotional individuation'.

There are three initial problems for the stance of emotional individuation.

(a) It is not enough to claim a connection between the individuation of a moral concept and some or other emotions. One has also to explain how this could provide any explanation of the existence of entitlements to make moral judgements on the basis of moral emotions. To use our apparatus of distinctions, this is to say that there must exist a Level-(3) explanation of why the entitlement exists. In the case of perception and observational concepts we argued that there is such an explanation, and that it has to do with the instance-individuation of basic perceptual contents, and the best complexity-reducing explanation of why there are experiences with such perceptual contents.

But moral concepts are not instance-individuated. For them to be so the moral concept would have not to be embedded in a wider theoretical conception of why the moral property in question is morally bad, or morally good (otherwise we would not have instance-individuation). This condition in particular is implausible.

Alternatively, someone might attempt to develop the stance of emotional individuation by treating moral concepts in a way analogous to classical treatments of secondary qualities. Under this view there is emotional individuation because what it is to have a moral property is to be disposed to produce, in some specified way and no doubt with certain further restrictions, certain moral emotions in us. This view, however, runs into the danger of conflict with the contentually a priori status of basic moral principles. One could not know truths about which action types or states of affairs are prima facie wrong, or unjust, independently of conscious emotional states if possession of those moral properties fundamentally consisted in the ability to produce such emotional states.

(b) If the emotional-individuation stance is correct, what are the roles of moral concepts in the emotions that individuate those concepts? It might be said: For the concept of justice, we admire the actions of the just person, and experience guilt when we ourselves are unjust, or experience contempt for others who are unjust; for the concept of benevolence, we admire the benevolent act . . . and so forth. All these emotions prima facie seem to presuppose that their experiencer already has the moral concept in question—that of fairness, benevolence, and so forth.

In the allegedly parallel perceptual case the response to this point would be that appearances are misleading, and that there is a level of non-conceptual representational content of perception to which appeal can be made in individuating observational concepts by their relation to perceptual experiences. But it is very hard to see what the analogous level of non-conceptual content is or might be in the case of the emotions and moral concepts. An array of conditions make the notion of non-conceptual perceptual representational content intelligible. These include, in the spatial case, scenario contents which in a certain sense have non-propositional correctness conditions; underlying mental representations which display Shepard's second-order isomorphisms; and the intuitive power of the case that the very same contents can be present in our experiences as in those of wholly non-conceptual creatures.[18] It is not clear that there are or could be analogues of any of these for any notion of non-conceptual representational content for an emotion, where the kind of content is supposed to underlie the presence of moral concepts in the emotions. For some moral concepts it seems to be intrinsically impossible. A notion of fairness must involve some sensitivity by those who employ the concept to the idea of two situations being the same in the relevant respects. This is a wholly conceptual idea, involving quantification over properties. Nor would it suffice to anchor the presence of moral concepts in the emotions by their relations to non-moral notions such as sympathy. That need not be circular, but when it is not it is also in danger of not giving the right correctness conditions for moral propositions.

(c) There is a general reason against the emotional-individuation stance that is implied by the general characterization of the emotions that I have already given. If a moral emotion is not irrational there is always some rationale for its representational content other than the occurrence of the emotion itself. This thesis of the 'independent rationale' simply follows from the No Addition Thesis, given the premises that moral emotions are a subclass of the emotions in general. The No Addition Thesis immediately implies that for any moral emotion that is not irrational we cannot by taking its representational content at face value learn something that we could not in principle have inferred from other information already available to us. (Here the qualification 'in principle' is of great importance, as I will soon be arguing.)

This seems to be borne out by consideration of examples. If I experience guilt about some omission of mine, the fact that I omitted to perform the act in question is information I already have, or is inferable from information I already have. Bernard Williams considers the case of a man who fails, through fear, to act on an agreement, made in advance, about what to do at a committee meeting. This can provoke the emotion of contempt, and Williams remarks that 'the mode in which this man's behaviour appeared bad may precisely

---

[18] On scenario content see my A Study of Concepts, ch. 3, 'Perceptual Content'; on second-order isomorphism see R. Shepard and S. Chipman, 'Second-Order Isomorphism of Internal Representations: Shapes of States', Cognitive Psychology, 1 (1970), 1–17.

have been that of its being contemptible'.[19] Here 'contemptible' must mean meriting contempt. The man's failure merits contempt because it involves going back on a freely made agreement, solely as a result of fear. This fact which grounds the badness of the action was available in advance of the betrayed person's experience of the emotion of contempt.

Precisely the opposite direction of individuation than that proposed by the emotional-individuation stance seems to me to hold between the emotions and moral concepts. Part of what makes a given moral emotion the kind of emotion it is is that it can be experienced only in relation to intentional contents that contain certain kinds of moral concepts. Part of what makes an emotion the emotion of guilt is that it can be experienced only as guilt about something the experiencer did or omitted to do, and which he takes to be wrong. In short, the opposite direction of individuation holds from that found in the case of perceptual experiences, where observational concepts are indeed individuated in part by their ability to feature in certain kinds of perceptual experiences.

This point about the individuation of moral emotions does not, so far as I can see, imply that there is a presumption that the reactive-affective representational content of an emotion is itself correct. It is one thing for a type of emotion to require that its intentional content have a certain kind of content involving moral concepts. It is another for that content to be true.

How then do emotions entitle us to make moral judgements? I suggest that the very fact that emotions have a reactive-affective relation to their representational contents means that the representational content of an emotion should be taken as true by the experiencer only if she has some independent reason for thinking that content is true. Does it follow that the course of our moral thought would be just the same if we never had moral emotions, so that the moral emotions have no effect on our moral thought? It does not follow at all. From the fact that for any moral emotion that is not irrational we could in principle infer its representational content from what we already accept it by no means follows that we always do what we could in principle do. On the contrary, since moral emotions can

[19] 'Morality and the Emotions', repr. in B. Williams, *Problems of the Self* (Cambridge: Cambridge University Press, 1973), at 214.

come to us unbidden, we may be struck by admiration, or guilt, and in being so struck realize for the first time the goodness or badness of some state of affairs. It need not be a question of the emotion show-ing us what we believed or thought all along (though that is a sig-nificant special case[20]). The emotion can have a content that something is good, or bad, and, though that content is inferable from what we already accepted, we might well not in fact have come to accept the moral content if we had not had the moral emotion. The moral emotion may surface in consciousness and thereby overcome self-deception, weakness, and other frailties of the mind that prevent the person from recognizing some moral truth. Some such cases are precisely those which Jonathan Glover so appropriately calls 'break-throughs', such as the experience of repugnance suffered by a doctor assigned the task of carrying out Nazi 'euthanasia' policies.[21]

On this position moral emotions can play a significant, psycholog-ically indispensable role in ordinary moral thought in a way that is entirely consistent with the theses of moral rationalism. The role as described here is consistent with fundamental moral truths being contentually a priori, and not at all mind-dependent. These features of moral rationalism are consistent with the fact that there are some moral truths each of us would not, in fact, reach without having the benefit of the moral emotions. Nothing here requires a mind-dependent account of moral truth. The moral emotions are facilitative in reaching moral truth; they are not constitutive of it.

Kant famously says in the *Critique of Practical Reason* that if a deter-mination of the will conformably with the moral law 'takes place . . . only by means of a feeling', 'so that the action is not done for the sake of the law', then the action does not contain morality.[22] Let us fix on a claim within the antecedent of this conditional. Does what comes after 'so that' follow from what precedes it? If a determination of the will takes place only by means of a feeling, does it follow that it is not done for the sake of the law? If Kant's use of 'feeling' is meant to include the moral emotions, it seems to me that it does not follow.

[20] See M. Stocker, 'Some Ways to Value Emotions', in *Understanding Emotions: Mind and Morals*, ed. P. Goldie (Aldershot: Ashgate, 2002), esp. 66 ff.

[21] *Humanity: A Moral History of the Twentieth Century* (New Haven, Conn.: Yale University Press, 2000), 345–8.   [22] Ch. III, 5: 72; I. Kant, *Practical Philosophy*, trans. and ed. Gregory, 198.

It may be true that if the moral emotion had not been experienced by the thinker then his will would not have been determined in the morally right direction. But on experiencing the emotion he may realize that its representational content, which involves moral notions, is correct. If the theses of these recent pages are right, this correctness of the moral content will be establishable by the thinker independently of the occurrence of this emotion. The thinker's appreciation of the rightness or wrongness of some course of action may have entirely a priori grounds, having to do with the moral law indeed: but those grounds would not have come to his attention without the occurrence of the moral emotion. The case is partially analogous to the consistency of the a priori status of belief in a logical proposition with the fact that the thinker would not have had the belief in the proposition without perception of a proof.

Perhaps Kant would say that he intends something stronger: 'only by means of a feeling' is meant to imply that the representational content of the emotion, with its normative content, is not directly relevant to the explanation of why the agent acts in accordance with the law. If so, what I have said does not contradict him; but it is important to see what a limited and curious kind of case his comments would then address. It would be a case in which an emotion explains an action independently of its content. There are cases of this, made possible by the fact that emotions have affect, and it need not be irrational. If certain emotions are very pleasant, or very unpleasant, that may explain someone's performing actions that produce them independently of any acceptance of their representational contents. But that rather special case, which Kant is surely right to say does not 'contain morality', is not at all the way in which our moral emotions ordinarily, and rightly, inform our moral thought. Our actions do contain morality when we rationally accept the content of a moral emotion, and moral rationalism can explain how this is possible.

Conclusion

In this short book I have done no more than make a start on articulating a general rationalist position. I have suggested a framework and attempted a treatment of certain subject matters within that framework. A fully developed rationalism would have to do much more.

A fully developed rationalism would, first and evidently, have to elucidate its application to other areas. The philosophy of mind is a salient example. The points of Chapters 3 through 5 have a bearing, for instance, on what would be the right kind of evidence for establishing that the behaviour of some organism is to be explained by states with intentional content. Suppose that the easiest way for it to be the case that a vast array of conditionals hold concerning the organism's behaviour in various counterfactual circumstances is for them to be explained by states with intentional content. The canons proposed in those chapters then imply that it is rational to accept that the conditionals are explained by intentional states. They also bear upon the kind of evidence one should seek in trying to confirm or refute hypotheses about the intentional states of a creature. One should seek precisely that evidence which would make it clear that the easiest way for the evidence to obtain is (or is not) for the hypotheses in question to be true. A full account of the correctness of this procedure would be founded in an account of what it is to be in the intentional states with the contents in question.

Not only other-ascription but also self-ascription of mental states needs to be exhibited as falling within the rationalist conception if the latter is to carry conviction. Correct, knowledge-yielding procedures for self-ascribing the striking panoply of different kinds of mental states need to be elucidated in terms of the identity of the states, contents, and concepts in question if the rationalist position is correct.

In carrying through a single overarching rationalist conception, as given by the three principles of rationalism in different domains—or some improvement or revision thereof—one does something towards showing the unity of reason over different domains, and that is a second task for further work. We may also have the ambition of showing more. Those who have hoped to show the unity of theoretical and practical reason may draw at various points on the apparatus and theses we have endorsed so far. In particular, the generalized rationalism I have outlined has been structured around a conception of judgements as mental actions, subject to norms and rational assessment. If judgements are actions, the more ambitious project of showing the unity of theoretical and practical reason becomes one of showing the unity of the notion of reason across two different subspecies of actions, the judgements on the one hand and the actions that are not judgements on the other.

A third, interdisciplinary task is that of showing how thinkers, with particular computational capacities, certain kinds of mental representations, and subpersonal procedures, are capable of conforming to the normative requirements of rationality. To resist any reduction of the normative to the non-normative certainly does not absolve one from answering the question 'How, empirically, are humans or other creatures capable of conforming to demands of these norms?'. We should also be prepared for such investigations to show that we may have mischaracterized the norms in various ways.

Finally, we should, in pursuing the rationalist agenda across more domains and more issues, aim to achieve a better understanding of the notion of knowing what it is for a given content to be true. I have argued that we cannot characterize rationality without invoking this notion. It informs our conception of what it is for a transition to be rational. The notion of knowing what it is for a given content to be true itself ties together the metaphysical and the epistemological. Failures to achieve the integration, in a given domain, of our metaphysics with our epistemology characteristically show up as manifestly defective accounts of knowledge of what it is for a content concerning that domain to be true. To understand knowledge of what it is for something to be the case would be to have a key not only to the epistemology and metaphysics of a domain but to the nature of ourselves as rational thinkers. Understanding our grasp of truth is an essential part of understanding ourselves.

Appendix: Main Principles and Definitions (with page of first occurrence)

PRINCIPLE I: *The Special Truth-Conduciveness Thesis*
A fundamental and irreducible part of what makes a transition one to which a thinker is entitled is that the transition tends to lead to true judgements (or, in case the transition relies on premisses, tends to do so when its premisses are true) in a distinctive way characteristic of rational transitions (p. 11).

PRINCIPLE II: *The Rationalist Dependence Thesis*
The rational truth-conduciveness of any given transition to which a thinker is entitled is to be philosophically explained in terms of the nature of the intentional contents and states involved in the transition (p. 52).

PRINCIPLE III: *The Generalized Rationalist Thesis*
All instances of the entitlement relation, both absolute and relative, are fundamentally a priori (p. 148).

The Rationalist Account of the A Priori
The a priori status of a transition is explained by its truth-preserving character being derivable from the nature of the concepts, contents, and states involved in the transition (p. 152).

p is *judgementally valid* with respect to a way W of coming to judge that *p* if the judgement that *p* is true in any circumstances in which it comes to be made in way W (p. 160).

p is *judgementally a priori* with respect to a way W just in case it is judgementally valid with respect to W, and W is an a priori way (p. 160).

p is *contentually a priori* with respect to a way W if W is an a priori way of coming to know *p*, and W is also a way that ensures the following: the content *p* of the judgement it yields is true in the actual world, whichever world is labelled as the actual world, and is true regardless of whether that way W is used, and of whether the conditions of its use are met, in the world that is labelled as the actual world (p. 163).

p is *contentually a priori* if there is a way with respect to which it is contentually a priori (p. 164).

The Initial Thesis on the Status of Moral Principles

Every moral principle that we know, or are entitled to accept, is either itself a priori or it is derivable from known a priori moral principles in conjunction with non-moral propositions which we know (p. 199).

The Sharpened Thesis on the Status of Moral Principles

Every moral principle that we know, or that we are entitled to accept, is either contentually a priori or follows from contentually a priori moral principles that are known in conjunction with non-moral propositions that we also know (p. 202–3).

Bibliography

ADAMS, E. (1975), *The Logic of Conditionals: An Application of Probability to Deductive Logic* (Dordrecht, Reidel).

ALSTON, W. (1967), 'Emotion and Feeling', in P. Edwards (ed.), *The Encyclopedia of Philosophy*, ii, (New York, Macmillan), 479–86.

—— 'An Internalist Externalism', *Synthese*, 74: 265–83.

AYER, A. J. (1946), *Language, Truth and Logic* (London, Gollancz).

BEALER, G. (1987), 'The Philosophical Limits of Scientific Essentialism', in J. Tomberlin (ed.), *Philosophical Perspectives, i. Metaphysics* (Atascadero, Calif., Ridgeview).

—— (1993), 'The Incoherence of Empiricism', in S. Wagner and R. Warner (eds.), *Naturalism: A Critical Appraisal* (Notre Dame, Ind., Notre Dame University Press).

BELNAP, N. (1962), 'Tonk, Plonk, and Plink', *Analysis*, 22: 130–4.

BENACERAFF, P. (1973), 'Mathematical Truth', *Journal of Philosophy*, 70: 661–79.

BENTLEY, W. (2000), *Snowflakes in Photographs* (Mineola, NY, Dover).

BLACKBURN, S. (1993), 'Filling in Space', in *Essays in Quasi-Realism* (New York, Oxford University Press).

—— (1998), *Ruling Passions: A Theory of Practical Reason* (Oxford, Oxford University Press).

BOGHOSSIAN, P. (1997), 'Analyticity', in R. Hale and C. Wright (eds.) *A Companion to the Philosophy of Language*. (Oxford, Blackwell).

—— AND C. PEACOCKE (2000) (eds.), *New Essays on the A Priori* (Oxford, Oxford University Press).

BONJOUR, L. (1985), *The Structure of Empirical Knowledge* (Cambridge, Mass., Harvard University Press).

—— (1998), *In Defense of Pure Reason* (Cambridge, Cambridge University Press).

BOOLOS, G., and JEFFREY, R. (1974), *Computability and Logic* (Cambridge, Cambridge University Press).

BRANDOM, R. (1994), *Making It Explicit: Reasoning, Representing and Discursive Commitment* (Cambridge, Mass., Harvard University Press).

—— (2000), *Articulating Reasons: An Introduction to Inferentialism* (Cambridge, Mass., Harvard University Press).

BREWER, B. (1995), 'Compulsion by Reason', *Proceedings of the Aristotelian Society, Suppl. vol.* 69: 237–53.

—— (1999), *Perception and Reason* (Oxford, Oxford University Press).

BURGE, T. (1979), 'Individualism and the Mental', *Midwest Studies in Philosophy*, 4: 73–121.

—— (1993), 'Content Preservation', *Philosophical Review*, 102/4: 457–88.

CARNAP, R. (1964), *The Logical Syntax of Language* (London, Routledge & Kegan Paul).

CASSAM, Q. (2000), 'Rationalism, Empiricism, and the A Priori', in P. Boghossian and C. Peacocke (eds.), *New Essays on the A Priori* (Oxford, Oxford University Press).

CHOMSKY, N. (1965), *Aspects of the Theory of Syntax* (Cambridge, Mass., MIT Press).

COLLINS, J. (2000), 'Preemptive Prevention', *Journal of Philosophy*, 97: 223–34.

CORNMAN, J. (1980), *Skepticism, Justification and Explanation* (Dordrecht, Reidel).

DAVEY, R., and STANLEY, D. (1993), 'All About Ice', *New Scientist*, 140, 18 Dec. 1993, 33–7.

DAVIDSON, D. (2001), 'How is Weakness of the Will Possible?', in *Essays on Actions and Events* (Oxford, Oxford University Press).

—— (2001), 'On the Very Idea of a Conceptual Scheme', in *Inquiries into Truth and Interpretation* 2nd edn., (Oxford, Oxford University Press).

DAVIES, M., and HUMBERSTONE, L. (1980), 'Two Notions of Necessity', *Philosophical Studies*, 38: 1–30.

DAWKINS, R. (1986), *The Blind Watchmaker* (Harlow, Longman).

DENNETT, D. (1978), *Brainstorms* (Montgomery, Bradford Books).

—— (2001), 'In Darwin's Wake, Where Am I ?', *Proceedings and Addresses of the American Philosophical Association*, 75 (2001), at 23.

DESCARTES, R. (1984), *Philosophical Writings of Descartes*, ii, trans. J. Cottingham, R. Storthof, and D. Murdoch (Cambridge, Cambridge University Press).

DUMMETT, M. (1973), *Frege: Philosophy of Language* (London, Duckworth).

—— (1978), 'The Justification of Deduction', in *Truth and Other Enigmas* (London, Duckworth).

—— (1978), 'The Significance of Quine's Indeterminacy Thesis', in *Truth and Other Enigmas* (London, Duckworth).

—— (1981), *The Interpretation of Frege's Philosophy* (London, Duckworth).

—— (1991), *The Logical Basis of Metaphysics* (Cambridge, Mass., Harvard University Press).

EVANS, G. (1982), *The Varieties of Reference* (Oxford, Oxford University Press).

FIELD, H. (1989), *Realism, Mathematics and Modality* (Oxford, Blackwell).

—— (2000), 'Apriority as an Evaluative Notion', in P. Boghossian and C. Peacocke (eds.), *New Essays on the A Priori* (Oxford, Oxford University Press).

FODOR, J. (1981), 'Methodological Solipsism Considered as a Research Strategy in Cognitive Psychology', in *Representation: Philosophical Essays on the Foundations of Cognitive Science* (Brighton, Harvester Press).

FORSTER, M., and SOBER, E. (1991), 'How to Tell When Simpler, More Unified, or Less *Ad Hoc* Theories will Provide More Accurate Predictions', *British Journal for the Philosophy of Science*, 45: 1–35.

FREGE, G. (1953), *The Foundations of Arithmetic* (Oxford, Blackwell).

—— (1977) 'Thoughts', in *Logical Investigations* trans. P. Geach and R. Storthoff, ed. P. Geach (Oxford, Blackwell).

—— (1998), *Grundgesetze der Arithmetik* (Hildesheim, Olms).

FRIEDMAN, M. (2001), *Dynamics of Reason* (Stanford, Calif., CSLI Publications).

GIBBARD, A. (2002), 'Normative and Recognitional Concepts', *Philosophy and Phenomenological Research*, 64: 151–67.

GLOVER, J. (2000), *Humanity: A Moral History of the Twentieth Century* (New Haven, Conn., Yale University Press).

GÖDEL, K. (1983), 'What is Cantor's Continuum Hypothesis?', in P. Benaceraff and H. Putnam (eds.), *Philosophy of Mathematics: Selected Readings* (Cambridge, Cambridge University Press).

—— (1995), *Collected Works* iii, ed. S. Feferman, J. Dawson, jun., W. Croldfarb, C. Parsons, R. Solovay (New York, Oxford University Press).

GODFREY-SMITH, P. (1996), *Complexity and the Function of Mind in Nature* (Cambridge, Cambridge University Press).

GOLDMAN, A. (1986), *Epistemology and Cognition* (Cambridge, Mass., Harvard University Press).

GOODMAN, N. (1965), *Fact, Fiction and Forecast*, 2nd edn. (Indianapolis, Ind., Bobbs-Merrill).

—— (1977), *The Structure of Appearance*, 3rd edn. (Dordrecht, Reidel).

GRICE, H. P. (1967), 'The Causal Theory of Perception', in G. Warnock (ed.), *The Philosophy of Perception* (Oxford: Oxford University Press).

HABERMAS, J. (1990), *Moral Consciousness and Communicative Action*, trans. C. Lenhardt and S. Weber Nicholsen (Cambridge, Mass., MIT Press).

HALL, N. (2000), 'Causation and the Price of Transitivity', *Journal of Philosophy* 97: 198–222.

HARDIN, C. (1988), *Color for Philosophers: Unweaving the Rainbow* (Indianapolis, Ind., Hackett).

HARMAN, G. (1965), 'The Inference to the Best Explanation', *Philosophical Review*, 74: 88–95.

—— (1973), *Thought* (Princeton, NJ, Princeton University Press).

—— (1977), *The Nature of Morality: An Introduction to Ethics* (New York, Oxford University Press).

HORWICH, P. (1982), *Probability and Evidence* (Cambridge, Cambridge University Press).

HUME, D. (2000), *A Treatise of Human Nature*, ed. D. Norton and M. Norton (Oxford, Oxford University Press).

JOHNSTON, M. (1989), 'Dispositional Theories of Value', *Proceedings of the Aristotelian Society, Suppl. Vol.* 63: 139–74.

KANT, I. (1996), *Critique of Pure Reason* (Indianapolis, Ind., Hackett).

—— (1996), *Practical Philosophy*, trans. and ed. M. Gregor (Cambridge, Cambridge University Press).

KAPLAN, D. (1989), 'Demonstratives', in J. Almog, J. Perry, and H. Wettstein (eds.), *Themes from Kaplan* (New York, Oxford University Press).

KEPLER, J. (1976), *The Six-Cornered Snowflake* (Oxford, Oxford University Press).

KIM, J. (1982), 'Psychophysical Supervenience', *Philosophical Studies*, 41: 51–70.

KITCHER, PHILIP. (1980), 'A Priori Knowledge', *The Philosophical Review*, 89: 3–23.

—— (2000), 'A Priori Knowledge Revisited', in P. Boghossian and C. Peacocke (eds.), *New Essays on the A Priori* (Oxford, Oxford University Press).

KORSGAARD, C. (1996), *The Sources of Normativity*, ed. O. O'Neill (Cambridge, Cambridge University Press).

KRANTZ, D., LUCE, R. et al. (1971) (eds.), *Foundations of Measurement*, i (New York, Academic Press).

KRIPKE, S. (1980), *Naming and Necessity* (Oxford, Blackwell).

LANGTON, R., and LEWIS, D. (1998), 'Defining "Intrinsic"', *Philosophy and Phenomenological Research*, 58: 333–45.

LEIBNIZ, G. (1981), *New Essays on Human Understanding*, trans. J. Bennett and P. Remnant (Cambridge, Cambridge University Press).

LEWIS, C. I. (1956), *Mind and the World Order: Outline of a Theory of Knowledge* (New York, Dover).

LEWIS, D. (1973), *Counterfactuals* (Oxford, Blackwell).

—— (1976), 'Probabilities of Conditionals and Conditional Probabilities', *Philosophical Review*, 85: 297–315.

—— (1983), 'How to Define Theoretical Terms', *Philosophical Papers*, i (New York, Oxford University Press).

—— (1986), 'Probabilities of Conditionals and Conditional Probabilities II', *Philosophical Review*, 95: 581–9.

—— (1989), 'Dispositional Theories of Value', *Proceedings of the Aristotelian Society, Suppl. Vol.* 63: 113–37.

LOCKE, J. (1976), *An Essay Concerning Human Understanding* (London, Dent).

LONGUENESSE, B. (1998), *Kant and the Capacity to Judge* (Princeton, NJ, Princeton University Press).

LYCAN, W. (1988), *Judgement and Justification* (Cambridge, Cambridge University Press).

LYCAN, W. (1998), 'Theoretical (Epistemic) Virtues', in E. Craig (ed.), *Routledge Encyclopedia of Philosophy*, ix (London, Routledge).

MARCEL, A. (2003), 'The Sense of Agency—Ownership and Awareness of Action', in J. Roessler and N. Eilan (eds.), *Agency and Self-Awareness* (Oxford, Oxford University Press).

McDOWELL, J. (1994), *Mind and World* (Cambridge, Mass., Harvard University Press).

—— (1998), 'Reply to Commentators', *Philosophy and Phenomenological Research*, 58: 403–31.

McGEE, V. (1985), 'A Counterexample to Modus Ponens', *Journal of Philosophy*, 82: 462–71.

MELLOR, D. H. (1991), 'In Defence of Dispositions', in *Matters of Metaphysics* (Cambridge, Cambridge University Press).

MOORE, G. E. (1922), *Philosophical Papers* (London, Routledge & Kegan Paul).

—— (1959), 'Proof of an External World', in *Philosophical Papers* (London, George Allen & Unwin).

—— (1993), *G. E. Moore: Selected Writings*, ed. T. Baldwin (London, Routledge).

—— (1993), *Principia Ethica*, ed. T. Baldwin (Cambridge, Cambridge University Press).

NICOLIS, G., and PRIGOGINE, I. (1989), *Exploring Complexity: An Introduction* (New York, Freeman).

NOZICK, R. (1981), *Philosophical Explanations* (Cambridge, Mass., Harvard University Press).

NUSSBAUM, M. (2001), *Upheavals of Thought: The Intelligence of Emotions* (Cambridge, Cambridge University Press).

PAUL, L. A. (2000), 'Aspect Causation', *Journal of Philosophy*, 97: 235–56.

PEACOCKE, C. (1983), *Sense and Content: Experience, Thought, and Their Relations* (Oxford, Oxford University Press).

—— (1987), 'Understanding Logical Constants: A Realist's Account', *Proceedings of the British Academy*, 73: 153–200.

—— (1992), *A Study of Concepts* (Cambridge, Mass., MIT Press).

—— (1993), 'Externalist Explanation', *Proceedings of the Aristotelian Society*, 93: 203–30.

—— (1993), 'How Are A Priori Truths Possible?', *European Journal of Philosophy*, 1: 175–99.

—— (1993), 'Proof and Truth', in J. Haldane and C. Wright (eds.), *Reality: Representation and Projection* (New York, Oxford University Press).

—— (1994), 'Content, Computation and Externalism', *Mind and Language*, 9: 303–35.

—— (1998), 'Implicit Conceptions, the A Priori, and the Identity of Concepts', *Philosophical Issues*, 9: 121–41.

—— (1998), 'Implicit Conceptions, Understanding and Rationality', *Philosophical Issues*, 9: 45–88.

—— (1998), 'The Philosophy of Language', in A. Grayling (ed.), *Philosophy; ii. Further Through the Subject*, ii (Oxford, Oxford University Press).

—— (1999), *Being Known* (Oxford, Oxford University Press).

—— (2000), 'Explaining the A Priori: The Programme of Moderate Rationalism', in P. Boghossian and C. Peacocke (eds.), *New Essays on the A Priori* (Oxford, Oxford University Press).

—— (2001), 'Does Perception have a Nonconceptual Content?', *Journal of Philosophy*, 98: 239–64.

—— (2001), 'Moralischer Rationalismus: Eine erste Skizze', *Deutsche Zeitschrift für Philosophie*, 49: 197–208.

—— (2001), 'The Past, Necessity, Externalism and Entitlement', *Philosophical Books*, 42: 106–17.

—— (2002), 'Three Principles of Rationalism', *European Journal of Philosophy*, 10: 375–97.

—— (2003), 'Action: Awareness, Ownership and Knowledge', in J. Roessler and N. Eilan (eds.), *Agency and Self-Awareness* (Oxford, Oxford University Press).

—— (2003), 'Explaining Perceptual Entitlement', in R. Schantz (ed.), *The Externalist Challenge* (Berlin, de Gruyter).

—— (2004), 'The A Priori', in F. Jackson and M. Smith (eds.), *The Oxford Handbook of Contemporary Philosophy* (Oxford, Oxford University Press).

PENROSE, R. (1995), *Shadows of the Mind: A Search for the Missing Science of Consciousness* (London, Viking).

PLANTINGA, A. (1993), *Warrant: The Current Debate* (New York, Oxford University Press).

POLLOCK, J. (1986), *Contemporary Theories of Knowledge* (Totowa, NJ, Rowman and Littlefield).

POPPER, K. (1957), *Observation and Interpretation in the Philosophy of Physics*, ed. S. Körner (New York, Dover).

PRICHARD, H. A. (1968), 'Does Moral Philosophy Rest on a Mistake?', in J. O. Urmson (ed.) *Moral Obligation, and Duty and Interest: Essays and Lectures by H. A. Prichard* (Oxford, Oxford University Press).

PRIOR, A. (1960), 'The Runabout Inference-Ticket', *Analysis*, 21: 38–9.

PRYOR, J. (2000), 'The Skeptic and the Dogmatist', *Noûs*, 34/4: 517–49.

PUTNAM, H. (1956), 'Reds, Greens and Logical Analysis', *Philosophical Review*, 65: 206–17.

PUTNAM, H. (1957), 'Red and Green All Over Again: A Rejoinder to Arthur Pap', *Philosophical Review*, 66: 100–3.

—— (1975), 'The Meaning of "Meaning"', in *Mind, Language and Reality* (Cambridge, Cambridge University Press).

—— (1995), *Pragmatism* (Oxford, Blackwell).

QUINE, W. (1961), 'Two Dogmas of Empiricism', in *From a Logical Point of View* (Cambridge, Mass., Harvard University Press).

—— (1974), *The Roots of Reference* (La Salle, Ill., Open Court).

—— (1976), *The Ways of Paradox and Other Essays,* rev. edn. (Cambridge, Mass., Harvard University Press).

—— (1981), *Theories and Things* (Cambridge, Mass., Harvard University Press).

RAILTON, P. (1997), 'Moral Realism', in S. Darwall, A. Gibbard, and P. Railton (eds.), *Moral Discourse and Practice: Some Philosophical Approaches* (New York, Oxford University Press).

RAWLS, J. (2000), *Lectures on the History of Moral Philosophy*, ed. B. Herman (Cambridge, Mass., Harvard University Press).

ROBERTS, ROBERT C. (1988), 'What An Emotion Is: A Sketch', *Philosophical Review*, 97: 183–209.

RUSSELL, B. (1973), *The Problems of Philosophy* (Oxford, Oxford University Press).

—— (1984), *Theory of Knowledge: The 1913 Manuscript*, ed. E. Eames (London, Routledge).

SCHAFFER, J. (2000), 'Trumping Preemption', *Journal of Philosophy*, 97: 165–81.

SCHIFFER, S. (forthcoming), 'Skepticism and the Vagaries of Justified Belief', *Philosophical Studies*.

SHEPARD, R., and CHIPMAN, S. (1970), 'Second-Order Isomorphism of Internal Representations: Shapes of States', *Cognitive Psychology*, 1: 1–17.

SMITH, M. (1989), 'Dispositional Theories of Value', *Proceedings of the Aristotelian Society, Suppl. vol.* 63: 89–111.

SOBER, E. (1975), *Simplicity* (Oxford, Oxford University Press).

—— (1998), 'Simplicity (in scientific theories)', in E. Craig (ed.), *Routledge Encyclopedia of Philosophy* (London, Routledge).

STALNAKER, R. (1968), A Theory of Conditionals, in N. Rescher (ed.), *Studies in Logical Theory* (Oxford, Blackwell).

—— (1999), *Context and Content* (Oxford, Oxford University Press).

STEWART, I. (1998), *Life's Other Secret: The New Mathematics of the Living World* (London, Allen Lane).

STOCKER, M. (2002), 'Some Ways to Value Emotions', in P. Goldie (ed.), *Understanding Emotions: Mind and Morals* (Aldershot, Ashgate).

STRAWSON, P. (1980), 'Reply to Evans', in Z. van Straaten (ed.), *Philosophical Subjects* (Oxford, Oxford University Press).

—— (1985), *Skepticism and Naturalism: Some Varieties* (London, Methuen).

STURGEON, N. (1985), 'Moral Explanations', in D. Copp and D. Zimmerman (eds.), *Morality, Reason and Truth: New Essays on the Foundations of Ethics* (Totowa, NJ, Rowman & Allanheld).

VAN FRAASSEN, B. (1980), *The Scientific Image* (Oxford, Oxford University Press).

—— (2002), *The Empirical Stance* (New Haven, Conn., Yale University Press).

VOGEL, J. (1990), 'Cartesian Skepticism and Inference to the Best Explanation', *Journal of Philosophy*, 87: 658–66.

WARNOCK, G. (1967) (ed.), *The Philosophy of Perception* (Oxford, Oxford University Press).

WEDGWOOD, R. (2002), 'Internalism Explained', *Philosophy and Phenomenological Research*, 65: 349–69.

WIGGINS, D. (1987), 'A Sensible Subjectivism?', in *Needs, Values and Truth*. (Oxford, Blackwell).

WILLIAMS, B. (1973), *Problems of the Self* (Cambridge, Cambridge University Press).

—— (2000), 'Philosophy as a Humanistic Discipline', *Philosophy*, 75: 477–96.

WILLIAMSON, T. (2000), *Knowledge and Its Limits* (Oxford, Oxford University Press).

WITTGENSTEIN, L. (1975), *Philosophical Remarks* (Oxford, Blackwell).

—— (1977), *Remarks on Colour* trans. L. McAlister and M. Schättle, ed. G. E. M. Anscombe, (Oxford, Blackwell).

—— (1980), *Remarks on the Philosophy of Psychology*, ii, trans. C. Luckhardt and M. Aue, ed. G. von Wright and H. Nyman, (Oxford, Blackwell).

WRIGHT, C. (1987), 'Strawson on Anti-Realism', in *Realism, Meaning and Truth* (Oxford, Blackwell).

—— (1992), *Truth and Objectivity* (Cambridge, Mass., Harvard University Press).

—— (forthcoming). '(Anti-)Sceptics Simple and Subtle: G. E. Moore and John McDowell', *Philosophy and Phenomenological Research*.

Index